Charles M. Parr, Ruth Parr, Howard Pyle, Alexandre O. Exquemelin, Charles Johnson

The Buccaneers and Marooners of America

Being an Account of the famous adventures and daring deeds of certain notorious freebooters of the Spanish Main. Second Edition

Charles M. Parr, Ruth Parr, Howard Pyle, Alexandre O. Exquemelin, Charles Johnson

The Buccaneers and Marooners of America
Being an Account of the famous adventures and daring deeds of certain notorious freebooters of the Spanish Main. Second Edition

ISBN/EAN: 9783337196271

Printed in Europe, USA, Canada, Australia, Japan

Cover: Foto ©Andreas Hilbeck / pixelio.de

More available books at **www.hansebooks.com**

MORGAN RECRUITING FOR THE ATTACK ON PORTO BELLO.
(From a Drawing by Howard Pyle.)

THE BUCCANEERS AND MAROONERS OF AMERICA

BEING AN ACCOUNT OF THE FAMOUS ADVENTURES AND DARING DEEDS OF CERTAIN NOTORIOUS FREEBOOTERS OF THE SPANISH MAIN

EDITED BY HOWARD PYLE

SECOND EDITION

LONDON: T. FISHER UNWIN, PATERNOSTER SQUARE. MDCCCXCII.

CONTENTS.

		PAGE
(1) EDITOR'S INTRODUCTION	. . . . . .	15
(2) THE TRANSLATOR'S PREFACE TO THE FIRST EDITION	.	43

PART I.

THE BUCCANEERS OF AMERICA.

CHAPTER I.

The Introduction—The Author sets forth for the Western Islands, in the service of the West India Company of France—They meet with an English frigate, and arrive at the Island of Tortuga 49

CHAPTER II.

A description of Tortuga—The fruits and plants there—How the French first settled there, at two several times, and forced out the Spaniards—The Author twice sold in the said island. 54

CHAPTER III.

A description of Hispaniola—A relation of the French Buccaneers 64

CHAPTER IV.

Original of the most famous pirates of the coasts of America—Famous exploit of Pierre le Grand 67

CONTENTS.

CHAPTER V.
How the pirates arm their vessels, and regulate their voyages . 80

CHAPTER VI.
Of the origin of Francis Lolonois, and the beginning of his robberies 95

CHAPTER VII.
Lolonois equips a fleet to land upon the Spanish islands of America, with intent to rob, sack, and burn whatsoever he met with 100

CHAPTER VIII.
Lolonois makes new preparations to take the city of St. James de Leon; as also that of Nicaragua; where he miserably perishes 115

CHAPTER IX.
The origin and descent of Captain Henry Morgan—his exploits, and the most remarkable actions of his life . . . 131

CHAPTER X.
Of the Island of Cuba—Captain Morgan attempts to preserve the Isle of St. Catherine as a refuge to the nest of pirates; but fails of his design—He arrives at, and takes, the village of El Puerto del Principe 140

CHAPTER XI.
Captain Morgan resolving to attack and plunder the City of Puerto Bello, equips a fleet, and with little expense and small forces takes it 149

CHAPTER XII.
Captain Morgan takes the City of Maracaibo, on the coast of Neuva Venezuela—Piracies committed in those seas—Ruin of three Spanish ships set forth to hinder the robberies of the pirates 158

CHAPTER XIII.

Captain Morgan goes to Hispaniola to equip a new fleet, with intent to pillage again on the coast of the West Indies . . 187

CHAPTER XIV.

What happened in the river De la Hacha 190

CHAPTER XV.

Captain Morgan leaves Hispaniola, and goes to St. Catherine's, which he takes 195

CHAPTER XVI.

Captain Morgan takes the Castle of Chagre, with four hundred men sent to this purpose from St. Catherine's . . . 202

CHAPTER XVII.

Captain Morgan departs from Chagre, at the head of twelve hundred men, to take the city of Panama 209

CHAPTER XVIII.

Captain Morgan sends canoes and boats to the South Sea—He fires the city of Panama—Robberies and cruelties committed there by the pirates, till their return to the Castle of Chagre 223

PART II.

A TRUE ACCOUNT OF FOUR NOTORIOUS PIRATES.

CHAPTER I. OF CAPTAIN TEACH *alias* BLACK-BEARD.

His beginning—His confederacy with Hornygold—The confederacy broken—Takes a large Guinea man—Engages the *Scarborough* man-of-war—His alliance with Major Stede Bonnet—Deposes his new ally—His advice to the Major—His progress and success—Takes prizes in sight of Charles Town—Sends ambassadors to the Governor of Carolina upon an impudent demand—Runs his ship aground designedly—His cruelty to some of his own companions—Surrenders to the King's Proclamation—The Governor of North Carolina's exceeding generosity to him—He marries—The number of his wives then living—Makes a second excursion in the way of pirating—Some State legerdemain betwixt him and the Governor—His frolics on shore—The merchants apply for a force against him, and where—A proclamation with a reward for taking or killing of pirates—Lieutenant Maynard sent in pursuit of him—Black-beard's good intelligence—The lieutenant engages Black-beard—A most execrable health drank by Black-beard—The fight bloody; the particulars of it—Black-beard killed—His sloop taken—The lieutenant's conduct—A reflection on the humours of seamen—Black-beard's correspondents discovered by his papers—Black-beard's desperate resolution before the fight—The lieutenant and Governor no very good friends—The prisoners hanged—Samuel Odell saved, and why—The good luck of Israel Hands—Black-beard's mischievous frolics—His beard described—Several instances of his wickedness—Some memoranda taken from his journal—The names of the pirates killed in the engagement—Of those executed—The value of the prize 239

Chapter II. Of Captain William Kid.

Commanded a privateer in the West Indies—Recommended to the Government by Lord Bellamont, &c.—Not encouraged—He is sent out in a private man-of-war with the King's commission—He sail for New York—In his way takes a French banker—Arrived there—Ships more hands—Sails to Madeira, Bonavista, Cape de Verde Islands, and Madagascar—Meets three English men-of-war—Meets with nothing at Madagascar—Goes to the Malabar coast—Cruises about Mohila and Johanna—Borrows money and repairs his ship—At Mabbee he takes some corn—From thence steers for Bab's Key—He sends a boat along the coast, and gains intelligence—He falls in with a fleet, but is obliged to sheer off—Goes to the Malabar coast—Takes a Moorish vessel—Treats the men cruelly, and discharges the vessel—Touches at Carawar, and is suspected of piracy—Engages a Portuguese man-of-war sent after him and gets off—Takes a Moor ship under pretence of her being French—Keeps company with a Dutch ship—Quarrels with and kills his gunner—Plunders a Portuguese ship on the Malabar coast and lets her go—His cooper is murdered in one of the Malabar Islands—He burns and pillages several houses—Commands a native to be shot—He takes the *Queda*, and shares £200 a man amongst his crew—

He cheats the Indians—Goes to Madagascar—Meets there
Culliford the pirate—Shifts into the *Queda*, and shares the
rest of her cargo—His men desert from him to forty—Goes
to Amboyna—hears he is declared a pirate in England—Lord
Bellamont prints his justification—A pardon granted to
pirates—Avery and Kid excepted—Kid goes to, and is secured
at, New York—Some of his crew depending on the pardon,
are confined—Sent to England and condemned—Three excepted—A distinction of the lawyers—Kid found guilty of the
murder of his gunner—Some plead the king's pardon to no
purpose—Mullins's plea—Kid's plea useless—He and his men
indicted—Executed 257

CHAPTER III. OF CAPTAIN BARTHOLOMEW ROBERTS AND HIS CREW.

His beginning—Elected captain in the room of Davis—The speech
of Lord Dennis at the election—Lord Sympton objects
against a papist—The death of Davis revenged—Roberts sails
southward in quest of adventures—The names of the prizes
taken by them—Brazil described—Roberts falls into a fleet
of Portuguese—Boards and takes the richest ship amongst
them—Make the Devil's Islands—An unfortunate adventure
of Roberts—Kennedy's treachery—Irishmen excluded by
Roberts and his crew—Articles sworn to by them—A copy of
them—Some account of the laws and customs of the pirates
—An instance of Roberts's cunning—He proceeds again
upon business, and takes prizes—Narrowly escapes being
taken—Sails for the Island Dominico—Another escape—Sails
for Newfoundland—Plunders, sinks, and burns twenty-two
sail in the harbour of Trepassi—Plunders ten sail of Frenchmen—The mad behaviour of the crew—A correspondence
hinted at—The pirates caressed at the island of St. Bartholomew—In extreme distress—Sail for Martinico—A stratagem
of Roberts—The insolent device in his colours—Odd compliment paid to Roberts—Three men desert the pirates, and
are taken by them—Their trial—Two executed and one
saved—The brigantine deserts them—Great divisions in the
company—A description of Serra Leone River—The names of
English settled there, and way of life—The *Onslow* belonging
to the African Company taken—The pirates' contempt of
soldiers—They are for entertaining a chaplain—Their skirmish with the Calabar negroes—The *King Solomon*, belonging to the African Company taken—The frolics of the pirates
—Take eleven sail in Whydah Road—A comical receipt
given by the pirates—A cruel action of Roberts—Sails for

Anna Bona—The progress of the *Swallow* man-of-war, in pursuit of Roberts—Roberts's consort taken—The bravery of Skyrme, a Welsh pirate—The surly humour of some of the prisoners—The *Swallow* comes up with Roberts—Roberts's dress described—Is killed—His character—His ship taken—The behaviour of the pirates when prisoners—A conspiracy of theirs discovered—Reflections on the manner of trying them—The form of the commission for trying the pirates—The oath taken by the commissioners—The names of those arraigned taken in the ship *Ranger*—The form of the indictment—The sum of the evidence against them—Their defence—The names of the prisoners of the *Royal Fortune*—Proceedings against them—Harry Glasby acquitted—The particular trial of Captain James Skyrme—Of John Walden—Of Peter Scudamore—Of Robert Johnson—Of George Wilson—Of Benjamin Jeffries—Of John Mansfield—Of William Davis—The names of those executed at Cape Corso—The petition of some condemned—The court's resolution—The form of an indenture of a pardoned pirate—The names of those pardoned upon indenture to serve seven years—The pirates how disposed of—The dying behaviour of those executed . . 275

Chapter IV. Of Captain Avery and his Crew.

Romantic reports of his greatness—His birth—Is mate of a Bristol man—For what voyage designed—Tampers with the seamen—Forms a plot for carrying off the ship—Executes it, and how—The pirates take a rich ship belonging to the Great Mogul—The Great Mogul threatens the English settlements—The pirates steer their course back for Madagascar—Call a council—Put all the treasure of board of Avery's ship—Avery and his crew treacherously leave his confederates—Go to the Isle of Providence in the West Indies—Sell the ship—Go to North America in a sloop—They disperse—Avery goes to New England—From thence to Ireland—Avery afraid to expose his diamonds to sale—Goes over to England—Puts his wealth into merchant's hands of Bristol—Changes his name—Lives at Bideford—The merchants send him no supplies—Importunes them—Goes privately to Bristol—They threaten to discover him—Goes over to Ireland—Solicits them from thence—Is very poor—Works his passage over to Plymouth—Walks to Bideford—Dies a beggar—An account of Avery's confederates—Their settlement at Madagascar—They meet other pirates—An account of them—The pirates deposed, and why—Marooned on the Island Mauritius—Some account of that island—The adventures of the company continued—Angria, an Indian pirate—His strength by land and sea—The East India Company's wars with him—The pirates go to the island of Melinda—Their barbarous behaviour there—Hear of Captain Mackra's designs against them—Their reflections thereupon—Sail for Cochin, a Dutch settlement—The pirates and the Dutch very good friends—Mutual presents made between the pirates and the Governor—The pirates in a fright—Almost starved—Take a prize of an immense value—Take an Ostend East Indiaman—A short description of Madagascar—A prodigious dividend made by the pirates—A fellow's way of increasing his diamonds—Some of the pirates quit, and join the remains of Avery—The proceedings of the men-of-war in those parts—Some Dutchmen petition to be among the pirates—The pirates divided in their measures—Break up—What became of them . . 381

LIST OF ILLUSTRATIONS.

(1) MORGAN RECRUITING FOR THE ATTACK ON PORTO BELLO (from a drawing by Howard Pyle) *Frontispiece*

(2) BARTHOLOMEW PORTUGUES (from the portrait in "De Americaensche Zee Roovers") ... *To face p.* 85

(3) LOLONOIS (from the portrait in "De Americaensche Zee Roovers") ... ... *To face p.* 96

(4) CAPTAIN HENRY MORGAN (from the portrait in "De Americaensche Zee Roovers") ... *To face p.* 178

(5) CAPTAIN TEACH (from the engraving in the second edition of Johnson's "General History of the Pyrates"). ... ... *To face p.* 239

(6) CAPTAIN BARTHOLOMEW ROBERTS (from the engraving in the second edition of Johnson's "General History of the Pyrates") ... ... *To face p.* 300

INTRODUCTION.

I.

HY is it that a little spice of deviltry lends not an unpleasantly titillating twang to the great mass of respectable flour that goes to make up the pudding of our modern civilization? And pertinent to this question another—Why is it that the pirate has, and always has had, a certain lurid glamour of the heroical enveloping him round about? Is there, deep under the accumulated *débris* of culture, a hidden ground-work of the old-time savage? Is there even in these well-regulated times an unsubdued nature in the respectable mental household of every one of us that still kicks against the pricks of law and order? To make my meaning more clear, would not every boy, for instance — that is every boy of any account—rather be a pirate captain than a Member of Parliament? And we ourselves; would we not rather read such a story as that of Captain Avery's capture of the East Indian treasure-ship, with its beautiful prin-

cess and load of jewels (which gems he sold by the handful, history sayeth, to a Bristol merchant), than—say one of Bishop Atterbury's sermons or the goodly Master Robert Boyle's religious romance of "Theodora and Didymus"? It is to be apprehended that to the unregenerate nature of most of us, there can be but one answer to such a query.

In the pleasurable warmth the heart feels in answer to tales of derring-do, Nelson's battles are all mightily interesting, but even in spite of their romance of splendid courage, I fancy that the majority of us would rather turn back over the leaves of history to read how Drake captured the Spanish treasure-ship in the South Sea, and of how he divided such a quantity of booty in the Island of Plate (so named because of the tremendous dividend there declared) that it had to be measured in quart bowls, being too considerable to be counted.

Courage and daring, no matter how mad and ungodly, have always a redundancy of *vim* and life to recommend them to the nether man that lies within us, and no doubt his desperate courage, his battle against the tremendous odds of all the civilized world of law and order have had much to do in making a popular hero of our friend of the black flag. But it is not altogether courage and daring that endears him to our hearts. There is another and perhaps a greater kinship in that lust for wealth that makes one's fancy revel more pleasantly in the story of the division of treasure in the pirate's island retreat, the hiding of his godless gains somewhere in the sandy stretch of tropic beach, there to remain hidden until the time should come to rake the dubloons up again and to spend them like a lord in polite society, than in the most thrilling tales of his wonderful escapes from commissioned cruisers through tortuous channels between the coral-reefs.

And what a life of adventure is his to be sure! A life of constant alertness, constant danger, constant escape! An ocean Ishmaelite, he wanders for ever aimlessly, homelessly; now unheard of for months, now careening his boat on some lonely uninhabited shore, now appearing suddenly to swoop down on some merchant-vessel with rattle of musketry, shouting, yells, and a hell of unbridled passions let loose to rend and tear.

What a Carlislean hero! What a setting of blood and lust and flame and rapine for such a hero!

II.

Piracy such as was practised in the flower of its days—that is, during the early eighteenth century—was no sudden growth. It was an evolution, from the semi-lawful buccaneering of the sixteenth century, just as buccaneering was upon its part, in a certain sense, an evolution from the unorganized, unauthorized warfare of the Tudor period.

For there was a deal of piratical smack in the anti-Spanish ventures of Elizabethan days. Many of the adventurers—of the Sir Francis Drake school, for instance—actually overstepped again and again the bounds of international law, entering into the realms of *de facto* piracy. Nevertheless, while their doings were not recognized officially by the Government, the perpetrators were neither punished nor reprimanded for their excursions against Spanish commerce at home or in the West Indies; rather were they commended, and it was considered not altogether a discreditable thing for men to get rich upon the spoils taken from Spanish galleons in times of nominal peace. Many of the most reputable citizens and merchants of London, when they felt that the Queen failed in her duty of pushing the fight against the great Catholic Power, fitted out fleets upon their own account and sent them to levy good Protestant war of a private nature upon the Pope's anointed.

Some of the treasures captured in such ventures were immense, stupendous, unbelievable. For an example, one can hardly credit the truth of the "purchase" gained by Drake in the famous capture of the plate-ship in the South Sea.

One of the old buccaneer writers of a century later says: "The Spaniards affirm to this day that he took at that time twelve-score tons of plate and sixteen bowls of coined money a man (his number being then forty-five men in all), insomuch that they were forced to heave much of it overboard, because his ship could not carry it all."

Maybe this was a very greatly exaggerated statement put by the author and his Spanish authorities, nevertheless there was enough truth in it to prove very conclusively to the bold minds of the age that tremendous profits—"purchases" they called them—were to be made from piracy. The Western World is filled with the names of daring mariners of those old days, who came flitting across the great trackless ocean in their little tub-like boats of a few hundred tons burden, partly to explore unknown seas, partly—largely, perhaps—in pursuit of Spanish treasure: Frobisher, Davis, Drake, and a score of others.

In this left-handed war against Catholic Spain many of the adventurers were, no doubt, stirred and incited by a grim, Calvinistic, Puritanical zeal for Protestantism. But equally beyond doubt the gold and silver and plate of the "Scarlet Woman" had much to do with the persistent energy with which these hardy mariners braved the mysterious unknown terrors of the great unknown ocean that stretched away to the sunset, there in far away waters to attack the huge, unwieldy treasure-ladened galleons that sailed up and down the Caribbean Sea and through the Bahama Channel.

III.

Of all ghastly and terrible things old-time religious war was the most ghastly and terrible. One can hardly credit nowadays the cold, callous cruelty of those times. Generally death was the least penalty that capture entailed. When the Spaniards made prisoners of the English, the Inquisition took them in hand, and what that meant all the world knows. When the English captured a Spanish vessel the prisoners were tortured, either for the sake of revenge or to compel them to disclose where treasure lay hidden. Cruelty begat cruelty, and it would be hard to say whether the Anglo-Saxon or the Latin showed himself to be most proficient in torturing his victim.

When Cobham, for instance, captured the Spanish ship in the Bay of Biscay, after all resistance was over and the heat of the battle had cooled, he ordered his crew to bind the captain and all of the crew and every Spaniard aboard— whether in arms or not—to sew them up in the mainsail and to fling them overboard. There were some twenty dead bodies in the sail when a few days later it was washed up on the shore.

Of course such acts were not likely to go unavenged, and many an innocent life was sacrificed to pay the debt of Cobham's cruelty.

Nothing could be more piratical than all this, nevertheless, as was said, it was winked at, condoned, if not sanctioned, by the law; and it was not beneath people of family and respectability to take part in it. But by and by Protestantism and Catholicism began to be at somewhat less deadly enmity with one another, religious wars were still far enough from being ended, but the scabbard of the sword was no longer flung away when the blade was drawn. And so followed a time of nominal peace, and a generation arose with whom it was no longer respectable and worthy—one might say a matter of duty—to fight a country with which one's own land was not at war. Nevertheless, the seed had been sown; it had been demonstrated that it was feasible to practice piracy against Spain and not to suffer therefor. Blood had been shed and cruelty practised, and once indulged no lust seems stronger than that of shedding blood and practising cruelty.

Though Spain might be ever so well grounded in peace at home, in the West Indies she was always at war with the whole world—English, French, Dutch. It was almost a matter of life or death with her to keep her hold upon the New World. At home she was bankrupt and, upon the earthquake of the Reformation, her power was already beginning to totter and to crumble to pieces. America was her treasure-house, and from it alone could she hope to keep her leaking purse full of gold and silver. So it was that she strove strenuously, desperately to keep out the world from her American possessions—a bootless task, for the old order upon which her power rested was broken and crumbled for ever. But still she strove, fighting against fate, and so it was that in the tropical America it was one continual war between her and all the world. Thus it came that long after piracy ceased to be allowed at home, it continued in those far away seas with unabated vigour, recruiting to its service all that lawless malign element which gathers together in every newly-opened country where the only law is lawlessness, where might is right and where a living is to be gained with no more trouble than cutting a throat.

IV.

Such were the conditions of life that gave rise to that peculiar class of outlaws and semi-outlaws known as the buccaneers—those pirates, hunters, and freebooters, whose very name has become a synonym of all that is lawless, desperate, godless.

Little or nothing is known of the lives and habits of these nomadic hunter-pirates beyond what is to be found in a short concise history of some of their greater exploits, written by one of their number—John Esquemeling by name—who lived with them, and was with Captain Morgan during his most deservedly famous attack upon the City of Panama.

The temptation is always great to an editor to interlope his own ideas of character and his own views of the results to the world of the world's happenings; but in the case of the Esquemeling history—though more serious historians are prone to say that the statements therein given are not to be depended upon—it should be decidedly hands off. One touch of the modern brush would destroy the whole tone of dim local colours of the past made misty by the lapse of time. It needs the quaint old archaic language of the seventeenth century to tell of those deeds of blood and rapine and cruelty, and the stiff, formal style of the author-translator seems in some way to remove those deeds out of the realms of actuality into the hazy light of romance. So told the adventures of those old buccaneers still remain a part of humbler history, but they do not sound so cruel, so revolting as they would be told in our nineteenth-century vernacular.

And as for the lives of the buccaneers themselves—the account of how they wrenched Tortuga from Spain, of how they peopled Western Hispaniola with cattle-killing hunters and desperadoes, of how they roamed through the tropical rankness of the forests, with their half-wild dogs and their huge, unwieldy firelock guns, now hunted by the Spaniards like wild beasts, and now like wild beasts turning at bay to rend and tear with savage quickness—it would be, if anything, still more a pity to mar the telling as he tells it with his pithy conciseness. And then, after all, it is such old histories alone that can bring one in full touch with the empty shell of a life that is past and gone, and such a history is doubly, trebly full of interest when told by an actor who actually lived it in the scenes of which he writes. And so we leave honest John Esquemeling to tell his own history in his own way.

However, of the differentiation of the buccaneer pirate from the buccaneer proper something may, perhaps, be added to aid the reader in a clearer understanding of the manner in which they came to graduate from cattle-stealing to throat-cutting.

V.

The buccaneers took their name from a peculiar method of curing beef by drying it in the sun, which was termed buchanning. The beef so cured was, itself wild or half-wild cattle, stolen from the neighbouring Spaniards of the great Island of Hispaniola—the San Domingo of our day. The chief rendezvous of these nomadic hunters and curers of meat was upon a little hunch of an island known as Tortuga de Mar, so called from its supposed resemblance to the sea-turtle. Of the manner in which the French settled upon this island of the sea-turtle, of their bloody fights with the Spaniards, of the conquest of the island by the one, of its recapture by the other, of its recapture again by the French, the author tells at length. Suffice it to be said here that, in spite of all the power of Spain, the buccaneers finally made conquest of Tortuga, and that a French governor was sent to rule over them.

No better situation could have been found for the trade in which they were busied. Tortuga, lying as it does off the north-west shore of Hispaniola and at the outlet of the Old Bahama Channel (a broad stretch of navigable water extending between the Island of Cuba and the great Bahama

Banks), was almost in the very centre of the main route of travel between the Western World and Europe, along which the commerce of the West Indies came and went, ebbed and flowed. It afforded, perhaps, one of the most convenient ports of the whole Western World in which home-returning vessels might provision and take in water. The captains and owners of the trading vessels asked no questions as to the means whereby cattle were procured. It sufficed them that the meat was well dried and well cured, and, having been stolen, was cheaper than that to be had at Porto Bello, Santa Catharina, and other Spanish ports. So buccaneering (in its proper sense) was quite a profitable business, and prospered accordingly; the step from stealing cattle to piracy was not so very great.

Among the buccaneers were to be found the off-scourings of all the French and English West Indies—a mad, savage, unkempt phase of humanity, wilder than the wildest Western cow-boys—fierce, savage, lawless, ungoverned, ungovernable. The Spaniards were merely the means whereby money was to be gained—money to spend in the wild debaucheries, for which the world has afforded few better opportunites than were to be found in the Spanish West Indies. The old days of legalized piracy had never been forgotten, and by and by it began to be felt by the wild cattle-hunters that beef-curing was too slow and laborious a means of earning duploons. It needed only the leadership of such a one as Pierre le Grand to awaken dormant piracy to a renewed vigour of life.

Our author only gives us meagre details concerning the result of that first bold expedition of the buccaneers under Pierre le Grande into the Carribbean Sea. He tells us but little of the capture of the great galleon by the pirate crew of the long-boat, and as to the gains made by the buccaneers upon the occasion he tells us only that " he (Pierre) set sail for France, carrying with him all the riches he found in that huge vessel, and that there he continued without ever returning to the parts of America again." But though our author does not tell just what was the plunder taken upon this memorable occasion, it must have been very considerable indeed, and one can imagine how the success of the venture set agog all the buccaneers of Tortuga and Hispaniola. One can fancy what a ferment the rumour of the great capture occasioned; what a hurrying hither and thither; what a crowding of crews of desperadoes into long-boats and hoys! It was so infinitely much easier, so vastly quicker and so much more congenial a means of getting rich upon ill-gotten gains than the dangerous and monotonous business of hunting and stealing cattle in an enemy's country. So, in a little while—a few years—the West Indian seas were alive with pirates—English, French, Dutch, and Portuguese.

Nearly always, though our author does not explicitly say so, the buccaneers appear to have sailed under some semi-official letters of marque, granted by the colonial governors. It was under such that the famous Captain Morgan sailed in his expedition against Porto Bello, Santa Catharina, and Panama. But such unauthorized letters of marque only made piracy all the more strenuous, unrelaxing, merciless giving as they did some sanction to the cruel and bloody warfare. French and English West Indian towns — such, for instance, as Port Royal, in Jamaica — grew fabulously rich with an unbelievable quickness. In ten or twelve years Spain had lost millions upon millions of dollars, which vast treasure was poured in a golden flood into those hot fever-holes of towns, where Jews and merchants and prostitutes battened on the burning lusts of the wild hunters whose blood was already set aflame with plunder and rapine. At last the risks of Spanish West Indian commerce became so great that no vessel dared venture out of port, excepting under escort of men-of-war. Even then they were not secure always of protection, for there are records that tell of the capture of rich prizes from the very midst of the surrounding plate fleet.

Cargoes of value from the Western provinces of Central and South America, instead of being sent to Spain across the Isthmus from Panama as heretofore, were carried more often by way of the Strait of Magellan, there being less danger in that long and toilsome voyage than in the pirate-infested Carribbean Sea in spite of its trade-winds and steady ocean currents. So it came that by and by the trade of freebooting no longer returned the great profits that had been one time realized by those who embarked in it. It seemed for awhile as though the business were likely to find its death in the very thing that had given it birth—the weakness of Spanish power, decaying to ruin.

It was in this time of its threatened decadence that Francis Lolonois gave a new impulse to the free trade—as it was sometimes called—of the times.

In the temporary paralysis of commerce vast wealth had gathered and accumulated in the great treasure-houses of the walled and fortified towns of the West Indies—Cartagena, Porto Bello, Maracaibo, Havana, and numerous other centres of Spanish power. It was Lolonois who conceived the scheme of descending upon these storehouses of treasure, there to gather in one swoop a prize such as a score of ventures in times past could not return.

It was upon Maracaibo that the first attack was made, and in the matter-of-fact way with which our author describes the sacking of that city and of the town of Gibraltar a picture of a phase of the times is given, so grim, so terrible, that were it not for the further bearing out of the impeachable records, we of these days of light might well doubt that such things could really be in lands calling themselves Christian. The result of the expedition was all—more than all—that Lolonois' most sanguine hopes could have anticipated; and when he returned in triumph to Tortuga, almost a howl of exultation went up from all the West Indies not under Spanish rule, for there were many other and richer towns than Maracaibo.

VI.

It was upon the lines marked out by Lolonois that the greatest of all the buccaneers reaped fame and wealth—Sir Henry Morgan, the hero of the author's book, the Alexander of his history. Of the birth, parentage, and family of Morgan but little is known, that little being quite apocryphal in its nature. Our author tells us that he was a Welshman, as was to be supposed from his name; that he was of good strain, as was also to be supposed; and that his father was a rich yeoman. The history further tells us that Captain Morgan was, upon his first coming to the Americas, sold for his passage, such being the customary manner of dealing with the steerage passengers of the day. Having served his time he went to Jamaica, where he entered into the service of one Mansvelt, a buccaneer of not a little note, and presently his name becomes famous in the nether history of the period.

Another history, not so picturesque as that written by Esquemeling, but perhaps more accurate, tell us of the great buccaneer's having been commissioned by Sir Thomas Modyford, then

Governor of Jamaica, to levy war upon Spain and other nationalites upon behalf of the King of England.

As was said before, the governors of the non-Spanish West India Islands were accustomed to issue such warrants to the buccaneer privateersmen, but during Sir Thomas Modyford's time some effort was beginning to be made by the home governments to put a stop to this semi-legal piracy. Sir Thomas, who, it was said, shared in the gains of the freebooters, was carried as prisoner to England to answer for the assumption of his authority in having declared war against a nation with whom the country was then at peace. Nevertheless the latent sympathy of the Government was still on the side of the buccaneers, and it was on account of his attack upon Panama that Captain Morgan was created Sir Henry Morgan by his Majesty King Charles II.

In the historical records of Jamaica his name appears twice as Lieutenant-Governor: once during the time that Sir Thomas Modyford, who had granted him commission, was a State prisoner in the Tower—once, succeeding Charles Earl, of Carlisle, in 1680.

It was perhaps a part of the paradoxical management of State affairs that he was finally recalled to England in 1683 by order of the Secretary of State, for breaking the peace with the Spaniards, contrary to his Majesty's express orders, and it seems a very fitting epilogue to the comedy of fate that he should have died in the Tower of London for the very deeds for which he was knighted.

Such are the bald and meagre details of his life. Of his renown the world has heard more or less blatant blasts upon the trumpet of Fame for two hundred years and more, the notes whereof are not a little attuned to the history of his deeds written by honest John Esquemeling, the first English edition of which is here edited.

VII.

If, as some assert, the popularity of a book is to be estimated according to the number of editions through which it passes, the history of Captain Sir Henry Morgan has, at least in past few generations, been very dear to English-speaking people.

At least this is true of the Esquemeling history; the first English edition was printed under date of 1684—about the time that the hero of it was a State prisoner standing his trial for levying war against Spain, contrary to his Majesty's express orders, and for the doing of those deeds of conquest for which he had once been honoured. Upon the title-page of the quaint old volume is given briefly and concisely the bibliography of the history to its then condition. That it was originally written in Dutch, thence translated into Spanish by Alonso de Bonne-Maison, and now faithfully rendered into English for the first time.

More particularly, the Dutch history from which

the Spanish translation was taken is a work published at Amsterdam in 1678, entitled, "De Americaensche Zee Roovers." A number of other translations beside the Spanish and English accounts were made cotemporarily with other European languages, the best known of which is, perhaps, the French "Histoire des Aventuriers qui se sont signaley dans les Indies," published originally in 1686. Another French edition, considerably enlarged and appearing in four volumes, was published in 1775.

In each new translation and each new edition the original narrative was expanded by additional matter. A year or two after the appearance of the earliest English edition—that of 1684—a second appeared in the same general form with the first, but with a supplement treating of the adventures of Captain Sharp, Sawkins, Coxon, and others on the coasts of the South Sea from the journal kept by Mr. Basil Ringrose. Both of these two editions are now of considerable rarity, and, being rather better printed than cotemporary volumes of the kind, and being, besides, well and interestingly illustrated by portraits of the more prominent freebooters, curious maps and quaint plates, they are in considerable esteem with collectors of old books. Of the two the second edition is the more valued because of the additional matter and maps, but for ordinary literary purposes the first edition is, perhaps, more preferable. The whole value of the history culminates and centres with Captain Morgan, and that part treating of the adventures of Captain Sparks and the others is not only dull, protracted, and prosy, but excessively tedious. Accordingly for the present purposes it has been deemed better to adhere to the scheme of the first edition, which is in reality a history of Captain Morgan's expeditions, rather than to unnecessarily extend the volume upon the lines more usually followed.

From these two earlier editions has sprung a host of successors. The second—that containing the adventures of Captain Sharp, Sawkins, Coxon, and others—with some further additions was reprinted in Walker's "British Classics" (12mo, 1810), besides which the history has appeared in a score of cheaper forms adapted to more popular reading and far too obscure and too numerous to trace and follow.

In the edition here presented some few changes have been made, some of the long and tedious bits of description have been omitted, but as a whole the history of Captain Morgan and his fellow-buccaneers stands almost exactly as originally told by the English translation of the Spanish translation of the Dutch Buccaneer Pirate Story.

VIII.

It was about 1680-5 that the English Government, as was shown in the case of Sir Henry Morgan and others, seriously took in hand the suppression of freebooting. Morgan was only one of many punished for having at one time or another levied private war upon Spain. Then came the Peace of Ryswick between France and Spain, which gave the finishing blow to buccaneering as a semi-legal venture; henceforth nothing remained but open piracy to those bold spirits, too active in the ferment of their passions to be contained by the bottle of law. Both France and England joined in stamping out freebooting, and for a little while it seemed as if they had succeeded—but it was only for a little while.

Filibustering and semi-piracy had become too much a part of the life of the West Indies, and was too thoroughly congenial to those who sought escape from the restraints of civilization to be thus easily put an end to. It was only the stem of buccaneering that had been lopped away by the sword of the law; from the roots sprung a new and more vigorous offshoot—the flower of Piracy itself. Under the new order it was no longer Spain alone that suffered, but the lawful commerce of all nations that became the prey of these ocean wolves. During the early eighteenth century the Spanish main and adjacent waters swarmed with pirate crafts, and the fame of their deeds forms a chapter of popular history that may almost take rank with that which tells of Robin Hood, Friar Rush, Schinderhannes, and other worthies of the like kidney of a more or less apocryphal nature.

Who has not heard tell of Black-beard? Who

does not know of the name of the renowned Captain Kid? Who has not heard the famous ballad which tells of his deeds of wickedness?—a rythmical chant such as has from the beginning of time been most taking to the popular ear:—

> "Oh! my name is Captain Kid,
>   As I sailed,
>   As I sailed,
> Oh! my name is Captain Kid,
>   As I sailed,
> Oh! my name is Captain Kid,
>   And God's laws I did forbid,
> And right wickedly I did
>   As I sailed."

So far as the knowledge of the editor of this work extends no such ballad has been written concerning the doings of that other famous knight of the black flag whose name is no less renowed in the history of his kind—Captain Edward Teach, better known as Black-beard. But, though so far as ballad fame is concerned he is at a disadvantage with the other, Captain Teach stands *par excellent* in an unique personality of his own. Perhaps there are few figures so picturesque as that suggested in the description of his get-up upon the occasions of public appearances—the plaited beard, the face smeared black with gunpowder, the lighted matches thrust under his hat brim, the burning sparks thereof hanging down about his face. The fiendish grimness of that figure has made fully as much impression upon the clay of the past as even that of Captain Kid, in spite of the celebrated song that emphasizes his fame. But the two together stand head and shoulders above all others of their kidney as the best-known pirates of the early eighteenth century. Even to this day it is safe to say that nowhere along the Atlantic coast of the whole United States, from Maine to Florida, are their names unknown, and that in all that stretch of sea-board there is hardly a lonesome sandy beach but is reputed to have held treasure hidden by the one or the other of them. Each is the hero of half a hundred legends and fantastically exaggerated tales, and it was Captain Kid who buried the treasure that Poe discovered in the delightful romance of "The Gold Bug."

But, nevertheless, though the fame of these two worthies is so pre-eminent, there are others only second to them in renown—others whose names and deeds have also been chronicled by Captain Johnson, the famous historian of scoundreldom. Captain Bartholomew Roberts, for instance, if he may not have had the fortune to be so famous as the two above-mentioned worthies, yet, in his marvellous escapes and deeds of daring, he well deserves to stand upon the same pedestal of renown. And Captain Avery, though his history is, perhaps, more apochryphal in its nature, nevertheless there is sufficint stamina of trust in the account of his exploits to grant him also place with his more famous brothers, for the four together—

Black-beard, Kid, Roberts, and Avery — form a galaxy the like of which is indeed hard to match in its own peculiar brilliancy.

IX.

Through circumstances the hunter name of buccaneers was given to the seventeenth-century pirates and freebooters; the term "marooners" was bestowed upon those who followed the same trade in the century succeeding. The name has in itself a terrible significance. The dictionary tells us that to maroon is to put ashore as upon a desert island, and it was from this that the title was derived.

These later pirates—the marooners—not being under the protection of the West Indian governors, and having no such harbour for retreat as that, for instance, of Port Royal, were compelled to adopt some means for the disposal of prisoners captured with their prizes other than taking them into a friendly port.

Occasionally such unhappy captives were set adrift in the ship's boats—with or without provisions, as the case might be. A method of disposing of them maybe more convenient, certainly more often used, was to set them ashore upon some desert coast or uninhabited island, with a supply of water perhaps, and perhaps a gun, a pinch of powder, and a few bullets—there to meet their fate, either in the slim chance of a passing vessel or more probably in death.

Nor was marooning the fate alone of the wretched captives of their piracy; sometimes it was resorted to as a punishment among themselves. Many a mutinous pirate sailor and not a few pirate captains have been left to the horrors of such a fate, either to die under the shrivelling glare of the tropical sun upon some naked sand-spit or to consume in the burning of a tropical fever amid the rank wilderness of mangroves upon some desert coast.

Hence the name marooners.

X.

As the marooners followed the buccaneers in actual fact, so should they follow them in the history that treats of West Indian freebooters.

Nor is it merely a matter of correctness of form to add the more unusual histories the four famous pirates here incorporated. There is another, a deeper, a more humanitarian reason for such a sequel. For is not the history of the savage outlawry of the marooners a verisemblance of the degeneration, the quick disintegration of humanity the moment that the laws of God and man are lifted? The Tudor sea-captains were little else than legalized pirates, and in them we may see that first small step that leads so quickly into the smooth downward path. The buccaneers, in their semi-legalized piracy, succeeded them as effect follows cause.

Then as the ultimate result followed the marooners—fierce, bloody, rapacious, human wild beasts lusting for blood and plunder, godless, lawless, the enemy of all men but their own wicked kind.

Is there not a profitable lesson to be learned in the history of such a human extreme of evil—all the more wicked from being the rebound from civilization?

Thus, in the present volume, it has been deemed best to add as a sequel to the redoubtable narrative of the honest Dutchman Esquemeling, the history, first of Captain Kid—who stood upon a sort of middle ground between the buccaneers and the marooners proper—and then the story of the lives of Black-beard, Roberts, and Avery: roaring, ranting, raving pirates *per se*.

As a rule it is generally difficult to find any actual data, any tangible history of the popular villain-hero. Now and then the curious collector of such ephemeral trifles gathers together a few chap-book histories of such, but as a rule any positive material passes quickly away and is lost in the oblivion of past things. Their deeds and actions are usually of small moment in the policy of nations, and it is only in popular romance and fiction that their name and fame is embalmed and preserved. But in the case of Kid and of Black-beard, however, and the more famous pirates and notorious rogues of their generation—both land-thieves and water-thieves, land-rats and water-rats—a Pliny has arisen, who has handed down their names and the history of their deeds to the present time — Captain Charles Johnson, who, in the earlier half of the eighteenth century collected and edited numberless chap-book histories of famous pirates and highwaymen.

As in the case of "The History of the Buccaneers," Johnson's works have gone through numberless editions, so that if by the quantity of books we measure the popular regard, Black-beard and Kid and Avery with their land-types—Duval, Shepherd, and Jonathan Wild—have a very dear place in the hearts of the people.

The first of these collected histories appeared under place and date, London, 1724, 8vo. It was entitled, "General History of the Pyrates of the New Providence," &c., and appeared again in a second edition of two volumes in 1727. In this history, most quaint and rare, appear the lives both of Black-beard and Kid, and it is now numbered among the more interesting and curious of Americana.

In 1734 was published in folio form "The History of Highwaymen and Pirates," &c.; but although the history of Black-beard appears in this edition, that of Captain Kid is, for some reason, omitted. In 1742 followed a second edition of this same history, printed from the original plates. Both this and the first edition (some of the copies of which bear the date 1736) are now grown quite rare and curious, being not often met with outside the libraries of the book-collector. From them so numerous a progeny had sprung that, as in the case of "The History of the Buccaneers," it is almost an impossible task to follow and particularize them. One of the more notable reprints appeared in 1839, another with additions by C. Whitehead in 1840, and again in 1853. These are but a few of a numerous tribe of the grand family in which these popular heroes act their life under the gaze of our far-away time.

To them the reader must turn if he would seek further in the dark passages of such lives as are here presented in the most notorious examples, perhaps, of all.

HOWARD PYLE.

Wilmington, Delaware,
   November, 1890.

THE TRANSLATOR

TO THE

READER (OF 1684).

THE present Volume, both for its Curiosity and Ingenuity, I dare recommend unto the perusal of our English Nation, whose glorious actions it containeth. What relateth unto the curiosity hereof, this Piece, both of Natural and Humane History, was no sooner published in the Dutch *Original, than it was snatch't up for the most curious Library's of* Holland; *it was Translated into* Spanish *(two impressions thereof being sent into* Spain *in one year); it was taken notice of by the learned Academy of Paris; and finally recommended as worthy our esteem, by the ingenious Author of the* Weekly Memorials for the Ingenious, *printed here at* London *about two years ago. Neither all this undeservedly, seeing it enlargeth our acquaintance of Natural History, so much prized and enquired for, by the Learned of this present Age, with several observations not easily to be found in other accounts already received from* America: *and besides, it informeth us (with huge novelty) of as great and bold attempts, in point of Military conduct and valour, as ever were performed by mankind; without excepting, here, either* Alexander *the Great, or* Julius Cæsar, *or the rest of the* Nine Worthy's of Fame. *Of all which actions, as we cannot confess ourselves to have been ignorant hitherto (the very name of* Bucaniers *being, as yet, known but unto few of the* Ingenious; *as their Lives, Laws, and Conversation, are in a manner unto none) so can they not choose but be admired, out of this ingenuous Author, by whosoever is curious to learn the various revolutions of humane affairs. But, more es-*

pecially by our English Nation; as unto whom these things more narrowly do appertain. We having here more than half the Book filled with the unparallel'd, if not inimitable, adventures and Heroick exploits of our own Country-men, and Relations; whose undaunted, and exemplary courage, when called upon by our King and Country, we ought to emulate.

From whence it hath proceeded, that nothing of this kind was ever, as yet, published in England, I cannot easily determine; except, as some will say, from some secret Ragion di Stato. Let the reason be as t'will; this is certain, so much the more we are obliged unto this present Author, who though a stranger unto our Nation, yet with that Candour and Fidelity hath recorded our Actions, as to render the Metal of our true English Valour to be the more believed and feared abroad, than if these things had been divulged by our selves at home. From hence peradventure will other Nations learn, that the English people are of their Genius more inclinable to act than to write; seeing as well they as we have lived unacquainted with these actions of our Nation, until such time as a Foreign Author to our Country came to tell them.

Besides the merits of this Piece for its curiosity, another point of no less esteem, is the truth and sincerity wherewith everything seemeth to be penned. No greater ornament or dignity can be added unto History, either humane or natural, than truth. All other embellishments, if this be failing, are of little or no esteem; if this be delivered, are either needless or superfluous. What concerneth this requisite in our Author, his lines do every-where declare the faithfulness and sincerity of his mind. He writeth not by hearsay, but was an eye witness, as he somewhere telleth you, unto all and every one of the bold and hazardous attempts which he relateth. And these he delivereth with such candour of stile, such ingenuity of mind, such plainness of words, such conciseness of periods, so much divested of Rhetorical Hyberboles, or the least flourishes of Eloquence, so hugely void of Passion or national Reflections, as that he strongly perswadeth all-along to the credit of what he saith; yea, raiseth the mind of the Reader to believe these things far greater than what he hath said; and having read him, leaveth onely this scruple or concern behind, that you can read him no longer. In a word, such are his deserts, that some persons peradventure would not stickle to compare him to the Father of Historians, Philip de Comines; at least thus much may be said, with all truth imaginable, that he resembleth that great Author in many of his excellent qualities.

I know some persons have objected against the greatness of these prodigious Adventures, intimating that the resistance our Bucaniers found in America, was every-where but small. For the Spaniards, say they, in the West Indies, are become of late years nothing less, but rather much more degenerate than in Europe. The continual Peace they have enjoyed in those parts, the defect of Military Discipline, and European Souldiers for their Commanders, much contributing hereunto. But more especially, and above all other reasons, the very luxury of the Soil and Riches, the extreme heat of those Countries, and influence of the Stars being such, as totally inclineth their bodies unto an infinite effeminacy and cowardize of minds.

Unto these Reasons I shall only answer in brief. This History will convince them to be manifestly false. For as to the continual Peace here alleadged, we know that no Peace could ever be established beyond the Line, since the first possession of the West-Indies by the Spaniards, till the burning of Panama. At that time, or few months before, Sir William Godolphin by his prudent negotiation in quality of Embassadour for our most Gracious Monarch, did conclude at Madrid a peace to be observed even beyond the Line, and through the whole extent of the Spanish Dominions in the West-Indies. This transaction gave the Spaniards new causes of complaints against our proceedings, that no sooner a Peace had been established for those parts of America, but our forces had taken and burnt both Chagre, St. Catherine, and Panama. But our reply was convincing, That whereas eight or ten months of time had been allowed by Articles for the publishing of the said Peace through all the Dominions of both Monarchies in America, those Hostilities had been committed, not onely without orders from his Majesty of England, but also within the space of the said eight or ten months of time. Until that time the Spanish Inhabitants of America being, as it were, in a perpetual War with Europe, certain it is that no Coasts nor Kingdoms in the World have been more frequently infested nor alarm'd with the invasions of several Nations than theirs. Thus from the very beginning of their Conquests in America, both English, French, Dutch, Portuguese, Swedes, Danes, Curlanders, and all other nations that navigate the Ocean, have frequented the West-Indies, and filled them with their Robberies and Assaults. From these occasions have they been in continual watch and ward, and kept their Militia in constant exercise, as also their Garrisons pretty well provided and paid; as fearing every sail they discovered at Sea, to be Pirats of one Nation or another. But much more especially, since that Curasao, Tortuga, and Jamaica have been inhabited by English, French, and Dutch, and bred up that race of Hunts-men, than which, no other ever was more desperate, nor more mortal enemies to the Spaniards, called Bucaniers. Now shall we say, that these People, through too long continuation of Peace, have utterly abolished the exercises of War, having been all-along incessantly vexed with the Tumults and Alarms thereof?

In like manner is it false, to accuse their defect of Military Discipline for want of European Commanders. For who knoweth not that all places, both Military and Civil, through those vast dominions of the West-Indies, are provided out of Spain? And those of the Militia most commonly given unto expert Commanders, trained up from their infancy in the Wars of Europe, either in Africa, Milan, Sicily, Naples, or Flanders, fighting against either English, French, Dutch, Portuguese, or Moors? Yea, their very Garrisons, if you search them in those parts, will peradventure be found to be stock'd three parts to four with Souldiers both born and bred in the Kingdom of Spain.

From these Considerations it may be inferr'd, what little difference ought to be allowed betwixt the Spanish Souldiers, Inhabitants of the West-Indies, and those of Europe. And how little the Soil or Climate hath influenced or caused their Courage to degenerate towards cowardize or baseness of mind. As if the very same Argument, deduced from the nature of that Climate, did not equally militate against the valour of our famous Bucaniers, and represent this to be of as degenerate Metal as theirs.

But nothing can be more clearly evinced, than is the Valour of the American Spaniards, either Souldiers or Officers, by the sequel of this History. What men ever fought more desperately than the Garrison of Chagre? Their number being 314, and of all these, only thirty remaining; of which number scarce ten were unwounded; and among them, not one officer found alive? Were not 600 killed upon the spot at Panama, 500 at Gibraltar, almost as many more at Puerto del Principe, all dying with their Arms in their hands, and facing bravely the Enemy for the defence of their Country and private Concerns? Did not those of the Town of San Pedro both fortifie themselves, lay several Ambuscades, and lastly sell their lives as dear as any European Souldier could do; Lolonois being forced to gain step by step his advance unto the Town, with huge loss both of bloud and men? Many other instances might be produced out of this compendious Volume, of the generous resistance the Spaniards made in several places, though Fortune favoured not their Arms.

Next, as to the personal Valour of many of their Commanders, What man ever behaved himself more briskly than the Governour of Gibraltar, than the Governour of Puerto del Principe, both dying for the defence of their Towns; than Don Alonso del Campo, and others? Or what examples can easily parallel the desperate courage of the Governour of Chagre? who, though the Palizada's were fired, the Terraplens were sunk into the Ditch, the Breaches were entred, the Houses all burnt above him, the whole Castle taken, his men all killed; yet would not admit of any quarter, but chose rather to die under his Arms, being shot into the brain, than surrender himself as a Prisoner unto the Bucaniers. What Lion ever fought to the last gasp more obstinately than the Governour of Puerto Velo? who, seeing the Town enter'd by surprizal in the night, one chief Castle blown up into the Air, all the other Forts and Castles taken, his own assaulted several ways, both Religious men and women placed at the front of the Enemy to fix the Ladders against the Walls; yet spared not to kill as many of the said Religious persons as he could. And at last, the walls being scaled, the Castle enter'd and taken, all his own men overcome by fire and smord, who had cast down their Arms, and begged mercy from the Enemy; yet would admit of none for his own life. Yea, with his own hands killed several of his Souldiers, to force them to stand to their Arms, though all were lost. Yea, though his own Wife and Daughter begged of him upon their knees that he would save his life by craving quarter, though the Enemy desired of him the same thing; yet would hearken to no cries nor perswasions, but they were forced to kill him, combating with his Arms in his hands, being not otherwise able to take him Prisoner, as they were desirous to do. Shall these men be said to be influenced with Cowardize, who thus acted to the very last Scene of their own Tragedies? Or shall we rather say that they wanted not Courage, but Fortune? It being certainly true, that he who is killed in a Battel, may be equally couragious with him that killeth. And that whosoever derogateth from the Valour of the Spaniards in the West-Indies, diminisheth in like manner the Courage of the Bucanier,s his own Country-men, who have seemed to act beyond mortal men in America.

Now, to say something concerning John Esquemeling, *the first Author of this History. I take him to be a* Dutch-man, *or at least born in* Flanders, *notwithstanding that the Spanish Translation representeth him to be Native of the Kingdom of* France. *His printing this History originally in Dutch, which doubtless must be his native Tongue, who otherwise was but an illiterate man, together with the very sound of his name, convincing me thereunto. True it is, he set sail from* France, *and was some years at* Tortuga; *but neither of these two Arguments, drawn from the History, are prevalent. For were he to be a* French-man *born, how came he to learn the* Dutch *language so perfectly as to prefer it to his own? Especially that not being spoken at* Tortuga *nor* Jamaica, *where he resided all the while.*

I hope I have made this English Translation something more plain and correct than the Spanish. Some few notorious faults either of the Printer or the Interpreter, I am sure I have redressed. But the Spanish Translator complaining much of the intricacy of Stile in the Original (as flowing from a person who, as hath been said, was no Scholar) as he was pardonable, being in great haste, for not rendring his own Version so distinct and elaborate as he could desire; so must I be excused from the one, that is to say, Elegancy, if I have cautiously declined the other, I mean Confusion.

THE HISTORY

OF THE

BUCCANEERS OF AMERICA.

―•―

CHAPTER I.

The introduction—The author sets forth for the Western Islands, in the service of the West-India Company of France—They meet with an English frigate, and arrive at the Island of Tortuga.

E set sail from Havre-de-Grace in France, from whence we set sail in the ship called *St. John*, May 2, 1666. Our vessel was equipped with twenty-eight guns, twenty mariners, and two hundred and twenty passengers, including those whom the company sent as free passengers. Soon after we came to an anchor under the Cape of Barfleur, there to join seven other ships of the same West-India company, which were to come from Diep, under convoy of a man-of-war, mounted with thirty-seven guns, and two hundred and fifty men. Of these ships two were bound for Senegal, five for the Caribbee islands, and ours for Tortuga. Here gathered to us about twenty sail of other ships, bound for Newfoundland, with some Dutch vessels going for Nantz, Rochel, and St. Martin's, so that

in all we made thirty sail. Here we put ourselves in a posture of defence, having noticed that four English frigates, of sixty guns each, waited for us near Aldernay. Our admiral, the Chevalier Sourdis, having given necessary orders, we sailed thence with a favourable gale, and some mists arising, totally impeded the English frigates from discovering our fleet. We steered our course as near as we could to the coast of France, for fear of the enemy. As we sailed along, we met a vessel of Ostend, who complained to our admiral, that a French privateer had robbed him that very morning; whereupon we endeavoured to pursue the said pirate; but our labour was in vain, not being able to overtake him.

Our fleet, as we sailed, caused no small fears and alarms to the inhabitants of the coasts of France, these judging us to be English, and that we sought some convenient place for landing. To allay their fright, we hung out our colours; but they would not trust us. After this we came to an anchor in the bay of Conquet in Brittany, near Ushant, there to take in water. Having stored ourselves with fresh provisions here, we prosecuted our voyage, designing to pass by the Ras of Fontenau, and not expose ourselves to the Sorlingues, fearing the English that were cruising thereabouts. The river Ras is of a current very strong and rapid, which, rolling over many rocks, disgorges itself into the sea, on the coast of France, in 48 deg. 10 min. latitude; so that this passage is very dangerous, all the rocks, as yet, being not thoroughly known.

Here I shall mention the ceremony, which, at this passage, and some other places, is used by the mariners, and by them called baptism, though it may seem little to our purpose. The master's mate clothed himself with a ridiculous sort of garment, that reached to his feet, and on his head he put a suitable cap, made very burlesque;

in his right hand he had a naked wooden sword, and in his left a pot full of ink: his face was horribly blacked with soot, and his neck adorned with a collar of many little pieces of wood. Thus apparelled, he commanded every one to be called who had never passed through that dangerous place before; and then, causing them to kneel down, he made the sign of the cross on their foreheads, with ink, and gave every one a stroke on the shoulders with his wooden sword. Meanwhile, the standers-by cast a bucket of water upon each man's head; and so ended the ceremony. But that done, each of the baptized must give a bottle of brandy, placing it nigh the main-mast, without speaking a word; even those who have no such liquor not being excused. If the vessel never passed that way before, the captain is obliged to distribute some wine among the mariners and passengers; but as for other gifts, which the newly-baptized frequently offer, they are divided among the old seamen, and of them they make a banquet among themselves.

The Hollanders likewise, not only at this passage, but also at the rocks called Berlingues, nigh the coast of Portugal, in 39 deg. 40 min. (being a passage very dangerous, especially by night, when, in the dark, the rocks are not distinguishable, the land being very high) they use some such ceremony: but their manner of baptizing is very different from that of the French; for he that is to be baptized is fastened, and hoisted up thrice, at the main-yard's end, as if he were a criminal. If he be hoisted the fourth time, in the name of the Prince of Orange, or of the captain of the vessel, his honour is more than ordinary. Thus every one is dipped several times in the main ocean; but he that is dipped first has the honour of being saluted with a gun. Such as are not willing to fall, must pay twelve pence for ransom; if he be an officer, two shillings;

and if a passenger, at their own pleasure. If the ship never passed that way before, the captain is to give a small rundlet of wine, which, if he denies, the mariners may cut off the stem of the vessel. All the profit accruing by this ceremony is kept by the master's mate, who, after reaching their port, usually lays it out in wine, which is drank amongst the ancient seamen. Some say this ceremony was instituted by the Emperor Charles V. though it is not amongst his laws. But here I leave these sea customs, and return to our voyage.

Having passed the Ras, we had very good weather, till we came to Cape Finis Terræ: here a sudden tempest surprised us, and separated our ship from the rest that were in our company. This storm continued eight days; in which time it would move compassion to see how miserably the passengers were tumbled to and fro, on all sides of the ship; insomuch, that the mariners, in the performance of their duty, were compelled to tread upon them. This boisterous weather being over, we had very favourable gales again, till we came to the tropic of Cancer. This tropic is an imaginary circle, which astronomers have invented in the heavens, limiting the progress of the sun towards the north pole. It is placed in the latitude of 23 deg. 30 min. Here we were baptized a second time, as before. The French always perform this ceremony at the tropic of Cancer, as also under the tropic of Capricorn. In this part of the world we had very favourable weather, at which we were very glad, because of our great want of water; for that element was so scarce with us, that we were stinted to two half pints a man every day.

About the latitude of Barbadoes, we met an English frigate, or privateer, who first began to give us chase; but finding herself not to exceed us in force, presently got away: hereupon, we pursued her, firing several guns, eight-pounders, at her; but at length she escaped, and we returned to our course. Soon after, we came within sight of Martinico. We were bent to the coast of the isle of St. Peter, but were frustrated by a storm, which took us hereabouts. Hence we resolved to steer to Gaudaloupe, yet we could not reach this island, by reason of the said storm; so that we directed our course to the isle of Tortuga, being the very same land we were bound to. We passed along the coast of Punta Rica, which is extremely agreeable and delightful to the sight, being adorned with beautiful woods, even to the tops of the mountains. Then we discovered Hispaniola (of which I shall give a description), and we coasted about it till we came to Tortuga, our desired port. Here we anchored, July 7, in the same year, not having lost one man in the voyage. We landed the goods that belonged to the West-India company, and, soon after, the ship was sent to Cal de Sac with some passengers.

CHAPTER II.

A description of Tortuga—The fruits and plants there—How the French first settled there, at two several times, and forced out the Spaniards—The author twice sold in the said island.

THE island of Tortuga is situate on the north side of Hispaniola, in 20 deg. 30 min. latitude; its just extent is threescore leagues about. The Spaniards, who gave name to this island, called it so from the shape of the land, in some manner resembling a great sea-tortoise, called by them Tortuga-de-mar. The country is very mountainous, and full of rocks, and yet thick of lofty trees, that grow upon the hardest of those rocks, without partaking of a softer soil. Hence it comes that their roots, for the greatest part, are seen naked, entangled among the rocks like the branching of ivy against our walls That part of this island which stretches to the north is totally uninhabited: the reason is, first, because it is incommodious, and unhealthy: and, secondly, for the ruggedness of the coast, that gives no access to the shore, unless among rocks almost inaccessible: for this cause it is peopled only on the south part, which hath only one port indifferently good: yet this harbour has two entries, or channels, which afford passage to ships of seventy guns; the port itself being without danger, and capable of receiving a great number of vessels. The inhabited parts, of which the first is called the Low-Lands, or Low-Country: this is the chief among the rest, because it contains the port aforesaid. The town is called Cayona, and here live the chiefest and richest planters of the island. The second part is called the Middle Plantation : its soil is yet almost new, being only known to be good for tobacco. The third is named Ringot, and is situate towards the west part of the island. The fourth and last is called the Mountain, in which place were made the first plantations upon this island.

As to the wood that grows here, we have already said that the trees are exceeding tall, and pleasing to the sight ; whence no man will doubt, but they may be applied to several uses. Such is the yellow saunder, which by the inhabitants is called bois de chandel, or, in English, candle-wood, because it burns like a candle, and serves them with light while they fish by night. Here grows, also, lignum sanctum, or guiacum : its virtues are very well known, more especially to those who observe not the Seventh Commandment, and are given to impure copulations !—physicians drawing hence, in several compositions, the greatest antidote for venereal diseases ; as also for cold and viscous humours. The trees, likewise, which afford gummi elemi, grow here in great abundance ; as doth radix Chinæ, or China root : yet this is not so good as that of other parts of the western world. It is very white and soft, and serves for pleasant food to the wild boars, when they can find nothing else. This island, also, is not deficient in aloes, nor an infinite number of the other medicinal herbs, which may please the curiosity of such as are given to their contemplation : moreover, for building of ships, or any other sort of architecture, here are found several sorts of timber. The fruits, likewise, which grow here abundantly, are nothing inferior, in quantity or quality, to what other islands produce. I shall name only some of the most ordinary and common: such are magniot, potatoes, Abajou apples, yannas, bacones, paquays, carosoles, mamayns, annananes, and divers other sorts, which I omit to specify. Here grow likewise, in great numbers, those trees called palmitoes, or palmites, whence is drawn a certain juice which serves the inhabitants instead of wine, and whose leaves cover their houses instead of tiles.

In this island aboundeth, also, the wild boar. The governor hath prohibited the hunting of them with dogs, fearing lest, the island being but small, the whole race of them, in a short time, should be destroyed. The reason why he thought convenient to preserve these wild beasts was, that, in case of any invasion, the inhabitants might sustain themselves with their food, especially were they once constrained to retire to the woods and mountains. Yet this sort of game is almost impeded by itself, by reason of the many rocks and precipices, which, for the greatest part, are covered with little shrubs, very green and thick; whence the huntsmen have oftentimes fallen, and left us the sad remembrance of many a memorable disaster.

At a certain time of the year there resort to Tortuga large flocks of wild pigeons, and then the inhabitants feed on them very plentifully, having more than they can consume, and leaving totally to their repose all other sorts of fowl, both wild and tame; that so, in the absence of the pigeons, these may supply their place. But as nothing in the universe, though never so pleasant, can be found, but what hath something of bitterness with it; the very symbol of this truth we see in the aforesaid pigeons: for these, the season being past, can scarce be touched with the tongue, they become so extremely lean, and bitter even to admiration. The reason of this bitterness is attributed to a certain seed which they eat about that time, even as bitter as gall. About the sea-shores, everywhere, are found great multitudes of crabs, both of land and sea, and both sorts very big. These are good to feed servants and slaves, whose palates they please, but are very hurtful to the sight: besides, being eaten too often, they cause great giddiness in the head, with much weakness of the brain; so that, very frequently, they are deprived of sight for a quarter of an hour.

The French having settled in the isle of St. Christopher, planted there a sort of trees, of which, at present, there possibly may be greater quantities; with the timber whereof they made long-boats, and hoys, which they sent thence westward, well manned and victualled, to discover other islands. These setting sail from St. Christopher, came within sight of Hispaniola, where they arrived with abundance of joy. Having landed, they marched into the country, where they found large quantities of cattle; such as cows, bulls, horses, and wild boars: but finding no great profit in these animals, unless they could enclose them, and knowing, likewise, the island to be pretty well peopled by the Spaniards, they thought it convenient to enter upon and seize the island of Tortuga. This they performed without any difficulty, there being upon the island no more than ten or twelve Spaniards to guard it. These few men let the French come in peaceably, and possess the island for six months, without any trouble; meanwhile they passed and repassed, with their canoes, to Hispaniola, from whence they transported many people, and at last began to plant the whole island of Tortuga. The few Spaniards remaining there, perceiving the French to increase their number daily, began, at last, to repine at their prosperity, and grudge them the possession: hence they gave notice to others of their nation, their neighbours, who sent several boats, well armed and manned, to dispossess the French. This expedition succeeded according to their desires; for the new possessors, seeing the great number of Spaniards, fled with all they had to the woods, and hence, by night, they wafted over with canoes to the island of Hispaniola: this they the more easily performed, having no women or children with them, nor any great substance to carry away. Here they also retired into the woods, both to seek for food, and from thence, with secrecy, to give intelligence to others of their own faction; judging for certain, that within a little while they should be in a capacity to hinder the Spaniards from fortifying in Tortuga.

Meanwhile, the Spaniards of the great island ceased not to seek after their new guests, the French, with intent to root them out of the woods if possible, or cause them to perish with hunger; but this design soon failed, having found that the French were masters both of good guns, powder, and bullets. Here therefore the fugitives waited for a certain opportunity, wherein they knew the Spaniards were to come from Tortuga with arms, and a great number of men, to join with those of the greater island for their destruction. When this occasion offered, they in the meanwhile deserting the woods where they were, returned to Tortuga, and dispossessed the small number of Spaniards that remained at home. Having so done, they fortified themselves the best they could, thereby to prevent the return of the Spaniards in case they should attempt it. Moreover, they sent immediately to the governor of St. Christopher's, craving his aid and relief, and demanding of him a governor, the better to be united among themselves, and strengthened on all occasions. The governor of St. Christopher's received their petition with much satisfaction, and, without delay, sent Monsieur le Passeur to them in quality of a governor, together with a ship full of men, and all necessaries for their establishment and defence. No sooner had they received this recruit, but the governor commanded a fortress to be built upon the top of a high rock, from whence he could hinder the entrance of any ships or other vessels to the port. To this fort no other access could be had, than by almost climbing through a very narrow passage that was capable only of receiving two persons at once, and those not without difficulty. In the middle of this rock was a great cavity, which now serves for a storehouse: besides, here was great convenience for raising a battery. The fort being finished, the governor commanded two guns to be mounted, which could not be done without great toil and labour; as also a house to be built within the fort, and afterwards the narrow way, that led to the said fort, to be broken and demolished, leaving no other ascent thereto than by a ladder. Within the fort gushes out a plentiful fountain of pure fresh water, sufficient to refresh a garrison of a thousand men. Being possessed of these conveniences, and the security these things might promise, the French began to people the island, and each of them to seek their living; some by hunting, others by planting tobacco, and others by cruizing and robbing upon the coasts of the Spanish islands, which trade is continued by them to this day.

The Spaniards, notwithstanding, could not behold, but with jealous eyes, the daily increase of the French in Tortuga, fearing lest, in time, they might by them be dispossessed also of Hispaniola. Thus taking an opportunity (when many of the French were abroad at sea, and others employed in hunting), with eight hundred men, in several canoes, they landed again in Tortuga, almost without being perceived by the French; but finding that the governor had cut down many trees for the better discovery of any enemy in case of an assault, as also that nothing of consequence could be done without great guns, they consulted about the fittest place for raising a battery. This place was soon concluded to be the top of a mountain which was in sight, seeing that from thence alone they could level their guns at the fort, which now lay open to them since the cutting down of the trees by the new possessors. Hence they resolved to open a way for the carriage of some pieces of ordnance to the top. This mountain is somewhat high, and the upper part thereof plain, from whence the whole island may be viewed: the sides thereof are very rugged, by reason a great number of inaccessible rocks do surround it; so that the ascent was very difficult, and would always have been the same, had not the Spaniards undergone the immense labour and toil of making the way before mentioned, as I shall now relate.

The Spaniards had with them many slaves and Indians, labouring men, whom they call matades, or, in English, half-yellow men; these they ordered with iron tools to dig a way through the rocks. This they performed with the greatest speed imaginable; and through this way, by the help of many ropes and pulleys, they at last made shift to get up two pieces of ordnance, wherewith they made a battery next day, to play on the fort. Meanwhile, the French knowing these designs, prepared for a defence (while the Spaniards were busy about the battery) sending notice everywhere to their companions for help. Thus the hunters of the island all joined together, and with them all the pirates who were not already too far from home. These landed by night at Tortuga, lest they should be seen by the Spaniards; and, under the same obscurity of the night, they all together, by a back way, climbed the mountain where the Spaniards were posted, which they did the more easily being acquainted with these rocks. They came up at the very instant that the Spaniards, who were above, were preparing to shoot at the fort, not knowing in the least of their coming. Here they set upon them at their backs with such fury as forced the greatest part to precipitate themselves from the top to the bottom, and dash their bodies in pieces: few or none escaped; for if any remained alive, they were put to the sword. Some Spaniards did still keep the bottom of the mountain; but these, hearing the shrieks and cries of them that were killed, and believing some tragical revolution to be above, fled immediately towards the sea, despairing ever to regain the island of Tortuga.

The governors of this island behaved themselves as proprietors and absolute lords thereof till 1664, when the West-India company of France took possession thereof, and sent thither, for their governor, Monsieur Ogeron. These planted the colony for themselves by their factors and servants, thinking to drive some considerable trade from thence with the Spaniards, even as the Hollanders do from Curacao: but this design did not answer; for with other nations they could drive no trade, by reason they could not establish any secure commerce from the beginning with their own; forasmuch as at the first institution of this company in France they agreed with the pirates, hunters, and planters, first possessors of Tortuga, that these should buy all their necessaries from the said company upon trust. And though this agreement was put in execution, yet the factors of the company soon after found that they could not recover either monies or returns from those people, that they were constrained to bring some armed men into the island, in behalf of the company, to get in some of their payments. But neither this endeavour, nor any other, could prevail towards the settling a second trade with those of the island. Hereupon, the company recalled their factors, giving them orders to sell all that was their own in the said plantation, both the servants belonging to the company (which were sold, some for twenty, and others for thirty pieces of eight), as also all other merchandizes and proprieties. And thus all their designs fell to the ground.

On this occasion I was also sold, being a servant under the said company in whose service I left France: but my fortune was very bad, for I fell into the hands of the most cruel and perfidious man that ever was born, who was then governor, or rather lieutenant-general, of that island. This man treated me with all the hard usage imaginable, yea, with that of hunger, with which I thought I should have perished inevitably. Withal, he was willing to let me buy my freedom and liberty, but not under the rate of three hundred pieces of eight, I not being master of one at a time in the world. At last, through the manifold miseries I endured, as also affliction of mind, I was thrown into a dangerous sickness. This misfortune, added to the rest, was the cause of my happiness: for my wicked master, seeing my condition, began to fear lest he should lose his monies with my life. Hereupon he sold me a second time to a surgeon, for seventy pieces of eight. Being with this second master, I began soon to recover my health through the good usage I received, he being much more humane and civil than my first patron. He gave me both clothes and very good food; and after I had served him but one year, he offered me my liberty, with only this condition, that I should pay him one hundred pieces of eight when I was in a capacity so to do; which kind proposal of his I could not but accept with infinite joy and gratitude.

Being now at liberty, though like Adam when he was first created — that is, naked and destitute of all human necessaries — not knowing how to get my living,

I determined to enter into the order of the pirates or robbers at sea. Into this society I was received with common consent, both of the superior and vulgar sort, where I continued till 1672. Having assisted them in all their designs and attempts, and served them in many notable exploits (of which hereafter I shall give the reader a true account), I returned to my own native country. But before I begin my relation, I shall say something of the island Hispaniola, which lies towards the western part of America; as also give my reader a brief description thereof, according to my slender ability and experience.

CHAPTER III.

A Description of Hispaniola.—A Relation of the French Buccaneers.

THE large and rich island called Hispaniola is situate from 17 degrees to 19 degrees latitude; the circumference is 300 leagues; the extent from east to west 120; its breadth almost 50, being broader or narrower at certain places. This island was first discovered by Christopher Columbus, A.D. 1492; he being sent for this purpose by Ferdinand, king of Spain; from which time to this present the Spaniards have been continually possessors thereof. There are upon this island very good and strong cities, towns, and hamlets, as well as a great number of pleasant country houses and plantations, the effects of the care and industry of the Spaniards its inhabitants.

The chief city and metropolis hereof is Santo Domingo; being dedicated to St. Dominic, from whom it derives its name. It is situate towards the south, and affords a most excellent prospect; the country round about being embellished with innumerable rich plantations, as also verdant meadows and fruitful gardens; all which produce plenty and variety of excellent pleasant fruits, according to the nature of those countries. The governor of the island resides in this city, which is, as it were, the storehouse of all the cities, towns, and villages, which hence export and provide themselves with all necessaries for human life;

and yet hath it this particularity above many other cities, that it entertains no commerce with any nation but its own, the Spaniards. The greatest part of the inhabitants are rich and substantial merchants or shopkeepers.

Another city of this island is San Jago, or St. James, being consecrated to that apostle. This is an open place, without walls or castle, situate in 19 deg. latitude. The inhabitants are generally hunters and planters, the adjacent territory and soil being very proper for the said exercises: the city is surrounded with large and delicious fields, as much pleasing to the view as those of Santo Domingo; and these abound with beasts both wild and tame, yielding vast numbers of skins and hides, very profitable to the owners.

In the south part of this island is another city, called Nuestra Sennora de Alta Gracia. This territory produces great quantities of cacao, whereof the inhabitants make great store of the richest chocolate. Here grows also ginger and tobacco, and much tallow is made of the beasts which are hereabouts hunted.

The inhabitants of this beautiful island of Hispaniola often resort in their canoes to the isle of Savona, not far distant, where is their chief fishery, especially of tortoises. Hither those fish constantly resort in great multitudes, at certain seasons, there to lay their eggs, burying them in the sands of the shoal, where, by the heat of the sun, which in those parts is very ardent, they are hatched. This island of Savona has little or nothing that is worthy consideration, being so very barren by reason of its sandy soil. True it is, that here grows some small quantity of lignum sanctum, or guaiacum, of whose use we say something in another place.

Westward of Santo Domingo is another great village called El Pueblo de Aso, or the town of Aso: the inhabitants thereof drive great traffic with those of another village, in the very middle of the island, and is called San Juan de Goave, or St. John of Goave. This is environed with a magnificent prospect of gardens, woods, and meadows. Its territory extends above twenty leagues in length, and grazes a great number of wild bulls and cows. In this village scarce dwell any others than hunters and butchers, who flay the beasts that are killed. These are for the most part a mongrel sort of people; some of which are born of white European people and negroes, and called mulattoes: others of Indians and white people, and termed mesticos: but others come of negroes and Indians, and are called alcatraces. Besides which sorts of people there are several other species and races, both here and in other places of the West Indies, of whom this account may be given—That the Spaniards love better the negro women in those western parts, or the tawny Indian females, than their own white European race; when as, peradventure, the negroes and Indians have greater inclinations to the white women, or those that come near them, the tawny, than their own. From the said village are exported yearly vast quantities of tallow and hides, they exercising no other traffic: for as to the lands in this place, they are not cultivated, by reason of the excessive dryness of the soil. These are the chiefest places that the Spaniards possess in this island, from the Cape of Lobos towards St. John de Goave, unto the Cape of Samana nigh the sea, on the north side, and from the eastern part towards the sea, called Punta de Espada. All the rest of the island is possessed by the French, who are also planters and hunters.

This island hath very good ports for ships, from the Cape of Lobos to the Cape of Tiburon, on the west side thereof. In this space there are no less than four ports, exceeding in goodness, largeness, and security, even the very best of England. Besides these, from the Cape of Tiburon to the Cape of Donna Maria, there are two very excellent ports; and from this cape to the Cape of St. Nicholas, there are no less than twelve others. Every one of these ports hath also the confluence of two or three good rivers, in which are great plenty of several sorts of fish very pleasing to the palate. The country hereabouts is well watered with large and deep rivers and brooks, so that this part of the land may easily be cultivated without any great fear of droughts, because of these excellent streams. The sea-coasts and shores are also very pleasant, to which the tortoises resort in large numbers to lay their eggs.

This island was formerly very well peopled, on the north side, with many towns and villages; but these, being ruined by the Hollanders, were at last, for the greatest part, deserted by the Spaniards.

The spacious fields of this island commonly are five or six leagues in length, the beauty whereof is so pleasing to the eye, that, together with the great variety of their natural productions, they captivate the senses of the beholder. For here at once they not only with diversity of objects recreate the sight, but with many of the same do also please the smell, and with most contribute delights to the taste; also they flatter and excite the appetite, especially with the multitudes of oranges and lemons here growing, both sweet and sour, and those that participate of both tastes, and are only pleasantly tartish. Besides here abundantly grow several sorts of fruit, such are citrons, toronjas, and limas; in English not improperly called crab lemons.

Beside the fruits which this island produces, whose plenty, as is said, surpasses all the islands of America; it abounds also with all sorts of quadrupeds, as horses, bulls, cows, wild boars, and others, very useful to mankind, not only for food, but for cultivating the ground, and the management of commerce.

Here are vast numbers of wild dogs: these destroy yearly many cattle; for no sooner hath a cow calved, or a mare foaled, but these wild mastiffs devour the young, if they find not resistance from keepers and domestic dogs. They run up and down the woods and fields, commonly fifty, threescore, or more, together; being withal so fierce, that they will often assault an entire herd of wild boars, not ceasing to worry them till they have fetched down two or three. One day a French buccaneer showed me a strange action of this kind: being in the fields a-hunting together, we heard a great noise of dogs which had surrounded a wild boar: having tame dogs with us, we left them to the custody of our servants, being desirous to see the sport. Hence my companion and I climbed up two several trees, both for security and prospect. The wild boar, all alone, stood against a tree, defending himself with his tusks from a great number of dogs that enclosed him; killed with his teeth, and wounded several of them. This bloody fight continued about an hour; the wild boar, meanwhile, attempting many times to escape. At last flying, one dog, leaping upon his back, fastened on his testicles, which at one pull he tore in pieces. The rest of the dogs, perceiving the courage of their companion, fastened likewise on the boar, and presently killed him. This done, all of them, the first only excepted, laid themselves down upon the ground about the prey, and there peaceably continued, till he, the first and most courageous of the troop, had ate as much as he could: when this dog had left off, all the rest fell in to take their share, till nothing was left. What ought we to infer from this notable action, performed by wild

animals, but this: that even beasts themselves are not
destitute of knowledge, and that they give us documents
how to honour such as have deserved well; even since
these irrational animals did reverence and respect him
that exposed his life to the greatest danger against the
common enemy?

The governor of Tortuga, Monsieur Ogeron, finding that
the wild dogs killed so many of the wild boars, that the
hunters of that island had much ado to find any; fearing
lest that common sustenance of the island should fail, sent
for a great quantity of poison from France to destroy the
wild mastiffs: this was done, A.D. 1668, by commanding
horses to be killed, and empoisoned, and laid open at
certain places where the wild dogs used to resort. This
being continued for six months, there were killed an
incredible number; and yet all this could not exterminate
and destroy the race, or scarce diminish them; their
number appearing almost as large as before. These wild
dogs are easily tamed among men, even as tame as
ordinary house dogs. The hunters of those parts, whenever they find a wild bitch with whelps, commonly take
away the puppies, and bring them home; which being
grown up, they hunt much better than other dogs.

But here the curious reader may perhaps inquire how
so many wild dogs came here. The occasion was, the
Spaniards having possessed these isles, found them peopled
with Indians, a barbarous people, sensual and brutish,
hating all labour, and only inclined to killing, and making
war against their neighbours; not out of ambition, but
only because they agreed not with themselves in some
common terms of language; and perceiving the dominion
of the Spaniards laid great restrictions upon their lazy
and brutish customs, they conceived an irreconcilable
hatred against them; but especially because they saw

them take possession of their kingdoms and dominions. Hereupon, they made against them all the resistance they could, opposing everywhere their designs to the utmost: and the Spaniards finding themselves cruelly hated by the Indians, and nowhere secure from their treacheries, resolved to extirpate and ruin them, since they could neither tame them by civility, nor conquer them with the sword. But the Indians, it being their custom to make the woods their chief places of defence, at present made these their refuge, whenever they fled from the Spaniards. Hereupon, those first conquerors of the New World made use of dogs to range and search the intricatest thickets of woods and forests for those their implacable and unconquerable enemies: thus they forced them to leave their old refuge, and submit to the sword, seeing no milder usage would do it; hereupon they killed some of them, and quartering their bodies, placed them in the highways, that others might take warning from such a punishment; but this severity proved of ill consequence, for instead of frighting them and reducing them to civility, they conceived such horror of the Spaniards, that they resolved to detest and fly their sight for ever; hence the greatest part died in caves and subterraneous places of the woods and mountains, in which places I myself have often seen great numbers of human bones. The Spaniards finding no more Indians to appear about the woods, turned away a great number of dogs they had in their houses, and they finding no masters to keep them, betook themselves to the woods and fields to hunt for food to preserve their lives; thus by degrees they became unacquainted with houses, and grew wild. This is the truest account I can give of the multitudes of wild dogs in these parts.

But besides these wild mastiffs, here are also great numbers of wild horses everywhere all over the island:

they are but low of stature, short bodied, with great heads, long necks, and big or thick legs: in a word, they have nothing handsome in their shape. They run up and down commonly in troops of two or three hundred together, one going always before to lead the multitude; when they meet any person travelling through the woods or fields, they stand still, suffering him to approach till he can almost touch them: and then suddenly starting, they betake themselves to flight, running away as fast as they can. The hunters catch them only for their skins, though sometimes they preserve their flesh likewise, which they harden with smoke, using it for provisions when they go to sea.

Here would be also wild bulls and cows in great number, if by continual hunting they were not much diminished; yet considerable profit is made to this day by such as make it their business to kill them. The wild bulls are of a vast bigness of body, and yet they hurt not any one except they be exasperated. Their hides are from eleven to thirteen feet long.

It is now time to speak of the French who inhabit great part of this island. We have already told how they came first into these parts: we shall now only describe their manner of living, customs, and ordinary employments. The callings or professions they follow are generally but three, either to hunt or plant, or else to rove the seas as pirates. It is a constant custom among them all, to seek out a comrade or companion, whom we may call partner in their fortunes, with whom they join the whole stock of what they possess towards a common gain. This is done by articles agreed to, and reciprocally signed. Some constitute their surviving companion absolute heir to what is left by the death of the first: others, if they be married, leave their estates to their wives and children; others, to other relations. This done, every one applies himself to his calling, which is always one of the three afore-mentioned.

The hunters are again subdivided into two sorts; for some of these only hunt wild bulls and cows, others only wild boars. The first of these are called bucaniers, and not long ago were about six hundred on this island, but now they are reckoned about three hundred. The cause has been the great decrease of wild cattle, which has been such, that, far from getting, they now are but poor in their trade. When the bucaniers go into the woods to hunt for wild bulls and cows, they commonly remain there a twelvemonth or two years, without returning home. After the hunt is over, and the spoil divided, they commonly sail to Tortuga, to provide themselves with guns, powder, and shot, and other necessaries for another expedition; the rest of their gains they spend prodigally, giving themselves to all manner of vices and debauchery, particularly to drunkenness, which they practise mostly with brandy: this they drink as liberally as the Spaniards do water. Sometimes they buy together a pipe of wine; this they stave at one end, and never cease drinking till it is out. Thus sottishly they live till they have no money left, and as freely gratify their lusts; for which they find more women than they can use; for all the tavern-keepers and strumpets wait for these lewd bucaniers just as they do at Amsterdam for the arrival of the East India fleet. The said bucaniers are very cruel and tyrannical to their servants, so that commonly they had rather be galley-slaves, or saw Brazil wood in the rasphouses of Holland, than serve such barbarous masters.

The second sort hunt nothing but wild boars; the flesh of these they salt, and sell it so to the planters. These hunters have the same vicious customs, and are as much addicted to debauchery as the former; but their manner of hunting is different from that in Europe; for these bucaniers have certain places designed for hunting, where they live for three or four months, and sometimes a whole year. Such places are called deza boulan; and in these, with only the company of five or six friends, they continue all the said time in mutual friendship. The first bucaniers many times agree with planters to furnish them with meat all the year at a certain price: the payment hereof is often made with two or three hundredweight of tobacco in the leaf; but the planters commonly into the bargain furnish them with a servant, whom they send to help. To the servant they afford sufficient necessaries for the purpose, especially of powder and shot to hunt withal.

The planters here have but very few slaves; for want of which, themselves and their servants are constrained to do all the drudgery. These servants commonly bind themselves to their masters for three years; but their masters, having no consciences, often traffic with their bodies, as with horses at a fair, selling them to other masters as they sell negroes. Yea, to advance this trade, some persons go purposely into France (and likewise to England, and other countries) to pick up young men or boys, whom they inveigle and transport; and having once got them into these islands, they work them like horses, the toil imposed on them being much harder than what they enjoin the negroes, their slaves; for these they endeavour to preserve, being their perpetual bondmen: but for their white servants, they care not whether they live or die, seeing they are to serve them no longer than three years. These miserable kidnapped people are frequently subject to a disease, which in these parts is called coma, being a total privation of their senses. This distemper is judged to proceed from their hard usage, and

the change of their native climate; and there being often
among these some of good quality, tender education, and
soft constitutions, they are more easily seized with this
disease, and others of those countries, than those of harder
bodies, and laborious lives. Beside the hard usage in
their diet, apparel, and rest, many times they beat them
so cruelly, that they fall down dead under the hands of
their cruel masters. This I have often seen with great
grief. Of the many instances, I shall only give you the
following history, it being remarkable in its circumstances.

A certain planter of these countries exercised such
cruelty towards one of his servants, as caused him to run
away. Having absconded, for some days, in the woods,
at last he was taken, and brought back to the wicked
Pharaoh. No sooner had he got him, but he commanded
him to be tied to a tree; here he gave him so many
lashes on his naked back, as made his body run with an
entire stream of blood; then, to make the smart of his
wounds the greater, he anointed him with lemon-juice,
mixed with salt and pepper. In this miserable posture he
left him tied to the tree for twenty-four hours, which being
past, he began his punishment again, lashing him, as
before, so cruelly, that the miserable wretch gave up the
ghost, with these dying words: " I beseech the Almighty
God, creator of heaven and earth, that he permit the
wicked spirit to make thee feel as many torments before
thy death, as thou hast caused me to feel before mine."
A strange thing, and worthy of astonishment and admiration! Scarce three or four days were past, after this
horrible fact, when the Almighty Judge, who had heard
the cries of the tormented wretch, suffered the evil one
suddenly to possess this barbarous and inhuman homicide,
so that those cruel hands which had punished to death
his innocent servant, were the tormentors of his own body:

for he beat himself, and tore his flesh, after a miserable manner, till he lost the very shape of a man; not ceasing to howl and cry, without any rest by day or night. Thus he continued raving mad, till he died. Many other examples of this kind I could rehearse; but these not belonging to our present discourse, I omit them.

The planters of the Carribbee islands are rather worse, and more cruel to their servants, than the former. In the isle of St. Christopher dwells one named Bettesa, well known to the Dutch merchants, who has killed above a hundred of his servants with blows and stripes. The English do the same with their servants; and the mildest cruelty they exercise towards them is, that when they have served six years of their time (they being bound among the English for seven) they use them so cruelly, as to force them to beg of their masters to sell them to others, though it be to begin another servitude of seven years, or at least three or four. And I have known many, who have thus served fifteen or twenty years, before they could obtain their freedom. Another law, very rigorous in that nation, is, if any man owes another above twenty-five shillings English, if he cannot pay it, he is liable to be sold for six or eight months. Not to trouble the reader any longer with relations of this kind, I shall now describe the famous actions and exploits of the greatest pirates of my time, during my residence in those parts: these I shall relate without the least passion or partiality, and assure my reader that I shall give him no stories upon trust, or hearsay, but only those enterprises to which I was myself an eye-witness.

CHAPTER IV.

Original of the most famous pirates of the coasts of America—Famous exploit of Pierre le Grand.

I HAVE told you in the preceding chapters how I was compelled to adventure my life among the pirates of America; which sort of men I name so, because they are not authorized by any sovereign prince: for the kings of Spain having on several occasions sent their ambassadors to the kings of England and France, to complain of the molestations and troubles those pirates often caused on the coasts of America, even in the calm of peace; it hath always been answered, "that such men did not commit those acts of hostility and piracy as subjects to their majesties; and therefore his Catholic Majesty might proceed against them as he should think fit." The king of France added, "that he had no fortress nor castle upon Hispaniola, neither did he receive a farthing of tribute from thence." And the king of England adjoined, "that he had never given any commissions to those of Jamaica, to commit hostilities against the subjects of his Catholic Majesty." Nor did he only give this bare answer, but out of his royal desire to pleasure the court of Spain, recalled the governor of Jamaica, placing another in his room; all which could not prevent these pirates from acting as heretofore. But before I relate their bold actions, I shall say something of their rise and exercises; as also of the chiefest of them, and their manner of arming themselves before they put to sea.

The first pirate that was known upon Tortuga was Pierre le Grand, or Peter the Great. He was born at Dieppe in Normandy. That action which rendered him famous was his taking the vice-admiral of the Spanish flota, near the Cape of Tiburon, on the west side of Hispaniola; this he performed with only one boat, and twenty-eight men. Now till that time the Spaniards had passed and repassed with all security, through the channel of Bahama; so that Pierre le Grand setting out to sea by the Caycos, he took this great ship with all the ease imaginable. The Spaniards they found aboard they set ashore, and sent the vessel to France. The manner how this undaunted spirit attempted and took this large ship I shall give you, out of the journal of the author, in his own words. "The boat," says he, "wherein Pierre le Grand was with his companions, had been at sea a long time without finding any prize worth his taking; and their provisions beginning to fail, they were in danger of starving. Being almost reduced to despair, they spied a great ship of the Spanish flota, separated from the rest; this vessel they resolved to take, or die in the attempt. Hereupon, they sailed towards her, to view her strength. And though they judged the vessel to be superior to theirs, yet their covetousness, and the extremity they were reduced to, made them venture. Being come so near that they could not possibly escape, they made an oath to their captain, Pierre le Grand, to stand by him to the last. 'Tis true, the pirates did believe they should find the ship unprovided to fight, and thereby the sooner master her. It was in the dusk of the evening they began to attack; but before they engaged, they ordered the surgeon of the boat to bore a hole in the sides of it, that their own vessel sinking under them, they might be compelled to attack more vigorously, and endeavour more hastily to board the ship. This was done accordingly, and without any other arms than a pistol in one hand and a sword in the other, they immediately climbed up the sides of the ship, and ran altogether into the great cabin, where they found the captain, with several of his companions, playing at cards. Here they set a pistol to his breast, commanding him to deliver up the ship. The Spaniards, surprised to see the pirates on board their ship, cried 'Jesus bless us! are these devils, or what are they?' Meanwhile some of them took possession of the gun-room, and seized the arms, killing as many as made any opposition; whereupon the Spaniards presently surrendered. That very day the captain of the ship had been told by some of the seamen that the boat which was in view, cruising, was a boat of pirates; whom the captain slightly answered, 'What then, must I be afraid of such a pitiful thing as that is? No, though she were a ship as big and as strong as mine is.' As soon as Pierre le Grand had taken this rich prize, he detained in his service as many of the common seamen as he had need of, setting the rest ashore, and then set sail for France, where he continued, without ever returning to America again."

The planters and hunters of Tortuga had no sooner heard of the rich prize those pirates had taken, but they resolved to follow their example. Hereupon, many of them left their employments, and endeavoured to get some small boats, wherein to exercise piracy; but not being able to purchase, or build them at Tortuga, they resolved to set forth in their canoes, and seek them elsewhere. With these they cruised at first upon Cape de Alvarez, where the Spaniards used to trade from one city to another in small vessels, in which they carry hides, tobacco, and other commodities, to the Havannah, and to which the Spaniards from Europe do frequently resort.

Here it was that those pirates at first took a great many boats laden with the aforesaid commodities; these they used to carry to Tortuga, and sell the whole purchase to the ships that waited for their return, or accidentally happened to be there. With the gains of these prizes they provided themselves with necessaries, wherewith to undertake other voyages, some of which were made to Campechy, and others toward New Spain; in both which the Spaniards then drove a great trade. Upon those coasts they found great numbers of trading vessels, and often ships of great burden. Two of the biggest of these vessels, and two great ships which the Spaniards had laden with plate in the port of Campechy, to go to the Caraccas, they took in less than a month's time, and carried to Tortuga; where the people of the whole island, encouraged by their success, especially seeing in two years the riches of the country so much increased, they augmented the number of pirates so fast, that in a little time there were, in that small island and port, above twenty ships of this sort of people. Hereupon the Spaniards, not able to bear their robberies any longer, equipped two large men-of-war, both for the defence of their own coasts, and to cruise upon the enemies.

CHAPTER V.

How the pirates arm their vessels, and regulate their voyages.

BEFORE the pirates go to sea, they give notice to all concerned, of the day on which they are to embark; obliging each man to bring so many pounds of powder and ball as they think necessary. Being all come aboard, they consider where to get provisions, especially flesh, seeing they scarce eat anything else; and of this the most common sort is pork; the next food is tortoises, which they salt a little: sometimes they rob such or such hog-yards, where the Spaniards often have a thousand head of swine together. They come to these places in the night, and having beset the keeper's lodge, they force him to rise, and give them as many heads as they desire, threatening to kill him if he refuses, or makes any noise; and these menaces are oftentimes executed on the miserable swine-keepers, or any other person that endeavours to hinder their robberies.

Having got flesh sufficient for their voyage, they return to their ship: here they allow, twice a day, every one as much as he can eat, without weight or measure; nor does the steward of the vessel give any more flesh, or anything else, to the captain, than to the meanest mariner. The ship being well victualled, they deliberate whither they shall go to seek their desperate fortunes, and likewise agree upon certain articles, which are put in writing, which every one is bound to observe; and all of them, or the chiefest part, do set their hands to it. Here they set down distinctly what sums of money each particular person ought to have for that voyage, the fund of all the payments being what is gotten by the whole expedition; for otherwise it is the same law among these people as with other pirates, No prey, no pay. First, therefore, they mention how much the captain is to have for his ship; next, the salary of the carpenter, or shipwright, who careened, mended, and rigged the vessel: this commonly amounts to one hundred or one hundred and fifty pieces of eight, according to the agreement. Afterwards, for provisions and victualling, they draw out of the same common stock about two hundred pieces of eight; also a salary for the surgeon, and his chest of medicaments, which usually is rated at two hundred or two hundred and fifty pieces of eight. Lastly, they agree what rate each one ought to have that is either wounded or maimed in his body, suffering the loss of any limb; as, for the loss of a right arm, six hundred pieces of eight, or six slaves; for the left arm, five hundred pieces of eight, or five slaves; for a right leg, five hundred pieces of eight, or five slaves; for the left leg, four hundred pieces of eight, or four slaves; for an eye, one hundred pieces of eight, or one slave; for a finger, the same as for an eye. All which sums are taken out of the common stock of what is gotten by their piracy, and a very exact and equal dividend is made of the remainder. They have also regard to qualities and places: thus the captain, or chief, is allotted five or six portions, to what the ordinary seamen have: the master's mate only two, and other officers proportionably to their employ: after which, they draw equal parts from the highest to the lowest mariner, the boys not being omitted, who draw half a share; because when they take a better vessel than their own, it is in the boys' duty to fire their former vessel, and then retire to the prize.

They observe among themselves very good orders; for in the prizes which they take, it is severely prohibited, to every one, to take anything to themselves: hence all they take is equally divided, as hath been said before: yea, they take a solemn oath to each other, not to conceal the least thing they find among the prizes; and if any one is found false to the said oath, he is immediately turned out of the society. They are very civil and charitable to each other; so that if any one wants what another has, with great willingness they give it one to another. As soon as these pirates have taken a prize, they immediately set ashore the prisoners, detaining only some few, for their own help and service: whom, also, they release, after two or three years. They refresh themselves at one island or another, but especially at those on the south of Cuba; here they careen their vessels, while some hunt, and others cruise in canoes for prizes.

The inhabitants of New Spain and Campechy lade their best merchandize in ships of great bulk: the vessels from Campechy sail in the winter to Caraccas, Trinity isles, and that of Margarita, and return back again in the summer. The pirates knowing these seasons (being very diligent in their inquiries) always cruise between the places abovementioned; but in case they light on no considerable booty, they commonly undertake some more hazardous enterprises: one remarkable instance of which I shall here give you.

A certain pirate called Pierre Francois, or Peter Francis, waiting a long time at sea with his boat and twenty-six men, for the ships that were to return from Maracaibo to Campheoy, and not being able to find any prey, at last he resolved to direct his course to Rancheiras, near the River de la Plata, in 12 deg. and a half north latitude. Here lies a rich bank of pearl, to the fishery whereof they yearly sent from Carthagena twelve vessels with a man-of-war for their defence. Every vessel has at least two negroes in it, who are very dextrous in diving to the depth of six fathoms, where they find good store of pearls. On this fleet, called the pearl-fleet, Pierre Francois resolved to venture, rather than go home empty; they then rid at anchor at the mouth of the River de la Hacha, the man-of-war scarce half a league distant from the small ships, and the wind very calm. Having spied them in this posture, he presently pulled down his sails, and rowed along the coast feigning to be a Spanish vessel coming from Maracaibo; but no sooner was he come to the pearl-bank, when suddenly he assaulted the vice-admiral of eight guns and sixty men, commanding them to surrender. The Spaniards made a good defence for some time, but at last were forced to submit.

Having thus taken the vice-admiral, he resolved to attempt the man-of-war, with which addition he hoped to master the rest of the fleet: to this end he presently sunk his own boat, putting forth the Spanish colours, and weighed anchor with a little wind which then began to stir, having with threats and promises compelled most of the Spaniards to assist him: but so soon as the man-of-war perceived one of his fleet to sail, he did so too, fearing lest the mariners designed to run away with the riches they had on board. The pirate on this immediately gave over the enterprise, thinking themselves unable to encounter force to force: hereupon they endeavoured to get out of the river and gain the open seas, by making as much sail as they could; which the man-of-war perceiving, he presently gave them chase, but the pirates having laid on too much sail, and a gust of wind suddenly rising, their main-mast was brought by the board, which disabled them from escaping.

This unhappy event much encouraged those in the man-of-war, they gaining upon the pirates every moment, and at last overtook them; but they finding they had twenty-two sound men, the rest being either killed or wounded, resolved to defend themselves as long as possible; this they performed very courageously for some time, till they were forced by the man-of-war, on condition that they should not be used as slaves to carry stones, or be employed in other labours for three or four years, as they served their negroes, but that they should be set safe ashore on free land. On these articles they yielded with all they had taken, which was worth, in pearls alone, above 100,000 pieces of eight, besides the vessel, provisions, goods, &c. All which would have made this a greater prize than he could desire, which he had certainly carried off, if his main-mast had not been lost, as we said before.

Another bold attempt like this, no less remarkable, I shall also give you. A certain pirate of Portugal, thence called Bartholomew Portugues, was cruising in a boat of thirty men and four small guns from Jamaica, upon the Cape de Corriente in Cuba, where he met a great ship from Maracaibo and Carthagena, bound for the Havannah, well provided with twenty great guns and seventy men, passengers and mariners; this ship he presently assaulted, which they on board as resolutely defended. The pirate escaping the first encounter, resolved to attack her more vigorously than before, seeing he had yet suffered no great damage: this he performed with so much resolution, that at last, after a long and dangerous fight, he became master of it. The Portuguese lost only ten men, and had four wounded; so that he had still remaining twenty fighting men, whereas the Spaniards had double the number.

BARTHOLOMEW PORTUGES.
(From the Portrait in "De Americaensche Roovers.")

Having possessed themselves of the ship, the wind being contrary to return to Jamaica, they resolved to steer to Cape St. Anthony (which lies west of Cuba), there to repair and take in fresh water, of which they were then in great want.

Being very near the cape abovesaid, they unexpectedly met with three great ships coming from New Spain, and bound for the Havannah; by these not being able to escape, they were easily retaken, both ship and pirates, and all made prisoners, and stripped of all the riches they had taken but just before. The cargo consisted in 120,000 weight of cocoa-nuts, the chief ingredient of chocolate, and 70,000 pieces of eight. Two days after this misfortune, there arose a great storm, which separated the ships from one another. The great vessel, where the pirates were, arrived at Campechy, where many considerable merchants came and saluted the captain; these presently knew the Portuguese pirate, being infamous for the many insolencies, robberies and murders he had committed on their coasts, which they kept fresh in their memory.

The next day after their arrival, the magistrates of the city sent to demand the prisoners from on board the ship, in order to punish them according to their desserts; but fearing the captain of the pirates should make his escape (as he had formerly done, being their prisoner once before) they judged it safer to leave him guarded on ship-board for the present, while they erected a gibbet to hang him on the next day, without any other process than to lead him from the ship to his punishment; the rumour of which was presently brought to Bartholomew Portugues, whereby he sought all possible means to escape that night: with this design he took two earthen jars, wherein the Spaniards carry wine from Spain to the West Indies, and stopped them very well, intending to use them for swimming, as those unskilled in that art do corks or empty bladders; having made this necessary preparation, he waited when all should be asleep; but not being able to escape his sentinel's vigilance, he stabbed him with a knife he had secretly purchased, and then threw himself into the sea with the earthen jars before-mentioned, by the help of which, though he never learned to swim, he reached the shore, and immediately took to the woods, where he hid himself for three days, not daring to appear, eating no other food than wild herbs.

Those of the city next day made diligent search for him in the woods, where they concluded him to be. This strict inquiry Portugues saw from the hollow of a tree, wherein he lay hid; and upon their return he made the best of his way to del Golpho Triste, forty leagues from Campechy, where he arrived within a fortnight after his escape: during which time, as also afterwards, he endured extreme hunger and thirst, having no other provision with him than a small calabaca with a little water: besides the fears of falling again into the hands of the Spaniards. He eat nothing but a few shell-fish, which he found among the rocks near the seashore; and being obliged to pass some rivers, not knowing well how to swim, he found at last an old board which the waves had driven ashore, wherein were a few great nails; these he took, and with no small labour whetted on a stone, till he had made them like knives, though not so well; with these, and nothing else, he cut down some branches of trees, which with twigs and osiers he joined together, and made as well as he could a boat to waft him over the rivers: thus arriving at the Cape of Golpho Triste, as was said, he found a vessel of pirates, comrades of his own, lately come from Jamaica.

To these he related all his adversities and misfortunes, and withal desired they would fit him with a boat and twenty men, with which company alone he promised to return to Campechy, and assault the ship that was in the river, by which he had been taken fourteen days before. They presently granted his request, and equipped him a boat accordingly. With this small company he set out to execute his design, which he bravely performed eight days after he left Golpho Triste ; for being arrived at Campechy, with an undaunted courage, and without any noise, he assaulted the said ship : those on board thought it was a boat from land that came to bring contraband goods, and so were in no posture of defence ; which opportunity the pirates laying hold of, assaulted them so resolutely, that in a little time they compelled the Spaniards to surrender.

Being masters of the ship, they immediately weighed anchor and set sail from the port, lest they should be pursued by other vessels. This they did with the utmost joy, seeing themselves possessors of so brave a ship ; especially Portugues, who by a second turn of fortune was become rich and powerful again, who was so lately in that same vessel a prisoner, condemned to be hanged. With this purchase he designed greater things, which he might have done, since there remained in the vessel so great a quantity of rich merchandise, though the plate had been sent to the city : but while he was making his voyage to Jamaica, near the isle of Pinos, on the south of Cuba, a terrible storm arose, which drove against the Jardines rocks, where she was lost ; but Portugues, with his companions, escaped in a canoe, in which he arrived at Jamaica, where it was not long ere he went on new adventures, but was never fortunate after.

Nor less considerable are the actions of another pirate who now lives at Jamaica, who on several occasions has performed very surprising things. He was born at Grouinghen in the United Provinces. His own name not being known, his companions gave him that of Roche Brasiliano, by reason of his long residence in Brasil: hence he was forced to fly, when the Portuguese retook those countries from the Dutch, several nations then inhabiting at Brasil (as English, French, Dutch, and others), being constrained to seek new fortunes.

This person fled to Jamaica, where, being at a stand how to get his living, he entered himself into the society of pirates, where he served as a private mariner for some time, and behaved himself so well, that he was beloved and respected by all. One day some of the mariners quarrelled with their captain to that degree, that they left the boat. Brasiliano following them, was chosen their leader, who having fitted out a small vessel, they made him captain.

Within a few days after, he took a great ship coming from New Spain, which had a great quantity of plate on board, and carried it to Jamaica. This action got him a great reputation at home; and though in his private affairs he governed himself very well, he would oftentimes appear brutish and foolish when in drink, running up and down the streets, beating and wounding those he met, no person daring to make any resistance.

To the Spaniards he was always very barbarous and cruel, out of an inveterate hatred against that nation. Of these he commanded several to be roasted alive on wooden spits, for not showing him hog-yards where he might steal swine. After many of these cruelties, as he was cruising on the coasts of Campechy, a dismal tempest surprised him so violently, that his ship was wrecked upon the coasts, the mariners only escaping with their muskets and some few bullets and powder, which were the only things they could save. The ship was lost between Campechy and the Golpho Triste: here they got ashore in a canoe, and, marching along the coast with all the speed they could, they directed their course towards Golpho Triste, the common refuge of the pirates. Being upon his journey, and all very hungry and thirsty, as is usual in desert places, they were pursued by a troop of an hundred Spaniards. Brasiliano, perceiving their imminent danger, encouraged his companions, telling them they were better soldiers, and ought rather to die under their arms fighting, as it became men of courage, than surrender to the Spaniards, who would take away their lives with the utmost torments. The pirates were but thirty; yet, seeing their brave commander oppose the enemy with such courage, resolved to do the like: hereupon they faced the troop of Spaniards, and discharged their muskets on them so dextrously, that they killed one horseman almost with every shot. The fight continued for an hour, till at last the Spaniards were put to flight. They stripped the dead, and took from them what was most for their use; such as were also not quite dead they dispatched with the ends of their muskets.

Having vanquished the enemy, they mounted on horses they found in the field, and continued their journey; Brasiliano having lost but two of his companions in this bloody fight, and had two wounded. Prosecuting their way, before they came to the port they spied a boat at anchor from Campechy, well manned, protecting a few canoes that were lading wood: hereupon they sent six of their men to watch them, who next morning, by a wile, possessed themselves of the canoes. Having given notice to their companions, they boarded them, and also took the little man-of-war, their convoy. Being thus masters of this fleet, they wanted only provisions, of which they found little aboard those vessels: but this defect was supplied by the horses, which they killed, and salted with salt, which by good fortune the wood-cutters had brought with them, with which they supported themselves till they could get better.

They took also another ship going from New Spain to Maracaibo, laden with divers sorts of merchandise and pieces of eight, designed to buy cocoa-nuts for their lading home : all these they carried to Jamaica, where they safely arrived, and, according to custom, wasted all in a few days in taverns and stews, giving themselves to all manner of debauchery. Such of these pirates will spend two or three thousand pieces of eight in a night, not leaving themselves a good shirt to wear in the morning. I saw one of them give a common strumpet five hundred pieces of eight to see her naked. My own master would buy sometimes a pipe of wine, and, placing it in the street, would force those that passed by to drink with him, threatening also to pistol them if they would not. He would do the like with barrels of beer or ale ; and very often he would throw these liquors about the streets, and wet peoples' clothes without regarding whether he spoiled their apparel.

Among themselves these pirates are very liberal : if any one has lost all, which often happens in their manner of life, they freely give him of what they have. In taverns and alehouses they have great credit ; but at Jamaica they ought not to run very deep in debt, seeing the inhabitants there easily sell one another for debt. This happened to my patron, to be sold for a debt of a tavern wherein he had spent the greatest part of his money. This man had, within three months before, three thousand pieces of eight in ready cash, all which he wasted in that little time, and became poor as I have told you.

But to return : Brasiliano, after having spent all, was forced to go to sea again to seek his fortune. He set forth towards the coast of Campechy, his common rendezvous : fifteen days after his arrival, he put himself into a canoe to espy the port of that city, and see if he could rob any Spanish vessel ; but his fortune was so bad, that both he and all his men were taken and carried before the governor, who immediately cast them into a dungeon, intending to hang them every one; and doubtless he had done so, but for a stratagem of Brasiliano, which saved their lives. He wrote a letter to the governor, in the names of other pirates that were abroad at sea, telling him he should have a care how he used those persons he had in custody; for if he hurt them in the least, they swore they would never give quarter to any Spaniard that should fall into their hands.

These pirates having been often at Campechy, and other places of the West Indies in the Spanish dominions, the governor feared what mischief their companions abroad might do, if he should punish them. Hereupon he released them, exacting only an oath on them that they would leave their exercise of piracy for ever; and withal he sent them as common mariners, in the galleons, to Spain. They got in this voyage, all together, five hundred pieces of eight; so that they tarried not long there after their arrival. Providing themselves with necessaries, they returned to Jamaica, from whence they set forth again to sea, committing greater robberies and cruelties than before; but especially abusing the poor Spaniards, who fell into their hands, with all sorts of cruelty.

The Spaniards, finding they could gain nothing on these people, nor diminish their number, daily resolved to lessen the number of their trading ships. But neither was this of any service; for the pirates, finding few ships at sea, began to gather into companies, and to land on their dominions, ruining cities, towns, and villages; pillaging, burning, and carrying away as much as they could.

The first pirate who began these invasions by land was Lewis Scot, who sacked the city of Campechy, which he almost ruined, robbing and destroying all he could; and after he had put it to an excessive ransom, he left it. After Scot came another named Mansvelt, who invaded Granada, and penetrated even to the South Sea; till at last, for want of provision, he was forced to go back. He assaulted the isle of St. Catherine, which he took, with a few prisoners. These directed him to Carthagena, a principal city in Nueva Granada. But the bold attempts and actions of John Davis, born at Jamaica, ought not to be forgotten, being some of the most remarkable; especially his rare prudence and valour showed in the fore-mentioned kingdom of Granada. This pirate, having long cruised in the Gulf of Pocatauro, on the ships expected to Carthagena, bound for Nicaragua, and not meeting any of them, resolved at last to land in Nicaragua, leaving his ship hid on the coast.

This design he soon executed; for taking eighty men out of ninety, which he had in all—and the rest he left to keep the ship—he divided them equally into three canoes. His intent was to rob the churches, and rifle the houses of the chief citizens of Nicaragua. Thus in the dark night they entered the river leading to that city, rowing in their canoes; by day they hid themselves and boats under the branches of trees, on the banks, which grow very thick along the river-sides in those countries, and along the sea-coast. Being arrived at the city the third night, the sentinel, who kept the post of the river, thought them to be fishermen that had been fishing in the lake: and most of the pirates understanding Spanish, he doubted not, as soon as he heard them speak. They had in their company an Indian who had run away from his master, who would have enslaved him unjustly. He went first ashore, and instantly killed the sentinel: this done, they entered the city, and went directly to three or four houses of the chief citizens, where they knocked softly. These, believing them to be friends, opened the doors; and the pirates, suddenly possessing themselves of the houses, stole all the money and plate they could find. Nor did they spare the churches and most sacred things; all which were pillaged and profaned, without any respect or veneration.

Meanwhile, great cries and lamentations were heard of some who had escaped them; so that the whole city was in an uproar, and all the citizens rallied in order to a defence; which the pirates preceiving, they instantly fled, carrying away their booty, and some prisoners: these they led away, that if any of them should be taken by the Spaniards, they might use them for ransom. Thus they got to their ship, and with all speed put to sea, forcing the prisoners, before they let them go, to procure them as much flesh as was necessary for their voyage to Jamaica. But no sooner had they weighed anchor, when they saw a troop of about five hundred Spaniards, all well armed, at the seaside: against these they let fly several guns, wherewith they forced them to quit the sands, and retire, with no small regret to see these pirates carry away so much plate of their churches and houses, though distant at least forty leagues from the sea.

These pirates got, on this occasion, above four thousand pieces of eight in money, besides much plate, and many jewels; in all, to the value of fifty thousand pieces of eight, or more: with all this they arrived at Jamaica soon after. But this sort of people being never long masters of their money, they were soon constrained to seek more by the same means; and Captain John Davis, presently after his return, was chosen admiral of seven or eight vessels, he being now esteemed an able conductor for such enterprises. He began his new command by directing his fleet to the north of Cuba, there to wait for the fleet from New Spain; but missing his design, they determined for Florida.

Being arrived there, they landed their men, and sacked a small city named St. Augustine of Florida. The castle had a garrison of two hundred men, but could not prevent the pillage of the city, they effecting it without the least damage from the soldiers or townsmen.

CHAPTER VI.

Of the origin of Francis Lolonois, and the beginning of his robberies.

FRANCIS LOLONOIS was a native of that territory in France which is called Les Sables d'Olone, or The Sands of Olone. In his youth he was transported to the Caribbee islands, in quality of servant, or slave, according to custom; of which we have already spoken. Being out of his time, he came to Hispaniola; here he joined for some time with the hunters, before he began his robberies upon the Spaniards, which I shall now relate, till his unfortunate death.

At first he made two or three voyages as a common mariner, wherein he behaved himself so courageously as to gain the favour of the governor of Tortuga, Monsieur de la Place; insomuch that he gave him a ship, in which he might seek his fortune, which was very favourable to him at first; for in a short time he got great riches. But his cruelties against the Spaniards were such, that the fame of them made him so well known through the Indies, that the Spaniards, in his time, would choose rather to die, or sink fighting, than surrender, knowing they should have no mercy at his hands. But Fortune, being seldom constant, after some time turned her back; for in a huge storm he lost his ship on the coast of Campechy. The men were all saved, but coming upon dry land, the Spaniards pursued them, and killed the greatest part wounding also Lolonois. Not knowing how to escape, he saved his life by a stratagem; mingling sand with the blood of his wounds, with which besmearing his face, and other parts of his body, and hiding himself dextrously among the dead, he continued there till the Spaniards quitted the field.

They being gone, he retired to the woods, and bound up his wounds as well as he could. These being pretty well healed, he took his way to Campechy, having disguised himself in a Spanish habit; here he enticed certain slaves, to whom he promised liberty if they would obey him and trust to his conduct. They accepted his promises, and stealing a canoe, they went to sea with him. Now the Spaniards, having made several of his companions prisoners, kept them close in a dungeon, while Lolonois went about the town and saw what passed. These were often asked, "What is become of your captain?" To whom they constantly answered, "He is dead:" which rejoiced the Spaniards, who made bonfires, and, knowing nothing to the contrary, gave thanks to God for their deliverance from such a cruel pirate. Lolonois, having seen these rejoicings for his death, made haste to escape, with the slaves above-mentioned, and came safe to Tortuga, the common refuge of all sorts of wickedness, and the seminary, as it were, of pirates and thieves. Though now his fortune was low, yet he got another ship with craft and subtlety, and in it twenty-one men. Being well provided with arms and necessaries, he set forth for Cuba, on the south whereof is a small village, called De los Cayos. The inhabitants drive a great trade in tobacco, sugar, and hides, and all in boats, not being able to use ships, by reason of the little depth of that sea.

Lolonois was persuaded he should get here some considerable prey; but by the good fortune of some fisher-

LOLONOIS.
(From the Portrait in "De Americaensche Roovers.")

men who saw him, and the mercy of God, they escaped him: for the inhabitants of the town dispatched immediately a vessel overland to the Havannah, complaining that Lolonois was come to destroy them with two canoes. The governor could very hardly believe this, having received letters from Campechy that he was dead: but, at their importunity, he sent a ship to their relief, with ten guns, and ninety men, well armed; giving them this express command, "that they should not return into his presence without having totally destroyed those pirates." To this effect he gave them a negro to serve for a hangman, and orders, "that they should immediately hang every one of the pirates, excepting Lolonois, their captain, whom they should bring alive to the Havannah." This ship arrived at Cayos, of whose coming the pirates were advertised beforehand, and instead of flying, went to seek it in the river Estera, where she rode at anchor. The pirates seized some fishermen, and forced them by night to show them the entry of the port, hoping soon to obtain a greater vessel than their two canoes, and thereby to mend their fortune. They arrived, after two in the morning, very nigh the ship; and the watch on board the ship asking them, whence they came, and if they had seen any pirates abroad? They caused one of the prisoners to answer, they had seen no pirates, nor anything else. Which answer made them believe that they were fled upon hearing of their coming.

But they soon found the contrary, for about break of day the pirates assaulted the vessel on both sides, with their two canoes, with such vigour, that though the Spaniards behaved themselves as they ought, and made as good defence as they could, making some use of their great guns, yet they were forced to surrender, being beaten by the pirates, with sword in hand, down under the hatches. From hence

Lolonois commanded them to be brought up, one by one, and in this order caused their heads to be struck off: among the rest came up the negro, designed to be the pirates' executioner; this fellow implored mercy at his hands very dolefully, telling Lolonois he was constituted hangman of that ship, and if he would spare him, he would tell him faithfully all that he should desire. Lolonois, making him confess what he thought fit, commanded him to be murdered with the rest. Thus he cruelly and barbarously put them all to death, reserving only one alive, whom he sent back to the governor of the Havannah, with this message in writing: "I shall never henceforward give quarter to any Spaniard whatsoever; and I have great hopes I shall execute on your own person the very same punishment I have done upon them you sent against me. Thus I have retaliated the kindness you designed to me and my companions." The governor, much troubled at this sad news, swore, in the presence of many, that he would never grant quarter to any pirate that should fall into his hands. But the citizens of the Havannah desired him not to persist in the execution of that rash and rigorous oath, seeing the pirates would certainly take occasion from thence to do the same, and they had an hundred times more opportunity of revenge than he; that being necessitated to get their livelihood by fishery, they should hereafter always be in danger of their lives. By these reasons he was persuaded to bridle his anger, and remit the severity of his oath.

Now Lolonois had got a good ship, but very few provisions and people in it; to purchase both which, he resolved to cruise from one port to another. Doing thus, for some time, without success, he determined to go to the port of Maracaibo. Here he surprised a ship laden with plate, and other merchandises, outward bound, to buy cocoa-nuts. With this prize he returned to Tortuga, where he was received with joy by the inhabitants; they congratulating his happy success, and their own private interest. He stayed not long there, but designed to equip a fleet sufficient to transport five hundred men, and necessaries. Thus provided, he resolved to pillage both cities, towns, and villages, and finally, to take Maracaibo itself. For this purpose he knew the island of Tortuga would afford him many resolute and courageous men, fit for such enterprises: besides, he had in his service several prisoners well acquainted with the ways and places designed upon.

CHAPTER VII.

Lolonois equips a fleet to land upon the Spanish islands of America, with intent to rob, sack, and burn whatsoever he met with.

OF this design Lolonois giving notice to all the pirates, whether at home or abroad, he got together, in a little while, above four hundred men; beside which, there was then in Tortuga another pirate, named Michael de Basco, who, by his piracy, had got riches sufficient to live at ease, and go no more abroad; having, withal, the office of major of the island. But seeing the great preparations that Lolonois made for this expedition, he joined him, and offered him, that if he would make him his chief captain by land (seeing he knew the country very well, and all its avenues) he would share in his fortunes, and go with him. They agreed upon articles to the great joy of Lolonois, knowing that Basco had done great actions in Europe, and had the repute of a good soldier. Thus they all embarked in eight vessels, that of Lolonois being the greatest, having ten guns of indifferent carriage.

All things being ready, and the whole company on board, they set sail together about the end of April, being, in all, six hundred and sixty persons. They steered for that part called Bayala, north of Hispaniola: here they took into their company some French hunters, who voluntarily offered themselves, and here they provided themselves with victuals and necessaries for their voyage.

From hence they sailed again the last of July, and steered directly to the eastern cape of the isle called Punta d'Espada. Hereabouts espying a ship from Puerto Rico, bound for New Spain, laden with cocoa-nuts, Lolonois commanded the rest of the fleet to wait for him near Savona, on the east of Cape Punta d'Espada, he alone intending to take the said vessel. The Spaniards, though they had been in sight full two hours, and knew them to be pirates, yet would not flee, but prepared to fight, being well armed, and provided. The combat lasted three hours, and then they surrendered. This ship had sixteen guns, and fifty fighting men aboard: they found in her 120,000 weight of cocoa, 40,000 pieces of eight, and the value of 10,000 more in jewels. Lolonois sent the vessel presently to Tortuga to be unladed, with orders to return as soon as possible to Savona, where he would wait for them: meanwhile, the rest of the fleet being arrived at Savona, met another Spanish vessel coming from Coman, with military provisions to Hispaniola, and money to pay the garrisons there. This vessel they also took, without any resistance, though mounted with eight guns. In it were 7,000 weight of powder, a great number of muskets, and like things, with 12,000 pieces of eight.

These successes encouraged the pirates, they seeming very lucky beginnings, especially finding their fleet pretty well recruited in a little time: for the first ship arriving at Tortuga, the governor ordered it to be instantly unladen, and soon after sent back, with fresh provisions, and other necessaries, to Lolonois. This ship he chose for himself, and gave that which he commanded to his comrade, Anthony du Puis. Being thus recruited with men in lieu of them he had lost in taking the prizes, and by sickness, he found himself in a good condition to set sail for Maracaibo, in the province of Neuva Venezuela, in the latitude of 12 deg. 10 min. north. This island is twenty leagues long, and twelve broad. To this port also belong the islands of Onega and Monges. The east side thereof is called Cape St. Roman, and the western side Cape of Caquibacoa: the gulf is called, by some, the Gulf of Venezuela, but the pirates usually call it the Bay of Maracaibo.

At the entrance of this gulf are two islands extending from east to west; that towards the east is called Isla de las Vigilias, or the Watch Isle; because in the middle is a high hill, on which stands a watch-house. The other is called Isla de la Palomas, or the Isle of Pigeons. Between these two islands runs a little sea, or rather lake of fresh water, sixty leagues long, and thirty broad; which disgorging itself into the ocean, dilates itself about the said two islands. Between them is the best passage for ships, the channel being no broader than the flight of a great gun, of about eight pounds. On the Isle of Pigeons standeth a castle, to impede the entry of vessels, all being necessitated to come very nigh the castle, by reason of two banks of sand on the other side, with only fourteen feet water. Many other banks of sand there are in this lake; as that called El Tablazo, or the Great Table, no deeper than ten feet, forty leagues within the lake; others there are, that have no more than six, seven, or eight feet in depth: all are very dangerous, especially to mariners unacquainted with them. West hereof is the city of Maracaibo, very pleasant to the view, its houses being built along the shore, having delightful prospects all round: the city may contain three or four thousand persons, slaves included, all which make a town of a reasonable bigness. There are judged to be about eight hundred persons able to bear arms, all Spaniards. Here are one parish church, well built and adorned, four monasteries, and one hospital. The city is governed by a deputy governor, substituted by the governor of the Caraccas. The trade here exercised is mostly in hides and tobacco. The inhabitants possess great numbers of cattle, and many plantations, which extend thirty leagues in the country especially towards the great town of Gibraltar, where are gathered great quantities of cocoa-nuts, and all other garden fruits, which serve for the regale and sustenance of the inhabitants of Maracaibo, whose territories are much drier than those of Gibraltar. Hither those of Maracaibo send great quantities of flesh, they making returns in oranges, lemons, and other fruits; for the inhabitants of Gibraltar want flesh, their fields not being capable of feeding cows or sheep.

Before Maracaibo is a very spacious and secure port, wherein may be built all sorts of vessels, having great convenience of timber, which may be transported thither at little charge. Nigh the town lies also a small island called Borrica, where they feed great numbers of goats, which cattle the inhabitants use more for their skins than their flesh or milk; they slighting these two, unless while they are tender and young kids. In the fields are fed some sheep, but of a very small size. In some islands of the lake, and in other places hereabouts, are many savage Indians, called by the Spaniards bravoes, or wild: these could never be reduced by the Spaniards, being brutish, and untameable. They dwell mostly towards the west side of the lake, in little huts built on trees growing in the water; so to keep themselves from the innumerable mosquitoes, or gnats, which infest and torment them night and day. To the east of the said lake are whole towns of fishermen, who likewise live in huts built on trees, as the former. Another reason of this dwelling, is the frequent inundations; for after great rains, the land is often overflown for two or three leagues, there being no less than twenty-five great rivers that feed this lake. The town of Gibraltar is also frequently drowned by these, so that the inhabitants are constrained to retire to their plantations.

Gibraltar, situate at the side of the lake about forty leagues within it, receives its provisions of flesh, as has been said, from Maracaibo. The town is inhabited by about 1,500 persons, whereof four hundred may bear arms; the greatest part of them keep shops, wherein they exercise one trade or other. In the adjacent fields are numerous plantations of sugar and cocoa, in which are many tall and beautiful trees, of whose timber houses may be built, and ships. Among these are many handsome and proportionable cedars, seven or eight feet about, of which they build boats and ships, so as to bear only one great sail; such vessels being called piraguas. The whole country is well furnished with rivers and brooks, very useful in droughts, being then cut into many little channels to water their fields and plantations. They plant also much tobacco, well esteemed in Europe, and for its goodness is called there tobacco de sacerdotes, or priest's tobacco. They enjoy nigh twenty leagues of jurisdiction, which is bounded by very high mountains perpetually covered with snow. On the other side of these mountains is situate a great city called Merida, to which the town of Gibraltar is subject. All merchandise is carried hence to the aforesaid city on mules, and that but at one season of the year, by reason of the excessive cold in those high mountains. On the said mules returns are made in flour of meal, which comes from towards Peru, by the way of Estaffe.

Thus far I thought good to make a short description of the lake of Maracaibo, that my reader might the better comprehend what I shall say concerning the actions of pirates in this place, as follows.

Lolonois arriving at the gulf of Venezuela, cast anchor with his whole fleet out of sight of the Vigilia or Watch Isle; next day very early he set sail thence with all his ships for the lake of Maracaibo, where they cast anchor again; then they landed their men, with design to attack first the fortress that commanded the bar, therefore called de la barra. This fort consists only of several great baskets of earth placed on a rising ground, planted with sixteen great guns, with several other heaps of earth round about for covering their men: the pirates having landed a league off this fort, advanced by degrees towards it; but the governor having espied their landing, had placed an ambuscade to cut them off behind, while he should attack them in front. This the pirates discovered, and getting before, they defeated it so entirely, that not a man could retreat to the castle: this done, Lolonois, with his companions, advanced immediately to the fort, and after a fight of almost three hours, with the usual desperation of this sort of people, they became masters thereof, without any other arms than swords and pistols: while they were fighting, those who were the routed ambuscade, not being able to get into the castle, retired into Maracaibo in great confusion and disorder, crying "The pirates will presently be here with two thousand men and more." The city having formerly been taken by this kind of people, and sacked to the uttermost, had still an idea of that misery; so that upon these dismal news they endeavoured to escape towards Gibraltar in their boats and canoes, carrying with them all the goods and money they could. Being come to Gibraltar, they told how the fortress was taken, and nothing had been saved, nor any persons escaped.

The castle thus taken by the pirates, they presently signified to the ships their victory, that they should come farther in without fear of danger: the rest of that day was spent in ruining and demolishing the said castle. They nailed the guns, and burnt as much as they could not carry away, burying the dead, and sending on board the fleet the wounded. Next day, very early, they weighed anchor, and steered altogether towards Maracaibo, about six leagues distant from the fort; but the wind failing that day, they could advance little, being forced to expect the tide. Next morning they came in sight of the town, and prepared for landing under the protection of their own guns, fearing the Spaniards might have laid an ambuscade in the woods: they put their men into canoes, brought for that purpose, and landed where they thought most convenient, shooting still furiously with their great guns: of those in the canoes, half only went ashore, the other half remained aboard; they fired from the ships as fast as possible, towards the woody part of the shore, but could discover nobody; then they entered the town, whose inhabitants, as I told you, were retired to the woods, and Gibraltar, with their wives, children, and families. Their houses they left well provided with victuals, as flour, bread, pork, brandy, wines, and poultry, with these the pirates fell to making good cheer, for in four weeks before they had no opportunity of filling their stomachs with such plenty.

They instantly possessed themselves of the best houses in the town, and placed sentinels wherever they thought convenient; the great church served them for their main guard. Next day they sent out an hundred and sixty men to find out some of the inhabitants in the woods thereabouts; these returned the same night, bringing with them 20,000 pieces of eight, several mules laden with household goods and merchandise, and twenty prisoners, men, women, and children. Some of these were put to the rack, to make them confess where they had hid the rest of the goods; but they could extort very little from them. Lolonois, who valued not murdering, though in cold blood, ten or twelve Spaniards, drew his cutlass, and hacked one to pieces before the rest, saying, "If you do not confess and declare where you have hid the rest of your goods, I will do the like to all your companions." At last, amongst these horrible cruelties and inhuman threats, one promised to show the place where the rest of the Spaniards were hid; but those that were fled, having intelligence of it, changed place, and buried the remnant of their riches underground, so that the pirates could not find them out, unless some of their own party should reveal them; besides, the Spaniards flying from one place to another every day, and often changing woods, were jealous even of each other, so as the father durst scarce trust his own son.

After the pirates had been fifteen days in Maracaibo, they resolved for Gibraltar; but the inhabitants having received intelligence thereof, and that they intended afterwards to go to Merida, gave notice of it to the governor there, who was a valiant soldier, and had been an officer in Flanders. His answer was, "he would have them take no care, for he hoped in a little while to exterminate the said pirates." Whereupon he came to Gibraltar with four hundred men well armed, ordering at the same time the inhabitants to put themselves in arms, so that in all he made eight hundred fighting men. With the same speed he raised a battery towards the sea, mounted with twenty guns, covered with great baskets of earth: another battery he placed in another place, mounted with eight guns. This done, he barricaded a narrow passage to the town through which the pirates must pass, opening at the same time another through much dirt and mud into the wood totally unknown to the pirates.

The pirates, ignorant of these preparations, having embarked all their prisoners and booty, took their way towards Gibraltar. Being come in sight of the place, they saw the royal standard hanging forth, and that those of the town designed to defend their houses. Lolonois seeing this, called a council of war what they ought to do, telling his officers and mariners, "That the difficulty of the enterprise was very great, seeing the Spaniards had had so much time to put themselves in a posture of defence, and had got a good body of men together, with much ammunition; but notwithstanding," said he, "have a good courage; we must either defend ourselves like good soldiers, or lose our lives with all the riches we have got. Do as I shall do who am your captain: at other times we have fought with fewer men than we have in our company at present, and yet we have overcome greater numbers than there possibly can be in this town: the more they are, the more glory and the greater riches we shall gain." The pirates supposed that all the riches of the inhabitants of Maracaibo were transported to Gibraltar, or at least the greatest part. After this speech, they all promised to follow, and obey him. Lolonois made answer, "'Tis well; but know ye, withal, that the first man who shall show any fear, or the least apprehension thereof, I will pistol him with my own hands."

With this resolution they cast anchor nigh the shore, near three-quarters of a league from the town: next day before sun-rising, they landed three hundred and eighty men well provided, and armed every one with a cutlass, and one or two pistols, and sufficient powder and bullet for thirty charges. Here they all shook hands in testimony of good courage, and began their march, Lolonois speaking thus, "Come, my brethren, follow me, and have good courage." They followed their guide, who, believing he led them well, brought them to the way which the governor had barricaded. Not being able to pass that way, they went to the other newly made in the wood among the mire, which the Spaniards could shoot into at pleasure; but the pirates, full of courage, cut down the branches of trees and threw them on the way, that they might not stick in the dirt. Meanwhile, those of Gibraltar fired with their great guns so furiously, they could scarce hear nor see for the noise and smoke. Being passed the wood, they came on firm ground, where they met with a battery of six guns, which immediately the Spaniards discharged upon them, all loaded with small bullets and pieces of iron; and the Spaniards sallying forth, set upon them with such fury, as caused the pirates to give way, few of them caring to advance towards the fort, many of them being already killed and wounded. This made them go back to seek another way; but the Spaniards having cut down many trees to hinder the passage, they could find none, but were forced to return to that they had left. Here the Spaniards continued to fire as before, nor would they sally out of their batteries to attack them any more. Lolonois and his companions not being able to grimp up the baskets of earth, were compelled to use an old stratagem, wherewith at last they deceived and overcame the Spaniards.

Lolonois retired suddenly with all his men, making show as if he fled; hereupon the Spaniards crying out "They flee, they flee, let us follow them," sallied forth with great disorder to the pursuit. Being drawn to some distance from the batteries, which was the pirates only design, they turned upon them unexpectedly with sword in hand, and killed above two hundred men; and thus fighting their way through those who remained, they possessed themselves of the batteries. The Spaniards that remained abroad, giving themselves over for lost, fled to the woods: those in the battery of eight guns surrendered themselves, obtaining quarter for their lives. The pirates being now become masters of the town, pulled down the Spanish colours and set up their own, taking prisoners as many as they could find. These they carried to the great church, where they raised a battery of several great guns, fearing lest the Spaniards that were fled should rally, and come upon them again; but next day, being all fortified, their fears were over. They gathered the dead to bury them, being above five hundred Spaniards, besides the wounded in the town, and those that died of their wounds in the woods. The pirates had also above one hundred and fifty prisoners, and nigh five hundred slaves, many women and children.

Of their own companions only forty were killed, and almost eighty wounded, whereof the greatest part died through the bad air, which brought fevers and other illness. They put the slain Spaniards into two great boats, and carrying them a quarter of a league to sea, they sunk the boats; this done, they gathered all the plate, household stuff, and merchandise they could, or thought convenient to carry away. The Spaniards who had anything left had hid it carefully: but the unsatisfied pirates, not contented with the riches they had got, sought for more goods and merchandise, not sparing those who lived in the fields, such as hunters and planters. They had scarce been eighteen days on the place, when the greatest part of the prisoners died for hunger. For in the town were few provisions, especially of flesh, though they had some, but no sufficient quantity of flour of meal, and this the pirates had taken for themselves, as they also took the swine, cows, sheep, and poultry, without allowing any share to the poor prisoners; for these they only provided some small quantity of mules' and asses' flesh; and many who could not eat of that loathsome provision died for hunger, their stomachs not being accustomed to such sustenance; only some women were allowed better cheer, because they served their sensual delights, to which those robbers are much given. Among these, some had been forced, others were volunteers, though almost all rather submitted through poverty and hunger than any other cause. Of the prisoners many also died under the torment they sustained to make them discover their money or jewels; and of these, some had none, nor knew of none, and others denying what they knew, endured such horrible deaths.

Finally, after having been in possession of the town four entire weeks, they sent four of the prisoners to the Spaniards that were fled to the woods, demanding of them a ransom for not burning the town. The sum demanded was 10,000 pieces of eight, which if not sent, they threatened to reduce it to ashes. For bringing in this money, they allowed them only two days; but the Spaniards not having been able to gather so punctually such a sum, the pirates fired many parts of the town; whereupon the inhabitants begged them to help quench the fire, and the ransom should be readily paid. The pirates condescended, helping as much as they could to stop the fire; but, notwithstanding all their best endeavours, one part of the town was ruined, especially the church belonging to the monastery was burnt down. After they had received the said sum, they carried aboard all the riches they had got, with a great number of slaves which had not paid the ransom; for all the prisoners had sums of money set upon them, and the slaves were also commanded to be redeemed. Hence they returned to Maracaibo, where being arrived, they found a general consternation in the whole city, to which they sent three or four prisoners to tell the governor and inhabitants, "they should bring them 30,000 pieces of eight aboard their ships, for a ransom of their houses, otherwise they should be sacked anew and burnt."

Among these debates a party of pirates came on shore, and carried away the images, pictures, and bells of the great church, aboard the fleet. The Spaniards who were sent to demand the sum aforesaid returned, with orders to make some agreement; who concluded with the pirates to give for their ransom and liberty 20,000 pieces of eight, and five hundred cows, provided that they should commit no farther hostilities, but depart thence presently after payment of money and cattle. The one and the other being delivered, the whole fleet set sail, causing great joy to the inhabitants of Maracaibo, to see themselves quit of them: but three days after they renewed their fears with admiration, seeing the pirates appear again, and re-enter the port with all their ships: but these apprehensions vanished, upon hearing one of the pirate's errand, who came ashore from Lolonois, "to demand a skilful pilot to conduct one of the greatest ships over the dangerous bank that lieth at the very entry of the lake." Which petition, or rather command, was instantly granted.

They had now been full two months in those towns, wherein they committed those cruel and insolent actions we have related. Departing thence, they took their course to Hispaniola, and arrived there in eight days, casting anchor in a port called Isla de la Vacca, or Cow Island. This island is inhabited by French bucaniers, who mostly sell the flesh they hunt to pirates and others, who now and then put in there to victual, or trade. Here they unladed their whole cargazon of riches, the usual storehouse of the pirates being commonly under the shelter of the bucaniers. Here they made a dividend of all their prizes and gains, according to the order and degree of every one, as has been mentioned before. Having made an exact calculation of all their plunder, they found in ready money 260,000 pieces of eight: this being divided, every one received for his share in money, as also in silk, linen, and other commodities, to the value of above 100 pieces of eight. Those who had been wounded received their first part, after the rate mentioned before, for the loss of their limbs: then they weighed all the plate uncoined, reckoning ten pieces of eight to a pound; the jewels were prized indifferently, either too high or too low, by reason of their ignorance: this done, every one was put to his oath again, that he had not smuggled anything from the common stock. Hence they proceeded to the dividend of the shares of such as were dead in battle, or otherwise: these shares were given to their friends, to be kept entire for them, and to be delivered in due time to their nearest relations, or their apparent lawful heirs.

The whole dividend being finished, they set sail for Tortuga: here they arrived a month after, to the great joy of most of the island; for as to the common pirates, in three weeks they had scarce any money left, having spent it all in things of little value, or lost it at play. Here had arrived, not long before them, two French ships, with wine and brandy, and suchlike commodities; whereby these liquors, at the arrival of the pirates, were indifferent cheap. But this lasted not long, for soon after they were enhanced extremely, a gallon of brandy being sold for four pieces of eight. The governor of the island bought of the pirates the whole cargo of the ship laden with cocoa, giving for that rich commodity scarce the twentieth part of its worth. Thus they made shift to lose and spend the riches they had got, in much less time than they were purchased: the taverns and stews, according to the custom of pirates, got the greatest part; so that, soon after, they were forced to seek more by the same unlawful means they had got the former.

CHAPTER VIII.

Lolonois makes new preparations to take the city of St. James de Leon; as also that of Nicaragua; where he miserably perishes.

LOLONOIS had got great repute at Tortuga by this last voyage, because he brought home such considerable profit; and now he need take no great care to gather men to serve under him, more coming in voluntarily than he could employ; every one reposing such confidence in his conduct that they judged it very safe to expose themselves, in his company, to the greatest dangers. He resolved therefore a second voyage to the parts of Nicaragua, to pillage there as many towns as he could.

Having published his new preparations, he had all his men together at the time, being about seven hundred. Of these he put three hundred aboard the ship he took at Maracaibo, and the rest in five other vessels of lesser burthen; so that they were in all six ships. The first port they went to was Bayaha in Hispaniola, to victual the fleet, and take in provisions; which done, they steered their course to a port called Matamana, on the south side of Cuba, intending to take here all the canoes they could; these coasts being frequented by the fishers of tortoises, who carry them hence to the Havannah. They took as many of them, to the great grief of those miserable people, as they thought necessary; for they had great use for these small bottoms, by reason the port they designed for had not depth enough for ships of any burthen. Hence they took their course towards the cape Gracias à Dios on the continent, in latitude 15 deg. north, one hundred leagues from the Island de los Pinos. Being at sea, they were taken with a sad and tedious calm, and, by the agitation of the waves alone, were thrown into the gulf of Honduras: here they laboured hard in vain to regain what they had lost, both the waters and the winds being contrary; besides, the ship wherein Lolonois was embarked could not follow the rest; and what was worse, they wanted provisions. Hereupon, they were forced to put into the first port they could reach, to revictual: so they entered with their canoes into the river Xagua, inhabited by Indians, whom they totally destroyed, finding great quantities of millet, and many hogs and hens: not contented with which, they determined to remain there till the bad weather was over, and to pillage all the towns and villages along the coast of the gulf. Thus they passed from one place to another, seeking still more provisions, with which they were not sufficiently supplied. Having searched and rifled many villages, where they found no great matter, they came at last to Puerto Cavallo: here the Spaniards have two storehouses to keep the merchandises that are brought from the inner parts of the country, till the arrival of the ships. There was then in the port a Spanish ship of twenty-four guns, and sixteen pedreros or mortar-pieces: this ship was immediately seized by the pirates, and then drawing nigh the shore, they landed, and burnt the two storehouses, with all the rest of the houses there. Many inhabitants likewise they took prisoners, and committed upon them the most inhuman cruelties that ever heathens invented; putting them to the cruellest tortures they could devise. It was the custom of Lolonois, that having tormented persons not confessing, he would instantly cut them in pieces with his hanger, and pull out their tongues, desiring to do so, if possible, to every Spaniard in the world. It often happened that some of these miserable prisoners, being forced by the rack, would promise to discover the places where the fugitive Spaniards lay hid, which not being able afterwards to perform, they were put to more cruel deaths than they who were dead before.

The prisoners being all dead but two (whom they reserved to show them what they desired), they marched hence to the town of San Pedro, or St. Peter, ten or twelve leagues from Puerto Cavallo, being three hundred men, whom Lolonois led, leaving behind him Moses van Vin his lieutenant, to govern the rest in his absence. Being come three leagues on their way, they met with a troop of Spaniards, how lay in ambuscade for their coming: these they set upon, with all the courage imaginable, and at last totally defeated. Howbeit, they behaved themselves very manfully at first; but not being able to resist the fury of the pirates, they were forced to give way, and save themselves by flight, leaving many pirates dead in the place, some wounded, and some of their own party maimed, by the way. These Lolonois put to death without mercy, having asked them what questions he thought fit for his purpose.

There were still remaining some few prisoners not wounded; these were asked by Lolonois, if any more Spaniards did lie farther on in ambuscade? They answered, there were. Then being brought before him, one by one, he asked if there was no other way to the town but that. This he did to avoid if possible those ambuscades. But they all constantly answered him they knew none. Having asked them all, and finding they could show him no other way, Lolonois grew outrageously passionate; so that he drew his cutlass, and with it cut open the breast of one of those poor Spaniards, and pulling out his heart began to bite and gnaw it with his teeth, like a ravenous wolf, saying to the rest, "I will serve you all alike, if you show me not another way."

Hereupon, those miserable wretches promised to show him another way, but withal, they told him, it was extremely difficult, and laborious. Thus to satisfy that cruel tyrant, they began to lead him and his army; but finding it not for his purpose as they had told him, he was forced to return to the former way, swearing with great choler and indignation, "Mort Dieu, les Espagnols me le payeront. By God's death, the Spaniards shall pay me for this."

Next day he fell into another ambuscade, which he assaulted with such horrible fury, that in less than an hour's time he routed the Spaniards, and killed the greatest part of them. The Spaniards thought by these ambuscades better to destroy the pirates, assaulting them by degrees, and for this reason had posted themselves in several places. At last he met with a third ambuscade, where was placed a party stronger, and more advantageously, than the former: yet notwithstanding, the pirates, by continually throwing little fire-balls in great numbers, for some time, forced this party, as well as the former, to flee, and this with so great loss of men, that before they could reach the town, the greatest part of the Spaniards were either killed or wounded. There was but one path which led to the town, very well barricaded with good defences; and the rest of the town round was planted with shrubs called raqueltes, full of thorns very sharp pointed. This sort of fortification seemed stronger than the triangles used in Europe, when an army is of necessity to pass by the place of an enemy; it being almost impossible for the pirates to traverse those shrubs. The Spaniards posted behind the said defences, seeing the pirates come, began to ply them with their great guns; but these perceiving them ready to fire, used to stoop down, and when the shot was made, to fall upon the defendants with fire-balls and naked swords, killing many of the town: yet notwithstanding, not being able to advance any farther, they retired, for the present: then they renewed the attack with fewer men than before, and observing not to shoot till they were very nigh, they gave the Spaniards a charge so dextrously, that with every shot they killed an enemy.

The attack continuing thus eager on both sides till night, the Spaniards were compelled to hang forth a white flag, and desired to come to a parley: the only conditions they required were, "that the pirates should give the inhabitants quarter for two hours." This little time they demanded with intent to carry away and hide as much of their goods and riches as they could, and to fly to some other neighbouring town. Granting this article, they entered the town, and continued there the two hours, without committing the least hostility on the inhabitants; but no sooner was that time past, than Lolonois ordered that the inhabitants should be followed, and robbed of all they had carried away; and not only their goods, but their persons likewise to be made prisoners; though the greatest part of their merchandise and goods were so hid, as the pirates could not find them, except a few leathern sacks, filled with anil, or indigo.

Having stayed here a few days, and, according to their custom, committed most horrid insolences, they at last quitted the place, carrying away all they possibly could, and reducing the town to ashes. Being come to the seaside, where they left a party of their own, they found these had been cruising upon the fishermen thereabouts, or who came that way from the river of Guatemala: in this river was also expected a ship from Spain. Finally, they resolved to go toward the islands on the other side of the gulf, there to cleanse and careen their vessels; but they left two canoes before the coast, or rather the mouth of the river of Guatemala, in order to take the ship, which, as I said, was expected from Spain.

But their chief intent in going hither was to seek provisions, knowing the tortoises of those places are excellent food. Being arrived, they divided themselves, each party choosing a fit post for that fishery. They undertook to knit nets with the rinds of certain trees called macoa, whereof they make also ropes and cables; so that no vessel can be in need of such things, if they can but find the said trees. There are also many places where they find pitch in so great abundance, that running down the sea-coasts, being melted by the sun, it congeals in the water in great heaps, like small islands. This pitch is not like that of Europe, but resembles, both in colour and shape, that froth of the sea called bitumen; but, in my judgment, this matter is nothing but wax mixed with sand, which stormy weather, and the rolling waves of great rivers hath cast into the sea; for in those parts are great quantities of bees who make their honey in trees, to the bodies of which the honeycomb being fixed, when tempests arise, they are torn away, and by the fury of the winds carried into the sea, as is said. Some naturalists say, that the honey and the wax are separated by the salt water; whence proceeds the good amber. This opinion seems the more probable, because the said amber tastes as wax doth.

But to return to my discourse. The pirates made in those islands all the haste they possibly could to equip their vessels, hearing that the Spanish ship was come which they expected. They spent some time cruising on the coasts of Jucatan, where inhabit many Indians, who seek for the said amber in those seas. And I shall here, by the by, make some short remarks on the manner of living of the Indians, and their religion.

They have now been above a hundred years under the Spaniards, to whom they performed all manner of services; for whensoever any of them needed a slave or servant, they sent for these to serve them as long as they pleased. By the Spaniards they were initiated in the principles of the Christian faith and religion, and they sent them every Sunday and holiday a priest to perform divine service among them; afterwards, for reasons not known, but certainly through temptations of the father of idolatry, the devil, they suddenly cast off the Christian religion, abusing the priest that was sent them: this provoked the Spaniards to punish them, by casting many of the chief into prison. Every one of those barbarians had, and hath still, a god to himself, whom he serves and worships. It is a matter of admiration, how they use a child newly born: as soon as it comes into the world, they carry it to the temple; here they make a hole, which they fill with ashes only, on which they place the child naked, leaving it there a whole night alone, not without great danger, nobody daring to come near it; meanwhile the temple is open on all sides, that all sorts of beasts may freely come in and out. Next day, the father, and relations of the infant, return to see if the track or step of any animal appears in the ashes: not finding any, they leave the child there till some beast has approached the infant, and left behind him the marks of his feet: to this animal, whatsoever it be, they consecrate the creature newly born, as to its god, which he is bound to worship all his life, esteeming the said beast his patron and protector. They offer to their gods sacrifices of fire, wherein they burn a certain gum called by them copal, whose smoke smells very deliciously. When the infant is grown up, the parents thereof tell him who he ought to worship, serve, and honour as his own proper god. Then he goes to the temple, where he makes offerings to the said beast. Afterwards, if in the course of his life, any one injure him, or any evil happen to him, he complains to that beast, and sacrifices to it for revenge. Hence it often comes, that those who have done the injury of which he complains are bitten, killed, or otherwise hurt by such animals.

After this superstitious and idolatrous manner live those miserable and ignorant Indians that inhabit the islands of the gulf of Honduras; as also many of them on the continent of Jucatan, in the territories whereof are most excellent ports, where those Indians most commonly build their houses. These people are not very faithful to one another, and use strange ceremonies at their marriages. Whensoever any one pretends to marry a young damsel, he first applies himself to her father or nearest relation: he examines him nicely about the manner of cultivating their plantations, and other things at his pleasure. Having satisfied the questions of his father-in-law, he gives the young man a bow and arrow, with which he repairs to the young maid, and presents her with a garland of green leaves and sweet-smelling flowers; this she is obliged to put on her head, and lay aside that which she wore before, it being the custom for virgins to go perpetually crowned with flowers. This garland being received, and put on her head, every one of the relations and friends go to advise with others, whether that marriage will be like to be happy or not; then they meet at the house of the damsel's father, where they drink of a liquor made of maize, or Indian wheat; and here, before the whole company, the father gives his daughter in marriage to the bridegroom. Next day the bride comes to her mother, and in her presence pulls off the garland, and tears it in pieces, with great cries and lamentations. Many other things I could relate of the manner of living and customs of those Indians, but I shall follow my discourse.

Our pirates therefore had many canoes of the Indians in the isle of Sambale, five leagues from the coasts of Jucatan. Here is great quantity of amber, but especially when any storm arises from towards the east; whence the waves bring many things, and very different. Through this sea no vessels can pass, unless very small, it being too shallow. In the lands that are surrounded by this sea, is found much Campechy wood, and other things that serve for dyeing, much esteemed in Europe, and would be more, if we had the skill of the Indians, who make a dye or tincture that never fades.

The pirates having been in that gulf three months, and receiving advice that the Spanish ship was come, hastened to the port where the ship lay at anchor unlading her merchandise, with design to assault her as soon as possible; but first they thought convenient to send away some of their boats to seek for a small vessel also expected very richly laden with plate, indigo, and cochineal. Meanwhile, the ship's crew having notice that the pirates designed upon them, prepared all things for a good defence, being mounted with forty-two guns, well furnished with arms and other necessaries, and one hundred and thirty fighting men. To Lolonois all this seemed but little, for he assaulted her with great courage, his own ship carrying but twenty-two guns, and having no more than a small saety or fly-boat for help: but the Spaniards defended themselves so well, as they forced the pirates to retire; but the smoke of the powder continuing thick, as a dark fog or mist, with four canoes well manned, they boarded the ship with great agility, and forced the Spaniards to surrender.

The ship being taken, they found not in her what they thought, being already almost unladen. All they got was only fifty bars of iron, a small parcel of paper, some earthen jars of wine, and other things of small importance.

Then Lolonois called a council of war, and told them, he intended for Guatemala: hereupon they divided into several sentiments, some liking the proposal, and others disliking it, especially a party of them who were but raw in those exercises, and who imagined at their setting forth from Tortuga that pieces of eight were gathered as easy as pears from a tree; but finding most things contrary to their expectation, they quitted the fleet, and returned; others affirmed they had rather starve than return home without a great deal of money.

But the major part judging the propounded voyage little to their purpose, separated from Lolonois and the rest: of these one Moses Vanclein was ringleader, captain of the ship taken at Puerto Cavallo: this fellow steered for Tortuga, to cruise to and fro in these seas. With him joined another comrade of his, by name Pierre le Picard, who seeing the rest leave Lolonois, thought fit to do the same. These runaways having thus parted company, steered homewards, coasting along the continent till they came to Costa Rica; here they landed a strong party nigh the river Veraguas, and marched in good order to the town of the same name: this they took and totally pillaged, though the Spaniards made a strong resistance. They brought away some of the inhabitants as prisoners, with all they had, which was of no great importance, by reason of the poverty of the place, which exerciseth no other trade than working in the mines, where some of the inhabitants constantly attend, while none seek for gold, but only slaves. These they compel to dig and wash the earth in the neighbouring rivers, where often they find pieces of gold as big as peas. The pirates gaining in this adventure but seven or eight pounds weight of gold, they returned, giving over the design to go to the town of Nata, situate on the coasts of the South Sea, whose inhabitants are rich merchants, and their slaves work in the mines of Veraguas; being deterred by the multitudes of Spaniards gathered on all sides to fall upon them, whereof they had timely advice.

Lolonois, thus left by his companions, remained alone in the gulf of Honduras. His ship being too great to get out at the reflux of those seas, there he sustained great want of provisions, so as they were constrained to go ashore every day to seek sustenance, and not finding anything else, they were forced to kill and eat monkeys, and other animals, such as they could find.

At last in the altitude of the cape of Gracias a Dios, near a certain little island called De las Pertas, his ship struck on a bank of sand, where it stuck so fast, as no art could get her off again, though they unladed all the guns, iron, and other weighty things as much as they could. Hereupon they were forced to break the ship in pieces, and with planks and nails build themselves a boat to get away; and while they are busy about it, I shall describe the said isles and their inhabitants.

The islands De las Pertas are inhabited by savage Indians, not having known or conversed with civil people: they are tall and very nimble, running almost as fast as horses; at diving also they are very dextrous and hardy. From the bottom of the sea I saw them take up an anchor of six hundredweight, tying a cable to it with great dexterity, and pulling it from a rock. Their arms are made of wood, without any iron point; but some instead thereof use a crocodile's tooth. They have no bows nor arrows, as the other Indians have, but their common weapon is a sort of lance a fathom and a half long. Here are many plantations surrounded with woods, whence they gather abundance of fruits, as potatoes, bananas, racoven, ananas, and many others. They have no houses to dwell in, as at other places in the Indies. Some say they eat human flesh, which is confirmed by what happened when Lolonois was there. Two of his companions, one a Frenchman and the other a Spaniard, went into the woods, where having straggled awhile, a troop of Indians pursued them. They defended themselves as well as they could with their swords, but at last were forced to flee. The nimble Frenchman escaped; but the Spaniard being not so swift, was taken and heard of no more. Some days after, twelve pirates set forth well armed to seek their companion, among whom was the Frenchman, who conducted them, and showed them the place where he left him; here they found that the Indians had kindled a fire, and at a small distance they found a man's bones well roasted, with some pieces of flesh ill scraped off the bones, and one hand, which had only two fingers remaining, whence they concluded they had roasted the poor Spaniard.

They marched on, seeking for Indians, and found a great number together, who endeavoured to escape, but they overtook some of them, and brought aboard their ships five men and four women; with these they took much pains to make themselves be understood, and to gain their affections, giving them trifles, as knives, beads, and the like; they gave them also victuals and drink, but nothing would they taste. It was also observable, that while they were prisoners, they spoke not one word to each other; so that seeing these poor Indians were much afraid, they presented them again with some small things, and let them go. When they parted, they made signs they would come again, but they soon forgot their benefactors, and were never heard of more; neither could any notice afterwards be had of these Indians, nor any others in the whole island, which made the pirates suspect that both those that were taken, and all the rest of the islanders, swam away by night to some little neighbouring islands, especially considering they could never set eyes on any Indian more, nor any boat or other vessel. Meanwhile the pirates were very desirous to see their long-boat finished out of the timber that struck on the sands; yet considering their work would be long, they began to cultivate some pieces of ground; here they sowed French beans, which ripened in six weeks, and many other fruits. They had good provision of Spanish wheat, bananas, racoven, and other things; with the wheat they made bread, and baked it in portable ovens, brought with them. Thus they feared not hunger in those desert places, employing themselves thus for five or six months; which past, and the long-boat finished, they resolved for the river of Nicaragua, to see if they could take some canoes, and return to the said islands for their companions that remained behind, by reason the boat could not hold so many men together; hereupon, to avoid disputes, they cast lots, determining who should go or stay.

The lot fell on one half of the people of the lost vessel, who embarked in the long-boat, and on the skiff which they had before, the other half remaining ashore. Lolonois having set sail, arrived in a few days at the river of Nicaragua: here that ill-fortune assailed him which of long time had been reserved for him, as a punishment due to the multitude of horrible crimes committed in his licentious and wicked life. Here he met with both Spaniards and Indians, who jointly setting upon him and his companions, the greatest part of the pirates were killed on the place. Lolonois, with those that remained alive, had much ado to escape aboard their boats: yet notwithstanding this great loss, he resolved not to return to those he had left at the isle of Pertas, without taking some boats, such as he looked for. To this effect he determined to go on to the coasts of Carthagena; but God Almighty, the time of His Divine justice being now come, had appointed the Indians of Darien to be the instruments and executioners thereof. These Indians of Darien are esteemed as bravoes, or wild savage Indians, by the neighbouring Spaniards, who never could civilize them. Hither Lolonois came (brought by his evil conscience that cried for punishment), thinking to act his cruelties; but the Indians within a few days after his arrival took him prisoner, and tore him in pieces alive, throwing his body limb by limb into the fire, and his ashes into the air, that no trace or memory might remain of such an infamous, inhuman creature. One of his companions gave me an exact account of this tragedy, affirming that himself had escaped the same punishment with the greatest difficulty; he believed also that many of his comrades, who were taken in that encounter by those Indians, were, as their cruel captain, torn in pieces and burnt alive. Thus ends the history, the life, and miserable death of that infernal wretch Lolonois, who full of horrid, execrable, and enormous deeds, and debtor to so much innocent blood, died by cruel and butcherly hands, such as his own were in the course of his life.

Those that remained in the island De las Pertas, waiting for the return of them who got away only to their great misfortune, hearing no news of their captain nor companions, at last embarked on the ship of a certain pirate, who happened to pass that way. This fellow came from Jamaica, with intent to land at Gracias a Dios, and from thence to enter the river with his canoes, and take the city of Carthagena. These two crews of pirates being now joined, were infinitely glad at the presence and society of one another. Those, because they found themselves delivered from their miseries, poverty, and necessities, wherein they had lived ten entire months. These, because they were now considerably strengthened, to effect with greater satisfaction their designs. Hereupon, as soon as they were arrived at Gracias a Dios, they all put themselves into canoes, and entered the river, being five hundred men, leaving only five or six persons in each ship to keep them. They took no provisions, being persuaded they should find everywhere sufficient; but these their hopes were found totally vain, not being grounded on Almighty God; for He ordained it so, that the Indians, aware of their coming, all fled, not leaving in their houses or plantations, which for the most part border on the sides of rivers, any necessary provisions or victuals: hereby, in a few days after they had quitted their ships, they were reduced to most extreme necessity and hunger; but their hopes of making their fortunes very soon, animating them for the present, they contented themselves with a few green herbs, such as they could gather on the banks of the river.

Yet all this courage and vigour lasted but a fortnight, when their hearts, as well as bodies, began to fail for hunger; insomuch as they were forced to quit the river, and betake themselves to the woods, seeking out some villages where they might find relief, but all in vain; for having ranged up and down the woods for some days, without finding the least comfort, they were forced to return to the river, where being come, they thought convenient to descend to the sea-coast where they had left their ships, not having been able to find what they sought for. In this laborious journey they were reduced to such extremity, that many of them devoured their own shoes, the sheaths of their swords, knives, and other such things, being almost ravenous, and eager to meet some Indians, intending to sacrifice them to their teeth. At last they arrived at the sea-coast, where they found some comfort and relief to their former miseries, and also means to seek more: yet the greatest part perished through faintness and other diseases contracted by hunger, which also caused the remaining part to disperse, till at last, by degrees, many or most of them fell into the same pit that Lolonois did; of whom, and of whose companions, having given a compendious narrative, I shall continue with the actions and exploits of Captain Henry Morgan, who may deservedly be called the second Lolonois, not being unlike or inferior to him, either in achievements against the Spaniards, or in robberies of many innocent people.

CHAPTER IX.

The origin and descent of Captain Henry Morgan—His exploits, and the most remarkable actions of his life.

CAPTAIN HENRY MORGAN was born in Great Britain, in the principality of Wales; his father was a rich yeoman, or farmer, of good quality, even as most who bear that name in Wales are known to be. Morgan, when young, had no inclination to the calling of his father, and therefore left his country, and came towards the sea-coasts to seek some other employment more suitable to his aspiring humour; where he found several ships at anchor, bound for Barbadoes. With these he resolved to go in the service of one, who, according to the practice of those parts, sold him as soon as he came ashore. He served his time at Barbadoes, and obtaining his liberty, betook himself to Jamaica, there to seek new fortunes: here he found two vessels of pirates ready to go to sea; and being destitute of employment, he went with them, with intent to follow the exercises of that sort of people: he soon learned their manner of living, so exactly, that having performed three or four voyages with profit and success, he agreed with some of his comrades, who had got by the same voyages a little money, to join stocks, and buy a ship. The vessel being bought, they unanimously chose him captain and commander.

With this ship he set forth from Jamaica to cruise on

the coasts of Campechy, in which voyage he took several ships, with which he returned triumphant. Here he found an old pirate, named Mansvelt (whom we have already mentioned), busied in equipping a considerable fleet, with design to land on the continent, and pillage whatever he could. Mansvelt seeing Captain Morgan return with so many prizes, judged him to be a man of courage, and chose him for his vice-admiral in that expedition: thus having fitted out fifteen ships, great and small, they sailed from Jamaica with five hundred men, Walloons and French. This fleet arrived, not long after, at the isle of St. Catherine, near the continent of Costa Rica, latitude 12 deg. 30 min. and distant thirty-five leagues from the river Chagre. Here they made their first descent, landing most of their men, who soon forced the garrison that kept the island to surrender all the forts and castles thereof; which they instantly demolished, except one, wherein they placed a hundred men of their own party, and all the slaves they had taken from the Spaniards: with the rest of their men they marched to another small island, so near St. Catherine's, that with a bridge they made in a few days, they passed thither, taking with them all the ordnance they had taken on the great island. Having ruined with fire and sword both the islands, leaving necessary orders at the said castle, they put to sea again, with their Spanish prisoners; yet these they set ashore not long after, on the firm land, near Puerto Velo: then they cruised on Costa Rica, till they came to the river Colla, designing to pillage all the towns in those parts, thence to pass to the village of Nata, to do the same.

The governor of Panama, on advice of their arrival, and of the hostilities they committed, thought it his duty to meet them with a body of men. His coming caused the pirates to retire suddenly, seeing the whole country was alarmed, and that their designs were known, and consequently defeated at that time. Hereupon, they returned to St. Catherine's, to visit the hundred men they left in garrison there. The governor of these men was a Frenchman, named Le Sieur Simon, who behaved himself very well in that charge, while Mansvelt was absent, having put the great island in a very good posture of defence, and the little one he had caused to be cultivated with many fertile plantations, sufficient to revictual the whole fleet, not only for the present, but also for a new voyage. Mansvelt was very much bent to keep the two islands in perpetual possession, being very commodiously situated for the pirates; being so near the Spanish dominions, and easily defended.

Hereupon, Mansvelt determined to return to Jamaica, to send recruits to St. Catherine's, that in case of an invasion the pirates might be provided for a defence. As soon as he arrived, he propounded his intentions to the governor there, who rejected his propositions, fearing to displease his master, the king of England; besides, that giving him the men he desired, and necessaries, he must of necessity diminish the forces of that island, whereof he was governor. Hereupon, Mansvelt, knowing that of himself he could not compass his designs, he went to Tortuga; but there, before he could put in execution what was intended, death surprised him, and put a period to his wicked life, leaving all things in suspense till the occasion I shall hereafter relate.

Le Sieur Simon, governor of St. Catherine's, receiving no news from Mansvelt, his admiral, was impatiently desirous to know the cause thereof: meanwhile, Don John Perez de Guzman, being newly come to the government of Costa Rica, thought it not convenient for the interest of Spain for that island to be in the hands of the pirates: hereupon, he equipped a considerable fleet, which he sent to retake it; but before he used violence, he writ a letter to Le Sieur Simon, telling him, that if he would surrender the island to his Catholic Majesty, he should be very well rewarded; but, in case of refusal, severely punished, when he had forced him to do it. Le Sieur Simon, seeing no probability of being able to defend it alone, nor any emolument that by so doing could accrue either to him, or his people, after some small resistance delivered it up to its true lord and master, under the same articles they had obtained it from the Spaniards; a few days after which surrender, there arrived from Jamaica an English ship, which the governor there had sent underhand, with a good supply of people, both men and women: the Spaniards from the castle having espied the ship, put forth English colours, and persuaded Le Sieur Simon to go aboard, and conduct the ship into a port they assigned him. This he performed and they were all made prisoners. A certain Spanish engineer has published in print an exact relation of the retaking of this isle by the Spaniards, which I have thought fit to insert here :—

> *A true relation, and particular account of the victory obtained by the arms of his Catholic Majesty against the English pirates, by the direction and valour of Don John Perez de Guzman, knight of the order of St. James, governor and captain-general of Terra Firma, and the Province of Veraguas.*

THE kingdom of Terra Firma, which of itself is sufficiently strong to repel and destroy great fleets, especially the pirates of Jamaica, had several ways notice imparted to the governor thereof, that fourteen English vessels cruised on the coasts belonging to his Catholic Majesty. July 14, 1665, news came to Panama, that they were arrived at Puerto de Naos, and had forced the Spanish garrison of the isle of St. Catherine, whose governor was Don Estevan del Campo, and possessed themselves of the said island, taking prisoners the inhabitants, and destroying all that they met. About the same time, Don John Perez de Guzman received particular information of these robberies from some Spaniards who escaped out of the island (and whom he ordered to be conveyed to Puerto Velo), that the said pirates came into the island May 2, by night, without being perceived; and that the next day, after some skirmishes, they took the fortresses, and made prisoners all the inhabitants and soldiers that could not escape. Upon this, Don John called a council of war, wherein he declared the great progress the said pirates had made in the dominions of his Catholic Majesty; and propounded "that it was absolutely necessary to send some forces to the isle of St. Catherine, sufficient to retake it from the pirates, the honour and interest of his Majesty of Spain being very narrowly concerned herein; otherwise the pirates by such conquests might easily, in course of time, possess themselves of all the countries thereabouts." To this some made answer, "that the pirates, not being able to subsist in the said island, would of necessity consume and waste themselves, and be forced to quit it, without any necessity of retaking it: that consequently it was not worth the while to engage in so many expenses and troubles as this would cost." Notwithstanding which, Don John being an expert and valiant soldier, ordered that provisions should be conveyed to Puerto Velo for the use of the militia, and transported himself thither, with no small danger of his life. Here he arrived July 2, with most things necessary to the expedition in hand, where he found in the port a good ship, and well mounted, called the *St. Vincent*, that belonged to the company of the negroes, which he manned and victualled very well, and sent to the isle of St. Catherine, constituting Captain Joseph Sanchez Ximenez, major of Puerto Velo, commander thereof. He carried with him two hundred and seventy soldiers, and thirty-seven prisoners of the same island, besides thirty-four Spaniards of the garrison of Puerto Velo, twenty-nine mulattoes of Panama, twelve Indians, very dextrous at shooting with bows and arrows, seven expert and able gunners, two lieutenants, two pilots, one surgeon, and one religious, of the order of St. Francis, for their chaplain.

Don John soon after gave orders to all the officers how to behave themselves, telling them that the governor of Carthagena would supply them with more men, boats, and all things else, necessary for that enterprise; to which effect he had already written to the said governor. July 24, Don John setting sail with a fair wind, he called before him all his people, and made them a speech, encouraging them to fight against the enemies of their country and religion, and especially against those inhuman pirates, who had committed so many horrid cruelties upon the subjects of his Catholic Majesty; withal, promising every one most liberal rewards, especially to such as should behave themselves well in the service of their king and country. Thus Don John bid them farewell, and the ship set sail under a favourable gale. The 22nd they arrived at Carthagena, and presented a letter to the governor thereof, from the noble and valiant Don John, who received it with testimonies of great affection to the person of Don John, and his Majesty's service: and seeing their resolution to be conformable to his desires, he promised them his assistance, with one frigate, one galleon, one boat, and one hundred and twenty-six men; one half out of his own garrison, and the other half mulattoes. Thus being well provided with necessaries, they left the port of Carthagena, August 2, and the 10th they arrived in sight of St. Catherine's towards the western point thereof; and though the wind was contrary, yet they reached the port, and anchored within it, having lost one of their boats by foul weather, at the rock called Quita Signos.

The pirates, seeing our ships come to an anchor, gave them presently three guns with bullets, which were soon answered in the same coin. Hereupon, Major Joseph Sanchez Ximenez sent ashore to the pirates one of his officers to require them, in the name of the Catholic King his master, to surrender the island, seeing they had taken it in the midst of peace between the two crowns of Spain and England; and that if they would be obstinate, he would certainly put them all to the sword. The pirates made answer, that the island had once before belonged unto the government and dominions of the king of England, and that instead of surrendering it, they preferred to lose their lives.

On Friday the 13th, three negroes, from the enemy, came swimming aboard our admiral; these brought intelligence, that all the pirates upon the island were only seventy-two in number, and that they were under a great consternation, seeing such considerable forces come against them. With this intelligence, the Spaniards resolved to land, and advance towards the fortresses, which ceased not to fire as many great guns against them as they possibly could; which were answered in the same manner on our side, till dark night. On Sunday, the 15th, the day of the Assumption of our Lady, the weather being very calm and clear, the Spaniards began to advance thus: The ship *St. Vincent*, riding admiral, discharged two whole broadsides on the battery called the Conception; the ship *St. Peter*, that was vice-admiral, discharged likewise her guns against the other battery named St. James: meanwhile, our people landed in small boats, directing their course towards the point of the battery last mentioned, and thence they marched towards the gate called Cortadura. Lieutenant Francis de Cazeres, being desirous to view the strength of the enemy, with only fifteen men, was compelled to retreat in haste, by reason of the great guns, which played so furiously on the place where he stood; they shooting, not only pieces of iron, and small bullets, but also the organs of the church, discharging in every shot threescore pipes at a time.

Notwithstanding this heat of the enemy, Captain Don Joseph Ramirez de Leyva, with sixty men, made a strong attack, wherein they fought on both sides very desperately, till at last he overcame, and forced the pirates to surrender the fort.

On the other side, Captain John Galeno, with ninety men, passed over the hills, to advance that way towards the castle of St. Teresa. Meanwhile Major Don Joseph Sanchez Ximenes, as commander-in-chief, with the rest of his men, set forth from the battery of St. James, passing the port with four boats, and landing, in despite of the enemy. About this same time, Captain John Galeno began to advance with the men he led to the forementioned fortress; so that our men made three attacks on three several sides, at one and the same time, with great courage; till the pirates seeing many of their men already killed, and that they could in no manner subsist any longer, retreated towards Cortadura, where they surrendered, themselves and the whole island, into our hands. Our people possessed themselves of all, and set up the Spanish colours, as soon as they had rendered thanks to God Almighty for the victory obtained on such a signalized day. The number of dead were six men of the enemies, with many wounded, and seventy prisoners: on our side was only one man killed, and four wounded.

There were found on the island eight hundred pounds of powder, two hundred and fifty pounds of small bullets, with many other military provisions. Among the prisoners were taken also, two Spaniards, who had bore arms under the English against his Catholic Majesty: these were shot to death the next day, by order of the major. The 10th day of September arrived at the isle an English vessel, which being seen at a great distance by the major, he ordered Le Sieur Simon, who was a Frenchman, to go and visit the said ship, and tell them that were on board, that the island belonged still to the English. He performed the command, and found in the said ship only fourteen men, one woman and her daughter, who were all instantly made prisoners.

The English pirates were all transported to Puerto Velo, excepting three, who by order of the governor were carried to Panama, there to work in the castle of St. Jerom. This fortification is an excellent piece of workmanship, and very strong, being raised in the middle of the port of a quadrangular form, and of very hard stone: its height is eighty-eight geometrical feet, the wall being fourteen, and the curtains seventy-five feet diameter. It was built at the expense of several private persons, the governor of the city furnishing the greatest part of the money; so that it cost his Majesty nothing.

CHAPTER X.

Of the Island of Cuba—Captain Morgan attempts to preserve the Isle of St. Catherine as a refuge to the nest of pirates, but fails of his design—He arrives at and takes the village of El Puerto del Principe.

CAPTAIN MORGAN seeing his predecessor and admiral Mansvelt were dead, used all the means that were possible, to keep in possession the isle of St. Catherine, seated near Cuba. His chief intent was to make it a refuge and sanctuary to the pirates of those parts, putting it in a condition of being a convenient receptacle of their preys and robberies. To this effect he left no stone unmoved, writing to several merchants in Virginia and New England, persuading them to send him provisions and necessaries, towards putting the said island in such a posture of defence, as to fear no danger of invasion from any side. But all this proved ineffectual, by the Spaniards retaking the said island: yet Captain Morgan retained his courage, which put him on new designs. First, he equipped a ship, in order to gather a fleet as great, and as strong as he could. By degrees he effected it, and gave orders to every member of his fleet to meet at a certain port of Cuba, there determining to call a council, and deliberate what was best to be done, and what place first to fall upon. Leaving these preparations in this condition, I shall give my reader some small account of the said isle of Cuba, in whose port this expedition was hatched, seeing I omitted to do it in its proper place.

Cuba lies from east to west, in north latitude, from 20 to 23 deg. in length one hundred and fifty German leagues, and about forty in breadth. Its fertility is equal to that of Hispaniola; besides which, it affords many things proper for trading and commerce; such as hides of several beasts, particularly those that in Europe are called hides of Havanna. On all sides it is surrounded with many small islands, called the Cayos: these little islands the pirates use as ports of refuge. Here they have their meetings, and hold their councils, how best to assault the Spaniards. It is watered on all sides with plentiful and pleasant rivers, whose entries form both secure and spacious ports; beside many other harbours for ships, which along the calm shores and coasts adorn this rich and beautiful island; all which contribute much to its happiness, by facilitating trade, whereto they invited both natives and aliens. The chief of these ports are San Jago, Byame, Santa Maria, Espiritu Santo, Trinidad, Zagoa, Cabo de Corientes, and others, on the south side of the island: on the north side are, La Havanna, Puerto Mariano, Santa Cruz, Mata Ricos, and Barracoa.

This island hath two chief cities, to which all the towns and villages thereof give obedience. The first is Santa Jago, or St. James, seated on the south side, and having under its jurisdiction one half of the island. The chief magistrates hereof are a bishop and a governor, who command the villages and towns of the said half. The chief of these are, on the south side, Espiritu Santo, Puerto del Principe, and Bayame. On the north it has Barracoa, and De los Cayos. The greatest part of the commerce driven here comes from the Canaries, whither they transport much tobacco, sugar, and hides, which sort of merchandise are drawn to the head city from the subordinate towns and villages. Formerly the city of Santa Jago was miserably sacked by the pirates of Jamaica and Tortuga, though it is defended by a considerable castle.

The city and port De la Havanna lies between the north and west side of the island: this is one of the strongest places of the West Indies; its jurisdiction extends over the other half of the island; the chief places under it being Santa Cruz on the north side, and La Trinidad on the south. Hence is transported huge quantities of tobacco, which is sent to New Spain and Costa Rica, even as far as the South Sea, besides many ships laden with this commodity, that are consigned to Spain and other parts of Europe, not only in the leaf, but in rolls. This city is defended by three castles, very great and strong, two of which lie towards the port, and the other is seated on a hill that commands the town. It is esteemed to contain about ten thousand families. The merchants of this place trade in New Spain, Campechy, Honduras, and Florida. All ships that come from the parts before mentioned, as also from Caraccas, Carthagena and Costa Rica, are necessitated to take their provisions in at Havanna to make their voyage for Spain; this being the necessary and straight course they must steer for the south of Europe, and other parts. The plate-fleet of Spain, which the Spaniards call Flota, being homeward bound, touches here yearly to complete their cargo with hides, tobacco, and Campechy wood.

Captain Morgan had been but two months in these ports of the south of Cuba, when he had got together a fleet of twelve sail, between ships and great boats, with seven hundred fighting men, part English and part French. They called a council, and some advised to assault the city of Havanna in the night, which they said might easily be done, if they could but take any few of the ecclesiastics;

yea, that the city might be sacked before the castles could put themselves in a posture of defence. Others propounded, according to their several opinions, other attempts; but the former proposal was rejected, because many of the pirates, who had been prisoners at other times in the said city, affirmed nothing of consequence could be done with less than one thousand five hundred men. Moreover, that with all these people, they ought first to go to the island De los Pinos, and land them in small boats about Matamona, fourteen leagues from the said city, whereby to accomplish their designs.

Finally, they saw no possibility of gathering so great a fleet, and hereupon, with what they had, they concluded to attempt some other place. Among the rest, one propounded they should assault the town of El Puerto del Principe. This proposition he persuaded to, by saying he knew that place very well, and that being at a distance from sea, it never was sacked by any pirates, whereby the inhabitants were rich, exercising their trade by ready money, with those of Havanna who kept here an established commerce, chiefly in hides. This proposal was presently admitted by Captain Morgan, and the chief of his companions. Hereupon they ordered every captain to weigh anchor and set sail, steering towards that coast nearest to El Puerto del Principe. Here is a bay named by the Spaniards El Puerto de Santa Maria: being arrived at this bay, a Spaniard, who was prisoner aboard the fleet, swam ashore by night to the town of el Puerto del Principe, giving an account to the inhabitants of the design of the pirates, which he overheard in their discourse, while they thought he did not understand English. The Spaniards upon this advice began to hide their riches, and carry away their movables; the governor immediately raised all the people of the town, freemen and slaves, and with part of them took a post by which of necessity the pirates must pass, and commanded many trees to be cut down and laid cross the ways to hinder their passage, placing several ambuscades strengthened with some pieces of cannon to play upon them on their march. He gathered in all about eight hundred men, of which detaching part into the said ambuscades, with the rest he begirt the town, drawing them up in a spacious field, whence they could see the coming of the pirates at length.

Captain Morgan, with his men, now on the march, found the avenues to the town unpassable; hereupon they took their way through the wood, traversing it with great difficulty, whereby they escaped divers ambuscades; at last they came to the plain, from its figure called by the Spaniards La Savanna, or the Sheet. The governor seeing them come, detached a troop of horse to charge them in the front, thinking to disperse them, and to pursue them with his main body; but this design succeeded not, for the pirates marched in very good order, at the sound of their drums, and with flying colours; coming near the horse they drew into a semicircle, and so advanced towards the Spaniards, who charged them valiantly for a while; but the pirates being very dextrous at their arms, and their governor, with many of their companions, being killed, they retreated towards the wood, to save themselves with more advantage; but before they could reach it, most of them were unfortunately killed by the pirates. Thus they left the victory to these new-come enemies, who had no considerable loss of men in the battle, and but very few wounded. The skirmish lasted four hours: they entered the town not without great resistance of such as were within, who defended themselves as long as possible, and many seeing the enemy in the town, shut themselves up in their own houses, and thence made several shots upon the pirates; who thereupon threatened them, saying, "If you surrender not voluntarily, you shall soon see the town in a flame, and your wives and children torn in pieces before your faces." Upon these menaces the Spaniards submitted to the discretion of the pirates, believing they could not continue there long.

As soon as the pirates had possessed themselves of the town, they enclosed all the Spaniards, men, women, children, and slaves, in several churches, and pillaged all the goods they could find; then they searched the country round about, bringing in daily many goods and prisoners, with much provision. With this they fell to making great cheer, after their old custom, without remembering the poor prisoners, whom they let starve in the churches, though they tormented them daily and inhumanly to make them confess where they had hid their goods, money, &c., though little or nothing was left them, not sparing the women and little children, giving them nothing to eat, whereby the greatest part perished.

Pillage and provisions growing scarce, they thought convenient to depart and seek new fortunes in other places; they told the prisoners, "they should find money to ransom themselves, else they should be all transported to Jamaica; and beside, if they did not pay a second ransom for the town, they would turn every house into ashes." The Spaniards hereupon nominated among themselves four fellow-prisoners to go and seek for the above-mentioned contributions; but the pirates, to the intent that they should return speedily with those ransoms, tormented several cruelly in their presence, before they departed. After a few days, the Spaniards returned, telling Captain Morgan, "We have ran up and down, and searched all the neighbouring woods and places we most suspected, and yet have not been able to find any of our own party, nor consequently any fruit of our embassy; but if you are pleased to have a little longer patience with us, we shall certainly cause all that you demand to be paid within fifteen days;" which Captain Morgan granted. But not long after, there came into the town seven or eight pirates who had been ranging in the woods and fields, and got considerable booty. These brought amongst other prisoners a negro, whom they had taken with letters. Captain Morgan having perused them, found that they were from the governor of Santa Jago, being written to some of the prisoners, wherein he told them, "they should not make too much haste to pay any ransom for their town or persons, or any other pretext; but on the contrary, they should put off the pirates as well as they could with excuses and delays, expecting to be relieved by him in a short time, when he would certainly come to their aid." Upon this intelligence Captain Morgan immediately ordered all their plunder to be carried aboard; and withal, he told the Spaniards, that the very next day they should pay their ransoms, for he would not wait a moment longer, but reduce the whole town to ashes, if they failed of the sum he demanded.

With this intimation, Captain Morgan made no mention to the Spaniards of the letters he had intercepted. They answered, "that it was impossible for them to give such a sum of money in so short a space of time, seeing their fellow-townsmen were not to be found in all the country thereabouts." Captain Morgan knew full well their intentions, but thought it not convenient to stay there any longer, demanding of them only five hundred oxen or cows, with sufficient salt to powder them, with this condition, that they should carry them on board his ships. Thus he departed with all his men, taking with him only six of the principal prisoners as pledges. Next day the

Spaniards brought the cattle and salt to the ships, and required the prisoners; but Captain Morgan refused to deliver them, till they had helped his men to kill and salt the beeves: this was performed in great haste, he not caring to stay there any longer, lest he should be surprised by the forces that were gathering against him; and having received all on board his vessels, he set at liberty the hostages. Meanwhile there happened some dissensions between the English and the French: the occasion was as follows: A Frenchman being employed in killing and salting the beeves, an English pirate took away the marrow-bones he had taken out of the ox, which these people esteem much; hereupon they challenged one another: being come to the place of duel, the Englishman stabbed the Frenchman in the back, whereby he fell down dead. The other Frenchmen, desirous of revenge, made an insurrection against the English; but Captain Morgan soon appeased them, by putting the criminal in chains to be carried to Jamaica, promising he would see justice done upon him; for though he might challenge his adversary, yet it was not lawful to kill him treacherously, as he did.

All things being ready, and on board, and the prisoners set at liberty, they sailed thence to a certain island, where Captain Morgan intended to make a dividend of what they had purchased in that voyage; where being arrived, they found nigh the value of fifty thousand pieces of eight in money and goods; the sum being known, it caused a general grief to see such a small purchase, not sufficient to pay their debts at Jamaica. Hereupon Captain Morgan proposed they should think on some other enterprise and pillage before they returned. But the French not being able to agree with the English, left Captain Morgan with those of his own nation, notwithstanding all the persuasions he used to reduce them to continue in his company. Thus they parted with all external signs of friendship, Captain Morgan reiterating his promises to them that he would see justice done on that criminal. This he performed; for being arrived at Jamaica, he caused him to be hanged, which was all the satisfaction the French pirates could expect.

CHAPTER XI.

Captain Morgan resolving to attack and plunder the city of Puerto Bello, equips a fleet, and with little expense and small forces takes it.

SOME may think that the French having deserted Captain Morgan, the English alone could not have sufficient courage to attempt such great actions as before. But Captain Morgan, who always communicated vigour with his words, infused such spirit into his men, as put them instantly upon new designs; they being all persuaded that the sole execution of his orders would be a certain means of obtaining great riches, which so influenced their minds, that with inimitable courage they all resolved to follow him, as did also a certain pirate of Campechy, who on this occasion joined with Captain Morgan, to seek new fortunes under his conduct. Thus Captain Morgan in a few days gathered a fleet of nine sail, either ships or great boats, wherein he had four hundred and sixty military men.

All things being ready, they put forth to sea, Captain Morgan imparting his design to nobody at present; he only told them on several occasions, that he doubted not to make a good fortune by that voyage, if strange occurrences happened not. They steered towards the continent, where they arrived in a few days near Costa Rica, all their fleet safe. No sooner had they discovered land but Captain Morgan declared his intentions to the captains, and presently after to the company. He told them he intended to plunder Puerto Bello by night, being resolved to put the whole city to the sack: and to encourage them he added, this enterprise could not fail, seeing he had kept it secret, without revealing it to anybody, whereby they could not have notice of his coming. To this proposition some answered, "they had not a sufficient number of men to assault so strong and great a city. But Captain Morgan replied, "If our number is small, our hearts are great; and the fewer persons we are, the more union and better shares we shall have in the spoil." Hereupon, being stimulated with the hope of those vast riches they promised themselves from their success, they unanimously agreed to that design. Now, that my reader may better comprehend the boldness of this exploit, it may be necessary to say something beforehand of the city of Puerto Bello.

This city is in the province of Costa Rica, 10 deg. north latitude, fourteen leagues from the gulf of Darien, and eight westwards from the port called Nombre de Dios. It is judged the strongest place the king of Spain possesses in all the West Indies, except Havanna and Carthagena. Here are two castles almost impregnable, that defend the city, situate at the entry of the port, so that no ship or boat can pass without permission. The garrison consists of three hundred soldiers, and the town is inhabited by about four hundred families. The merchants dwell not here, but only reside awhile, when the galleons come from or go for Spain, by reason of the unhealthiness of the air, occasioned by vapours from the mountains; so that though their chief warehouses are at Puerto Bello, their habitations are at Panama, whence they bring the plate upon mules, when the fair begins, and when the ships belonging to the company of negroes arrive to sell slaves.

Captain Morgan, who knew very well all the avenues of this city and the neighbouring coasts, arrived in the dusk of the evening at Puerto de Naos, ten leagues to the west of Puerto Bello. Being come hither, they sailed up the river to another harbour called Puerto Pontin, where they anchored: here they put themselves into boats and canoes, leaving in the ships only a few men to bring them next day to the port. About midnight they came to a place called Estera longa Lemos, where they all went on shore, and marched by land to the first posts of the city: they had in their company an Englishman, formerly a prisoner in those parts, who now served them for a guide: to him and three or four more they gave commission to take the sentinel, if possible, or kill him on the place: but they seized him so cunningly, as he had no time to give warning with his musket, or make any noise, and brought him, with his hands bound, to Captain Morgan, who asked him how things went in the city, and what forces they had; with other circumstances he desired to know. After every question they made him a thousand menaces to kill him, if he declared not the truth. Then they advanced to the city, carrying the said sentinel bound before them: having marched about a quarter of a league, they came to the castle near the city, which presently they closely surrounded, so that no person could get either in or out.

Being posted under the walls of the castle, Captain Morgan commanded the sentinel, whom they had taken prisoner, to speak to those within, charging them to surrender to his discretion; otherwise they should all be cut in pieces, without quarter. But they regarding none of these threats, began instantly to fire, which alarmed the city; yet notwithstanding, though the governor and soldiers of the said castle made as great resistance as could be, they were forced to surrender. Having taken the castle, they resolved to be as good as their words, putting the Spaniards to the sword, thereby to strike a terror into the rest of the city. Whereupon, having shut up all the soldiers and officers as prisoners into one room, they set fire to the powder (whereof they found great quantity) and blew up the castle into the air, with all the Spaniards that were within. This done, they pursued the course of their victory, falling upon the city, which, as yet, was not ready to receive them. Many of the inhabitants cast their precious jewels and money into wells and cisterns, or hid them in places underground, to avoid, as much as possible, being totally robbed. One party of the pirates, assigned to this purpose, ran immediately to the cloisters, and took as many religious men and women as they could find. The governor of the city, not being able to rally the citizens, through their great confusion, retired to one of the castles remaining, and thence fired incessantly at the pirates: but these were not in the least negligent either to assault him, or defend themselves, so that amidst the horror of the assault, they made very few shots in vain; for aiming with great dexterity at the mouths of the guns, the Spaniards were certain to lose one or two men every time they charged each gun anew.

This continued very furious from break of day till noon; yea, about this time of the day the case was very dubious which party should conquer, or be conquered. At last, the pirates perceiving they had lost many men, and yet advanced but little towards gaining either this, or the other castles, made use of fire-balls, which they threw with their hands, designing to burn the doors of the castles; but the Spaniards from the walls let fall great quantities of stones, and earthen pots full of powder, and other combustible matter, which forced them to desist. Captain Morgan seeing this generous defence made by the Spaniards, began to despair of success. Hereupon, many faint and calm meditations came into his mind; neither could he determine which way to turn himself in that strait. Being thus puzzled, he was suddenly animated to continue the assault, by seeing English colours put forth at one of the lesser castles, then entered by his men; of whom he presently after spied a troop coming to meet him, proclaiming victory with loud shouts of joy. This instantly put him on new resolutions of taking the rest of the castles, especially seeing the chiefest citizens were fled to them, and had conveyed thither great part of their riches, with all the plate belonging to the churches and divine service.

To this effect, he ordered ten or twelve ladders to be made in all haste, so broad, that three or four men at once might ascend them: these being finished, he commanded all the religious men and women, whom he had taken prisoners, to fix them against the walls of the castle. This he had before threatened the governor to do, if he delivered not the castle: but his answer was, "he would never surrender himself alive." Captain Morgan was persuaded the governor would not employ his utmost force, seeing the religious women, and ecclesiastical persons, exposed in the front of the soldiers to the greatest danger. Thus the ladders, as I have said, were put into the hands of religious persons of both sexes, and these were forced, at the head of the companies, to raise and apply them to the walls: but Captain Morgan was fully deceived in his judgment of this design; for the governor, who acted like a brave soldier in performance of his duty, used his utmost endeavour to destroy whosoever came near the walls. The religious men and women ceased not to cry to him, and beg of him, by all the saints of heaven, to deliver the castle, and spare both his and their own lives; but nothing could prevail with his obstinacy and fierceness. Thus many of the religious men and nuns were killed before they could fix the ladders; which at last being done, though with great loss of the said religious people, the pirates mounted them in great numbers, and with not less valour, having fire-balls in their hands, and earthen pots full of powder; all which things, being now at the top of the walls, they kindled and cast in among the Spaniards.

This effort of the pirates was very great, insomuch that the Spaniards could no longer resist nor defend the castle, which was now entered. Hereupon they all threw down their arms, and craved quarter for their lives; only the governor of the city would crave no mercy, but killed many of the pirates with his own hands, and not a few of his own soldiers; because they did not stand to their arms. And though the pirates asked him if he would have quarter; yet he constantly answered, "By no means, I had rather die as a valiant soldier, than be hanged as a coward." They endeavoured as much as they could to take him prisoner, but he defended himself so obstinately, that they were forced to kill him, notwithstanding all the cries and tears of his own wife and daughter, who begged him, on their knees, to demand quarter, and save his life. When the pirates had possessed themselves of the castle, which was about night, they enclosed therein all the prisoners, placing the women and men by themselves, with some guards: the wounded were put in an apartment by itself, that their own complaints might be the cure of their diseases; for no other was afforded them.

This done, they fell to eating and drinking, as usual; that is, committing in both all manner of debauchery and excess: these two vices were immediately followed by many insolent actions of rape and adultery, committed on many very honest women, as well married as virgins; who being threatened with the sword, were constrained to submit their bodies to the violence of those lewd and wicked men. Thus they gave themselves up to all sorts of debauchery, that fifty courageous men might easily have retaken the city, and killed all the pirates. Next day, having plundered all they could find, they examined some of the prisoners (who had been persuaded by their companions to say they were the richest of the town), charging them severely to discover where they had hid their riches and goods. Not being able to extort anything from them, they not being the right persons, it was resolved to torture them: this they did so cruelly, that many of them died on the rack, or presently after. Now the president of Panama being advertised of the pillage and ruin of Puerto Bello, he employed all his care and industry to raise forces to pursue and cast out the pirates thence; but these cared little for his preparations, having their ships at hand, and determining to fire the city, and retreat. They had now been at Puerto Bello fifteen days, in which time they had lost many of their men, both by the unhealthiness of the country, and their extravagant debaucheries.

Hereupon, they prepared to depart, carrying on board all the pillage they had got, having first provided the fleet with sufficient victuals for the voyage. While these things were doing, Captain Morgan demanded of the prisoners a ransom for the city, or else he would burn it down, and blow up all the castles; withal, he commanded them to send speedily two persons, to procure the sum, which was 100,000 pieces of eight. To this effect two men were sent to the president of Panama, who gave him an account of all. The president, having now a body of men ready, set forth towards Puerto Bello, to encounter the pirates before their retreat; but they, hearing of his coming, instead of flying away, went out to meet him at a narrow passage, which he must pass: here they placed a hundred men, very well armed, which at the first encounter put to flight a good party of those of Panama. This obliged the president to retire for that time, not being yet in a posture of strength to proceed farther. Presently after, he sent a message to Captain Morgan, to tell him, "that if he departed not suddenly with all his forces from Puerto Bello, he ought to expect no quarter for himself, nor his companions, when he should take them, as he hoped soon to do." Captain Morgan, who feared not his threats, knowing he had a secure retreat in his ships, which were at hand, answered, "he would not deliver the castles, before he had received the contribution money he had demanded; which if it were not paid down, he would certainly burn the whole city, and then leave it, demolishing beforehand the castles, and killing the prisoners."

The governor of Panama perceived by this answer that no means would serve to mollify the hearts of the pirates, nor reduce them to reason: hereupon, he determined to leave them, as also those of the city whom he came to relieve, involved in the difficulties of making the best agreement they could. Thus in a few days more the miserable citizens gathered the contributions required, and brought 100,000 pieces of eight to the pirates for a ransom of their cruel captivity: but the president of Panama was much amazed to consider that four hundred men could take such a great city, with so many strong castles, especially having no ordnance, wherewith to raise batteries, and, what was more, knowing the citizens of Puerto Bello had always great repute of being good soldiers themselves, and who never wanted courage in their own defence. This astonishment was so great, as made him send to Captain Morgan, desiring some small pattern of those arms wherewith he had taken with such vigour so great a city. Captain Morgan received this messenger very kindly, and with great civility; and gave him a pistol, and a few small bullets, to carry back to the president his master; telling him, withal, "he desired him to accept that slender pattern of the arms wherewith he had taken Puerto Bello, and keep them for a twelvemonth; after which time he promised to come to Panama, and fetch them away." The governor returned the present very soon to Captain Morgan, giving him thanks for the favour of lending him such weapons as he needed not; and, withal, sent him a ring of gold, with this message, "that he desired him not to give himself the labour of coming to Panama, as he had done to Puerto Bello: for he did assure him, he should not speed so well here, as he had done there."

After this, Captain Morgan (having provided his fleet with all necessaries, and taken with him the best guns of the castles, nailing up the rest) set sail from Puerto Bello with all his ships, and arriving in a few days at Cuba, he sought out a place wherein he might quickly make the dividend of their spoil. They found in ready money 250,000 pieces of eight, besides other merchandises; as cloth, linen, silks, &c. With this rich purchase they sailed thence to their common place of rendezvous, Jamaica. Being arrived, they passed here some time in all sorts of vices and debaucheries, according to their custom; spending very prodigally what others had gained with no small labour and toil.

CHAPTER XII.

Captain Morgan takes the city of Maracaibo on the coast of Neuva Venezuela—Piracies committed in those seas—Ruin of three Spanish ships, set forth to hinder the robberies of the pirates.

NOT long after their arrival at Jamaica, being that short time they needed to lavish away all the riches above mentioned, they concluded on another enterprise to seek new fortunes: to this effect Captain Morgan ordered all the commanders of his ships to meet at De la Vacca, or the Cow Isle, south of Hispaniola, as is said. Hither flocked to them great numbers of other pirates, French and English; the name of Captain Morgan being now famous in all the neighbouring countries for his great enterprises. There was then at Jamaica an English ship newly come from New England, well mounted with thirty-six guns: this vessel, by order of the governor of Jamaica, joined Captain Morgan to strengthen his fleet, and give him greater courage to attempt mighty things. With this supply Captain Morgan judged himself sufficiently strong; but there being in the same place another great vessel of twenty-four iron guns, and twelve brass ones, belonging to the French, Captain Morgan endeavoured also to join this ship to his own; but the French not daring to trust the English, denied absolutely to consent.

The French pirates belonging to this great ship had met at sea an English vessel; and being under great want of victuals, they had taken some provisions out of the English ship, without paying for them, having, perhaps, no ready money aboard : only they gave them bills of exchange for Jamaica and Tortuga, to receive money there. Captain Morgan having notice of this, and perceiving he could not prevail with the French captain to follow him, resolved to lay hold on this occasion, to ruin the French, and seek his revenge. Hereupon he invited, with dissimulation, the French commander, and several of his men, to dine with him on board the great ship that was come to Jamaica, as is said. Being come, he made them all prisoners, pretending the injury aforesaid done to the English vessel.

This unjust action of Captain Morgan was soon followed by Divine punishment, as we may conceive : the manner I shall instantly relate. Captain Morgan, presently after he had taken these French prisoners, called a council to deliberate what place they should first pitch upon in this new expedition. Here it was determined to go to the isle of Savona, to wait for the flota then expected from Spain, and take any of the Spanish vessels straggling from the rest. This resolution being taken, they began aboard the great ship to feast one another for joy of their new voyage, and happy council, as they hoped : they drank many healths, and discharged many guns, the common sign of mirth among seamen. Most of the men being drunk, by what accident is not known, the ship suddenly was blown up, with three hundred and fifty Englishmen, besides the French prisoners in the hold ; of all which there escaped but thirty men, who were in the great cabin, at some distance from the main force of the powder. Many more, it is thought, might have escaped, had they not been so much overtaken with wine.

This loss brought much consternation of mind upon the English ; they knew not whom to blame, but at last the accusation was laid on the French prisoners, whom they suspected to have fired the powder of the ship out of revenge, though with the loss of their own lives: hereupon they added new accusations to their former, whereby to seize the ship and all that was in it, by saying the French designed to commit piracy on the English. The grounds of this accusation were given by a commission from the governor of Barracoa, found aboard the French vessel, wherein were these words, "that the said governor did permit the French to trade in all Spanish ports," &c. "As also to cruise on the English pirates in what place soever they could find them, because of the multitudes of hostilities which they had committed against the subjects of his Catholic Majesty in time of peace betwixt the two crowns." This commission for trade was interpreted as an express order to exercise piracy and war against them, though it was only a bare licence for coming into the Spanish ports; the cloak of which permission were those words, "that they should cruise upon the English." And though the French did sufficiently expound the true sense of it, yet they could not clear themselves to Captain Morgan nor his council: but in lieu thereof, the ship and men were seized and sent to Jamaica. Here they also endeavoured to obtain justice, and the restitution of their ship, but all in vain; for instead of justice, they were long detained in prison, and threatened with hanging.

Eight days after the loss of the said ship, Captain Morgan commanded the bodies of the miserable wretches who were blown up to be searched for, as they floated on the sea; not to afford them Christian burial, but for their clothes and attire: and if any had gold rings on their fingers, these were cut off, leaving them exposed to the voracity of the monsters of the sea. At last they set sail for Savona, the place of their assignation. There were in all fifteen vessels, Captain Morgan commanding the biggest, of only fourteen small guns; his number of men was nine hundred and sixty. Few days after, they arrived at the Cabo de Lobos, south of Hispaniola, between Cape Tiburon and Cape Punta de Espada : hence they could not pass by reason of contrary winds for three weeks, notwithstanding all the utmost endeavours Captain Morgan used to get forth; then they doubled the cape, and spied an English vessel at a distance. Having spoken with her, they found she came from England, and bought of her, for ready money, some provisions they wanted.

Captain Morgan proceeded on his voyage till he came to the port of Ocoa ; here he landed some men, sending them into the woods to seek water and provisions, the better to spare such as he had already on board. They killed many beasts, and among others some horses. But the Spaniards, not well satisfied at their hunting, laid a stratagem for them, ordering three or four hundred men to come from Santo Domingo not far distant, and desiring them to hunt in all the parts thereabout near the sea, that so, if the pirates should return, they might find no subsistence. Within few days the same pirates returned to hunt, but finding nothing to kill, a party of about fifty straggled farther on into the woods. The Spaniards, who watched all their motions, gathered a great herd of cows, and set two or three men to keep them. The pirates having spied them, killed a sufficient number; and though the Spaniards could see them at a distance, yet they could not hinder them at present; but as soon as they attempted to carry them away, they set upon them furiously, crying, "Mata, mata," *i.e.*, "Kill, kill." Thus the pirates were compelled to quit the prey, and retreat to their ships; but they did it in good order, retiring by degrees, and when they had opportunity, discharging full volleys on the Spaniards, killing many of their enemies, though with some loss.

The Spaniards seeing their damage, endeavoured to save themselves by flight, and carry off their dead and wounded companions. The pirates perceiving them flee, would not content themselves with what hurt they had already done, but pursued them speedily into the woods, and killed the greatest part of those that remained. Next day Captain Morgan, extremely offended at what had passed, went himself with two hundred men into the woods to seek for the rest of the Spaniards, but finding nobody, he revenged his wrath on the houses of the poor and miserable rustics that inhabit those scattering fields and woods, of which he burnt a great number: with this he returned to his ships, somewhat more satisfied in his mind for having done some considerable damage to the enemy, which was always his most ardent desire.

The impatience wherewith Captain Morgan had waited a long while for some of his ships not yet arrived, made him resolve to sail away without them, and steer for Savona, the place he always designed. Being arrived, and not finding any of his ships come, he was more impatient and concerned than before, fearing their loss, or that he must proceed without them; but he waiting for their arrival a few days longer, and having no great plenty of provisions, he sent a crew of one hundred and fifty men to Hispaniola to pillage some towns near Santo Domingo; but the Spaniards, upon intelligence of their coming, were so vigilant, and in such good posture of defence, that the pirates thought not convenient to assault them, choosing rather to return empty-handed to Captain Morgan, than to perish in that desperate enterprise.

At last Captain Morgan, seeing the other ships did not come, made a review of his people, and found only about five hundred men; the ships wanting were seven, he having only eight in his company, of which the greatest part were very small. Having hitherto resolved to cruise on the coasts of Caraccas, and to plunder the towns and villages there, finding himself at present with such small forces, he changed his resolution by advice of a French captain in his fleet. This Frenchman having served Lolonois in the like enterprises, and at the taking of Maracaibo, knew all the entries, passages, forces, and means, how to put in execution the same again in company of Captain Morgan; to whom having made a full relation of all, he concluded to sack it the second time, being himself persuaded, with all his men, of the facility the Frenchman propounded. Hereupon they weighed anchor, and steered towards Curasao. Being come within sight of it, they landed at another island near it, called Ruba, about twelve leagues from Curasao to the west. This island, defended by a slender garrison, is inhabited by Indians subject to Spain, and speak Spanish, by reason of the Roman Catholic religion, here cultivated by a few priests sent from the neighbouring continent.

The inhabitants exercise commerce or trade with the pirates that go or come this way: they buy of the islanders sheep, lambs, and kids, which they exchange for linen, thread, and like things. The country is very dry and barren, the whole substance thereof consisting in those three things, and in a little indifferent wheat. This isle produces many venemous insects, as vipers, spiders, and others. These last are so pernicious, that a man bitten by them dies mad; and the manner of recovering such is to tie them very fast both hands and feet, and so to leave them twenty-four hours, without eating or drinking anything. Captain Morgan, as was said, having cast anchor before this island, bought of the inhabitants sheep, lambs, and wood, for all his fleet. After two days, he sailed again in the night, to the intent they might not see what course he steered.

Next day they arrived at the sea of Maracaibo, taking great care not to be seen from Vigilia, for which reason they anchored out of sight of it. Night being come, they set sail again towards the land, and next morning, by break of day, were got directly over against the bar of the said lake. The Spaniards had built another fort since the action of Lolonois, whence they now fired continually against the pirates, while they put their men into boats to land. The dispute continued very hot, being managed with great courage from morning till dark night. This being come, Captain Morgan, in the obscurity thereof, drew nigh the fort, which having examined, he found nobody in it, the Spaniards having deserted it not long before. They left behind them a match lighted near a train of powder, to have blown up the pirates and the whole fortress as soon as they were in it. This design had taken effect, had not the pirates discovered it in a quarter of an hour; but Captain Morgan snatching away the match, saved both his own and his companions' lives. They found here much powder, whereof he provided his fleet, and then demolished part of the walls, nailing sixteen pieces of ordnance, from twelve to twenty-four pounders. Here they also found many muskets and other military provisions.

Next day they commanded the ships to enter the bar, among which they divided the powder, muskets, and other things found in the fort: then they embarked again to continue their course towards Maracaibo; but the waters being very low, they could not pass a certain bank at the entry of the lake: hereupon they were compelled to go into canoes and small boats, with which they arrived next day before Maracaibo, having no other defence than some small pieces which they could carry in the said boats. Being landed, they ran immediately to the fort De la Barra, which they found as the precedent, without any person in it, for all were fled into the woods, leaving also the town without any people, unless a few miserable folks, who had nothing to lose.

As soon as they had entered the town, the pirates searched every corner, to see if they could find any people that were hid, who might offend them unawares; not finding anybody, every party, as they came out of their several ships, chose what houses they pleased. The church was deputed for the common corps du guard, where they lived after their military manner, very insolently. Next day after they sent a troop of a hundred men to seek for the inhabitants and their goods; these returned next day, bringing with them thirty persons, men, women, and children, and fifty mules laden with good merchandise. All these miserable people were put to the rack, to make them confess where the rest of the inhabitants were, and their goods. Among other tortures, one was to stretch their limbs with cords, and then to beat them with sticks and other instruments. Others had burning matches placed betwixt their fingers, which were thus burnt alive. Others had slender cords or matches twisted about their heads, till their eyes burst out. Thus all inhuman cruelties were executed on those innocent people. Those who would not confess, or who had nothing to declare, died under the hands of those villains. These tortures and racks continued for three whole weeks, in which time they sent out daily parties to seek for more people to torment and rob, they never returning without booty and new riches.

Captain Morgan having now gotten into his hands about a hundred of the chief families, with all their goods, at last resolved for Gibraltar, as Lolonois had done before: with this design he equipped his fleet, providing it sufficiently with all necessaries. He put likewise on board all the prisoners, and weighing anchor, set sail with resolution to hazard a battle. They had sent before some prisoners to Gibraltar, to require the inhabitants to surrender, otherwise Captain Morgan would certainly put them all to the sword, without any quarter. Arriving before Gibraltar, the inhabitants received him with continual shooting of great cannon bullets; but the pirates, instead of fainting hereat, ceased not to encourage one another, saying, "We must make one meal upon bitter things, before we come to taste the sweetness of the sugar this place affords."

Next day very early they landed all their men, and being guided by the Frenchman abovesaid, they marched towards the town, not by the common way, but crossing through woods, which way the Spaniards scarce thought they would have come; for at the beginning of their march they made as if they intended to come the next and open way to the town, hereby to deceive the Spaniards: but these remembering full well what Lolonois had done but two years before, thought it not safe to expect a second brunt, and hereupon all fled out of the town as fast as they could, carrying all their goods and riches, as also all the powder; and having nailed all the great guns, so as the pirates found not one person in the whole city, but one poor innocent man who was born a fool. This man they asked whither the inhabitants were fled, and where they had hid their goods. To all which questions and the like, he constantly answered, "I know nothing, I know nothing:" but they presently put him to the rack, and tortured him with cords; which torments forced him to cry out, "Do not torture me any more, but come with me, and I will show you my goods and my riches." They were persuaded, it seems, he was some rich person disguised under those clothes so poor, and that innocent tongue; so they went along with him, and he conducted them to a poor miserable cottage, wherein he had a few earthen dishes and other things of no value, and three pieces of eight, concealed with some other trumpery underground. Then they asked him his name, and he readily answered, "My name is Don Sebastian Sanchez, and I am brother unto the governor of Maracaibo." This foolish answer, it must be conceived, these inhuman wretches took for truth: for no sooner had they heard it, but they put him again upon the rack, lifting him up on high with cords, and tying huge weights to his feet and neck. Besides which, they burnt him alive, applying palm-leaves burning to his face.

The same day they sent out a party to seek for the inhabitants, on whom they might exercise their cruelties These brought back an honest peasant with two daughters of his, whom they intended to torture as they used others, if they showed not the places where the inhabitants were hid. The peasant knew some of those places, and seeing himself threatened with the rack, went with the pirates to show them; but the Spaniards perceiving their enemies to range everywhere up and down the woods, were already fled thence farther off into the thickest of the woods, where they built themselves huts, to preserve from the weather those few goods they had. The pirates judged themselves deceived by the peasant, and hereupon, to revenge themselves, notwithstanding all his excuses and supplication, they hanged him on a tree.

Then they divided into parties to search the plantations; for they knew the Spaniards that were absconded could not live on what the woods afforded, without coming now and then for provisions to their country houses. Here they found a slave, to whom they promised mountains of gold and his liberty, by transporting him to Jamaica, if he would show them where the inhabitants of Gibraltar lay hid. This fellow conducted them to a party of Spaniards, whom they instantly made prisoners, commanding this slave to kill some before the eyes of the rest; that by this perpetrated crime, he might never be able to leave their wicked company. The negro, according to their orders, committed many murders and insolencies upon the Spaniards, and followed the unfortunate traces of the pirates; who eight days after returned to Gibraltar with many prisoners, and some mules laden with riches. They examined every prisoner by himself (who were in all about two hundred and fifty persons), where they had hid the rest of their goods, and if they knew of their fellow-townsmen. Such as would not confess were tormented after a most inhuman manner. Among the rest, there happened to be a Portuguese, who by a negro was reported, though falsely, to be very rich; this man was commanded to produce his riches. His answer was, he had no more than one hundred pieces of eight in the world, and these had been stolen from him two days before by his servant; which words, though he sealed with many oaths and protestations, yet they would not believe him, but dragging him to the rack, without any regard to his age of sixty years, they stretched him with cords, breaking both his arms behind his shoulders.

This cruelty went not alone; for he not being able or willing to make any other declaration, they put him to another sort of torment more barbarous; they tied him with small cords by his two thumbs and great toes to four stakes fixed in the ground, at a convenient distance, the whole weight of his body hanging on those cords. Not satisfied yet with this cruel torture, they took a stone of above two hundred pounds, and laid it upon his belly, as if they intended to press him to death; they also kindled palm leaves, and applied the flame to the face of this unfortunate Portuguese, burning with them the whole skin, beard, and hair. At last, seeing that neither with these tortures, nor others, they could get anything out of him, they untied the cords, and carried him half dead to the church, where was their corps du guard; here they tied him anew to one of the pillars thereof, leaving him in that condition, without giving him either to eat or drink, unless very sparingly, and so little that would scarce sustain life for some days; four or five being past, he desired one of the prisoners might come to him, by whose means he promised he would endeavour to raise some money to satisfy their demands. The prisoner whom he required was brought to him, and he ordered him to promise the pirates five hundred pieces of eight for his ransom; but they were deaf and obstinate at such a small sum, and instead of accepting it, beat him cruelly with cudgels, saying, "Old fellow, instead of five hundred, you must say five hundred thousand pieces of eight; otherwise you shall here end your life." Finally, after a thousand protestations that he was but a miserable man, and kept a poor tavern for his living, he agreed with them for one thousand pieces of eight. These he raised, and having paid them, got his liberty; though so horribly maimed, that it is scarce to be believed he could survive many weeks.

Other tortures, besides these, were exercised upon others, which this Portuguese endured not: some were hanged up by the testicles, or privy-members, and left till they fell to the ground, those parts being torn from their bodies: if with this they minded to show mercy to those wretches, thus lacerated in the most tender parts, their mercy was, to run them through with their swords; otherwise they used to lie four or five days under the agonies of death, before they died. Others were crucified by these tyrants, and with kindled matches burnt between the joints of their fingers and toes: others had their feet put into the fire, and thus were left to be roasted alive. Having used these and other cruelties with the white men, they began to practise the same with the negroes, their slaves, who were treated with no less inhumanity than their masters.

Among these slaves was one who promised Captain Morgan to conduct him to a river of the lake, where he should find a ship and four boats, richly laden with goods of the inhabitants of Maracaibo: the same discovered likewise where the governor of Gibraltar lay hid, with the greatest part of the women of the town; but all this he revealed, upon great menaces to hang him, if he told not what he knew. Captain Morgan sent away presently two hundred men in two settees, or great boats, to this river, to seek for what the slave had discovered; but he himself, with two hundred and fifty more, undertook to go and take the governor. This gentleman was retired to a small island in the middle of the river, where he had built a little fort, as well as he could, for his defence; but hearing that Captain Morgan came in person with great forces to seek him, he retired to the top of a mountain not far off, to which there was no ascent but by a very narrow passage, so straight, that whosoever did attempt to gain the ascent, must march his men one by one. Captain Morgan spent two days before he arrived at this little island, whence he designed to proceed to the mountain where the governor was posted, had he not been told of the impossibility of ascent, not only for the narrowness of the way, but because the governor was well provided with all sorts of ammunition: beside, there was fallen a huge rain, whereby all the pirates' baggage and powder was wet. By this rain, also, they lost many men at the passage over a river that was overflown: here perished, likewise, some women and children, and many mules laden with plate and goods, which they had taken from the fugitive inhabitants; so that things were in a very bad condition with Captain Morgan, and his men much harassed, as may be inferred from this relation: whereby, if the Spaniards, in that juncture, had had but fifty men well armed, they might have entirely destroyed the pirates. But the fears the Spaniards had at first conceived were so great, that the leaves stirring on the trees they often fancied to be pirates. Finally, Captain Morgan and his people, having upon this march sometimes waded up to their middles in water for half, or whole miles together, they at last escaped, for the greatest part; but the women and children for the major part died.

Thus twelve days after they set forth to seek the governor they returned to Gibraltar, with many prisoners: two days after arrived also the two settees that went to the river, bringing with them four boats, and some prisoners; but the greatest part of the merchandise in the said boats they found not, the Spaniards having unladed and secured it, having intelligence of their coming; who designed also, when the merchandise was taken out, to burn the boats: yet the Spaniards made not so much haste to unlade these vessels, but that they left in the ship and boats great parcels of goods, which the pirates seized, and brought a considerable booty to Gibraltar. Thus, after they had been in possession of the place five entire weeks, and committed an infinite number of murders, robberies, rapes, and such-like insolencies, they concluded to depart; but first they ordered some prisoners to go forth into the woods and fields, and collect a ransom for the town, otherwise they would certainly burn it down to the ground. These poor afflicted men went as they were sent, and having searched the adjoining fields and woods, returned to Captain Morgan, telling him they had scarce been able to find anybody, but that to such as they had found they had proposed his demands; to which they had answered, that the governor had prohibited them to give any ransom for the town, but they beseeched him to have a little patience, and among themselves they would collect five thousand pieces of eight; and for the rest, they would give some of their own townsmen as hostages, whom he might carry to Maracaibo, till he had received full satisfaction.

Captain Morgan having now been long absent from Maracaibo, and knowing the Spaniards had had sufficient time to fortify themselves, and hinder his departure out of the lake, granted their proposition, and made as much haste as he could for his departure: he gave liberty to all the prisoners, first putting every one to a ransom; yet he detained the slaves. They delivered him four persons agreed on for hostages of what money more he was to receive, and they desired to have the slave mentioned above, intending to punish him according to his deserts; but Captain Morgan would not deliver him, lest they should burn him alive. At last, they weighed anchor, and set sail in all haste for Maracaibo: here they arrived in four days, and found all things as they had left them; yet here they received news from a poor distressed old man, whom alone they found sick in the town, that three Spanish men-of-war were arrived at the entry of the lake, waiting the return of the pirates: moreover, that the castle at the entry thereof was again put into a good posture of defence, well provided with guns and men, and all sorts of ammunition.

This relation could not choose but disturb the mind of Captain Morgan, who now was careful how to get away through the narrow entry of the lake: hereupon he sent his swiftest boat to view the entry, and see if things were as they had been related. Next day the boat came back, confirming what was said; assuring him, they had viewed the ships so nigh, that they had been in great danger of their shot: hereunto they added, that the biggest ship was mounted with forty guns, the second with thirty, and the smallest with twenty-four. These forces being much beyond those of Captain Morgan, caused a general consternation in the pirates, whose biggest vessel had not above fourteen small guns. Every one judged Captain Morgan to despond, and to be hopeless, considering the difficulty of passing safe with his little fleet amidst those great ships and the fort, or he must perish. How to escape any other way, by sea or land, they saw no way. Under these necessities, Captain Morgan resumed new courage, and resolving to show himself still undaunted, he boldly sent a Spaniard to the admiral of those three ships, demanding of him a considerable ransom for not putting the city of Maracaibo to the flames. This man (who was received by the Spaniards with great admiration of the boldness of those pirates) returned two days after, bringing to Captain Morgan a letter from the said admiral, as follows:—

The Letter of Don Alonso del Campo y Espinosa, Admiral of the Spanish Fleet, to Captain Morgan, Commander of the Pirates.

" Having understood by all our friends and neighbours, the unexpected news that you have dared to attempt and commit hostilities in the countries, cities, towns, and villages belonging to the dominions of his Catholic Majesty, my sovereign lord and master; I let you understand by these lines, that I am come to this place, according to my obligation, near that castle which you took out of the hands of a parcel of cowards; where I have put things into a very good posture of defence, and mounted again the artillery which you had nailed and dismounted. My intent is, to dispute with you your passage out of the lake, and follow and pursue you everywhere, to the end you may see the performance of my duty. Notwithstanding, if you be contented to surrender with humility all that you have taken, together with the slaves and all other prisoners, I will let you freely pass, without trouble or molestation; on condition that you retire home presently to your own country. But if you make any resistance or opposition to what I offer you, I assure you I will command boats to come from Caraccas, wherein I will put my troops, and coming to Maracaibo, will put you every man to the sword. This is my last and absolute resolution. Be prudent, therefore, and do not abuse my bounty with ingratitude. I have with me very good soldiers, who desire nothing more ardently than to revenge on you, and your people, all the cruelties, and base infamous actions, you have committed upon the Spanish nation in America. Dated on board the royal ship named the *Magdalen*, lying at anchor at the entry of the lake of Maracaibo, this 24th of April, 1669.

"Don Alonso del Campo y Espinosa."

As soon as Captain Morgan received this letter, he called all his men together in the market-place of Maracaibo, and after reading the contents thereof, both in French and English, asked their advice and resolution on the whole matter, and whether they had rather surrender all they had got to obtain their liberty, than fight for it.

They answered all, unanimously, they had rather fight to the last drop of blood, than surrender so easily the booty they had got with so much danger of their lives. Among the rest, one said to Captain Morgan, "Take you care for the rest, and I will undertake to destroy the biggest of those ships with only twelve men : the manner shall be, by making a brulot, or fire-ship, of that vessel we took in the river of Gibraltar ; which, to the intent she may not be known for a fireship, we will fill her decks with logs of wood, standing with hats and montera caps, to deceive their sight with the representation of men. The same we will do at the port-holes that serve for the guns, which shall be filled with counterfeit cannon. At the stern we will hang out English colours, and persuade the enemy she is one of our best men-of-war going to fight them." This proposition was admitted and approved by every one; howbeit, their fears were not quite dispersed.

For, notwithstanding what had been concluded there, they endeavoured the next day to come to an accommodation with Don Alonso. To this effect, Captain Morgan sent to him two persons, with these propositions : First, that he would quit Maracaibo, without doing any damage to the town, or exacting any ransom for the firing thereof. Secondly, that he would set at liberty one half of the slaves, and all the prisoners, without ransom. Thirdly, that he would send home freely the four chief inhabitants of Gibraltar, which he had in his custody as hostages for the contributions those people had promised to pay. These propositions were instantly rejected by Don Alonso, as dishonourable : neither would he hear of any other accommodation, but sent back this message: "That if they surrendered not themselves voluntarily into his hands, within two days, under the conditions which he had offered them by his letter, he would immediately come, and force them to do it."

No sooner had Captain Morgan received this message from Don Alonso, than he put all things in order to fight, resolving to get out of the lake by main force, without surrendering anything. First, he commanded all the slaves and prisoners to be tied, and guarded very well, and gathered all the pitch, tar, and brimstone, they could find in the whole town, for the fire-ship above-mentioned: then they made several inventions of powder and brimstone with palm leaves, well annointed with tar. They covered very well their counterfeit cannon, laying under every piece many pounds of powder; besides, they cut down many outworks of the ship, that the powder might exert its strength the better; breaking open, also, new port-holes, where, instead of guns, they placed little drums used by the negroes. Finally, the decks were handsomely beset with many pieces of wood, dressed up like men with hats, or monteras, and armed with swords, muskets, and bandeleers.

The fire-ship being thus fitted, they prepared to go to the entry of the port. All the prisoners were put into one great boat, and in another of the biggest they placed all the women, plate, jewels, and other rich things: into others they put the bales of goods and merchandise, and other things of bulk: each of these boats had twelve men aboard, very well armed; the brulot had orders to go before the rest of the vessels, and presently to fall foul with the great ship. All things being ready, Captain Morgan exacted an oath of all his comrades, protesting to defend themselves to the last drop of blood, without demanding quarter; promising withal, that whosoever behaved himself thus, should be very well rewarded.

With this courageous resolution they set sail to seek the Spaniards. On April 30, 1669, they found the Spanish fleet riding at anchor in the middle of the entry of the lake. Captain Morgan, it being now late and almost dark, commanded all his vessels to an anchor, designing to fight even all night if they forced him to it. He ordered a careful watch to be kept aboard every vessel till morning, they being almost within shot, as well as within sight of the enemy. The day dawning, they weighed anchor, and sailed again, steering directly towards the Spaniards; who seeing them move, did instantly the same. The fire-ship sailing before the rest fell presently upon the great ship, and grappled her; which the Spaniards (too late) perceiving to be a fire-ship, they attempted to put her off, but in vain: for the flame seizing her timber and tackling, soon consumed all the stern, the fore part sinking into the sea, where she perished. The second Spanish ship perceiving the admiral to burn, not by accident, but by industry of the enemy, escaped towards the castle, where the Spaniards themselves sunk her, choosing to lose their ship rather than to fall into the hands of those pirates. The third, having no opportunity to escape, was taken by the pirates. The seamen that sunk the second ship near the castle, perceiving the pirates come towards them to take what remains they could find of their shipwreck (for some part was yet above water), set fire also to this vessel, that the pirates might enjoy nothing of that spoil. The first ship being set on fire, some of the persons in her swam towards the shore; these the pirates would have taken up in their boats, but they would not ask or take quarter, choosing rather to lose their lives than receive them from their hands, for reasons which I shall relate.

The pirates being extremely glad at this signal victory so soon obtained, and with so great an inequality of forces, conceived greater pride than they had before, and all presently ran ashore, intending to take the castle. This they found well provided with men, cannon, and ammunition, they having no other arms than muskets, and a few hand granadoes: their own artillery they thought incapable, for its smallness, of making any considerable breach in the walls. Thus they spent the rest of the day, firing at the garrison with their muskets, till the dusk of the evening, when they attempted to advance nearer the walls, to throw in their fire-balls: but the Spaniards resolving to sell their lives as dear as they could, fired so furiously at them, that they having experimented the obstinacy of the enemy, and seeing thirty of their men dead, and as many more wounded, they retired to their ships.

The Spaniards believing the pirates would next day renew the attack with their own cannon, laboured hard all night to put things in order for their coming; particularly, they dug down, and made plain, some little hills and eminences, when possibly the castle might be offended.

But Captain Morgan intended not to come again, busying himself next day in taking prisoners some of the men who still swam alive, hoping to get part of the riches lost in the two ships that perished. Among the rest, he took a pilot, who was a stranger, and who belonged to the lesser ship of the two, of whom he inquired several things; as, What number of people those three ships had in them? Whether they expected any more ships to come? From what port they set forth last, when they came to seek them out? He answered, in Spanish, "Noble sir, be pleased to pardon and spare me, that no evil be done to me, being a stranger

HENRY MORGAN.
(*From the Portrait in "De Americaensche Roovers."*)

to this nation I have served, and I shall sincerely inform you of all that passed till our arrival at this lake. We were sent by orders from the Supreme Council of State in Spain, being six men-of-war well equipped, into these seas, with instructions to cruise upon the English pirates, and root them out from these parts by destroying as many of them as we could.

"These orders were given, upon the news brought to the court of Spain of the loss and ruin of Puerto Bello, and other places; of all which damages and hostilities committed here by the English, dismal lamentations have often been made to the catholic king and council, to whom belongs the care and preservation of this new world. And though the Spanish court hath many times by their ambassadors complained hereof to the king of England; yet it hath been the constant answer of his Majesty of Great Britain, that he never gave any letters patent, nor commissions, for acting any hostility against the subjects of the king of Spain. Hereupon the catholic king resolved to revenge his subjects, and punish these proceedings: commanded six men-of-war to be equipped, which he sent under the command of Don Augustine de Bustos, admiral of the said fleet. He commanded the biggest ship, named *N. S. de la Soleda*, of forty-eight great guns, and eight small ones. The vice-admiral was Don Alonso del Campo y Espinosa, who commanded the second ship called *La Conception*, of forty-four great guns, and eight small ones; beside four vessels more, whereof the first was named the *Magdalen*, of thirty-six great guns, and twelve small ones, with two hundred and fifty men. The second was called *St. Lewis*, with twenty-six great guns, twelve small ones, and two hundred men. The third was called *La Marquesa*, of sixteen great guns, eight small ones, and one hundred and fifty men. The fourth and last, *N. S. del Carmen*, with eighteen great guns, eight small ones, and one hundred and fifty men.

"Being arrived at Carthagena, the two greatest ships received orders to return to Spain, being judged too big for cruising on these coasts. With the four ships remaining, Don Alonso del Campo y Espinosa departed towards Campechy to seek the English: we arrived at the port there, where, being surprised by a huge storm from the north, we lost one of our ships, being that which I named last. Hence we sailed for Hispaniola, in sight of which we came in a few days, and steered for Santo Domingo: here we heard that there had passed that way a fleet from Jamaica, and that some men thereof had landed at Alta Gracia; the inhabitants had taken one prisoner, who confessed their design was to go and pillage the city of Caraccas. On this news, Don Alonso instantly weighed anchor, and, crossing over to the continent, we came in sight of the Caraccas: here we found them not, but met with a boat, which certified us they were in the lake of Maracaibo, and that the fleet consisted of seven small ships, and one boat.

"Upon this we came here, and arriving at the entry of the lake, we shot off a gun for a pilot from the shore. Those on land perceiving we were Spaniards, came willingly to us with a pilot, and told us the English had taken Maracaibo, and that they were now at the pillage of Gibraltar. Don Alonso, on this news, made a handsome speech to his soldiers and mariners, encouraging them to their duty, and promising to divide among them all they should take from the English: he ordered the guns we had taken out of the ship that was lost to be put into the castle, and mounted for its defence, with two eighteen-pounders more, out of his own ship. The pilots conducted us into the port, and Don Alonso commanded the people on shore to come before him, whom he ordered to repossess the castle, and reinforce it with one hundred men more than it had before its being taken. Soon after, we heard of your return from Gibraltar to Maracaibo, whither Don Alonso wrote you a letter, giving you an account of his arrival and design, and exhorting you to restore what you had taken. This you refusing, he renewed his promises to his soldiers and seamen, and having given a very good supper to all his people, he ordered them not to take or give any quarter, which was the occasion of so many being drowned, who dared not to crave quarter, knowing themselves must give none. Two days before you came against us, a negro came aboard Don Alonso's ship, telling him, 'Sir, be pleased to have great care of yourself; for the English have prepared a fire-ship, with design to burn your fleet.' But Don Alonso not believing this, answered, 'How can that be? Have they, peradventure, wit enough to build a fire-ship? Or what instruments have they to do it withal?'"

This pilot having related so distinctly these things to Captain Morgan, was very well used by him, and, after some kind proffers made to him, remained in his service. He told Captain Morgan, that, in the ship which was sunk, there was a great quantity of plate, to the value of forty thousand pieces of eight; which occasioned the Spaniards to be often seen in boats about it. Hereupon, Captain Morgan ordered one of his ships to remain there, to find ways of getting out of it what plate they could; meanwhile, himself, with all his fleet, returned to Maracaibo, where he refitted the great ship he had taken, and chose it for himself, giving his own bottom to one of his captains.

Then he sent again a messenger to the admiral, who was escaped ashore, and got into the castle, demanding of him a ransom of fire for Maracaibo; which being denied, he threatened entirely to consume and destroy it. The

Spaniards considering the ill-luck they had all along with those pirates, and not knowing how to get rid of them, concluded to pay the said ransom, though Don Alonso would not consent.

Hereupon, they sent to Captain Morgan, to know what sum he demanded. He answered, that on payment of 30,000 pieces of eight, and five hundred beeves, he would release the prisoners and do no damage to the town. At last they agreed on 20,000 pieces of eight, and five hundred beeves to victual his fleet. The cattle were brought the next day, with one part of the money; and, while the pirates were busied in salting the flesh, they made up the whole 20,000 pieces of eight, as was agreed.

But Captain Morgan would not presently deliver the prisoners, as he had promised, fearing the shot of the castle at his going forth out of the lake. Hereupon he told them he intended not to deliver them till he was out of that danger, hoping thus to obtain a free passage. Then he set sail with his fleet in quest of the ship he had left, to seek for the plate of the vessel that was burnt. He found her on the place, with 15,000 pieces of eight got out of the work, beside many pieces of plate, as hilts of swords, and the like; also a great quantity of pieces of eight melted and run together, by the force of the fire.

Captain Morgan scarce thought himself secure, nor could he contrive how to avoid the shot of the castle: hereupon he wished the prisoners to agree with the governor to permit a safe passage to his fleet, which, if he should not allow, he would certainly hang them all up in his ships. Upon this the prisoners met, and appointed some of their fellow-messengers to go to the said governor, Don Alonso: these went to him, beseeching and supplicating him to have compassion on those afflicted prisoners, who were, with their wives and children, in the hands of

Captain Morgan; and that to this effect he would be pleased to give his word to let the fleet of pirates freely pass, this being the only way to save both the lives of them that came with this petition, as also of those who remained in captivity; all being equally menaced with the sword and gallows, if he granted them not this humble request. But Don Alonso gave them for answer a sharp reprehension of their cowardice, telling them, " If you had been as loyal to your king in hindering the entry of these pirates, as I shall do their going out, you had never caused these troubles neither to yourselves nor to our whole nation, which hath suffered so much through your pusillanimity. In a word, I shall never grant your request, but shall endeavour to maintain that respect which is due to my king, according to my duty."

Thus the Spaniards returned with much consternation, and no hopes of obtaining their request, telling Captain Morgan what answer they had received: his reply was, " If Don Alonso will not let me pass, I will find means how to do it without him." Hereupon he presently made a dividend of all they had taken, fearing he might not have an opportunity to do it in another place, if any tempest should rise and separate the ships, as also being jealous that any of the commanders might run away with the best part of the spoil, which then lay much more in one vessel than another. Thus they all brought in according to their laws, and declared what they had, first making oath not to conceal the least thing. The accounts being cast up, they found to the value of 25,000 pieces of eight, in money and jewels, beside the huge quantity of merchandise and slaves, all which purchase was divided to every ship or boat, according to their share.

The dividend being made, the question still remained how they should pass the castle, and get out of the lake.

To this effect they made use of a stratagem, as follows: the day before the night wherein they determined to get forth, they embarked many of their men in canoes, and rowed towards the shore, as if they designed to land: here they hid themselves under branches of trees that hang over the coast awhile, laying themselves down in the boats; then the canoes returned to the ships, with the appearance of only two or three men rowing them back, the rest being unseen at the bottom of the canoes: thus much only could be perceived from the castle, and this false landing of men, for so we may call it, was repeated that day several times: this made the Spaniards think the pirates intended at night to force the castle by scaling it. This fear caused them to place most of their great guns on the land side, together with their main force, leaving the side towards the sea almost destitute of defence.

Night being come, they weighed anchor, and by moonlight, without setting sail, committed themselves to the ebbing tide, which gently brought them down the river, till they were near the castle; being almost over against it, they spread their sails with all possible haste. The Spaniards perceiving this, transported with all speed their guns from the other side, and began to fire very furiously at them; but these having a very favourable wind, were almost past danger before those of the castle could hurt them; so that they lost few of their men, and received no considerable damage in their ships. Being out of the reach of the guns, Captain Morgan sent a canoe to the castle with some of the prisoners, and the governor thereof gave them a boat to return to their own homes; but he detained the hostages from Gibraltar, because the rest of the ransom for not firing the place was yet unpaid. Just as he departed, Captain Morgan ordered seven great guns with bullets to be fired against the castle, as it were to take his leave of them, but they answered not so much as with a musket shot.

Next day after, they were surprised with a great tempest, which forced them to cast anchor in five or six fathom water: but the storm increasing, compelled them to weigh again, and put to sea, where they were in great danger of being lost; for if they should have been cast on shore, either into the hands of the Spaniards or Indians, they would certainly have obtained no mercy: at last, the tempest being spent, the wind ceased, to the great joy of the whole fleet.

While Captain Morgan made his fortune by these pillagings, his companions, who were separated from his fleet at the Cape de Lobos, to take the ship spoken of before, endured much misery, and were unfortunate in all their attempts. Being arrived at Savona, they found not Captain Morgan there, nor any of their companions, nor had they the fortune to find a letter which Captain Morgan at his departure left behind him in a place where in all probability they would meet with it. Thus, not knowing what course to steer, they concluded to pillage some town or other. They were in all about four hundred men, divided into four ships and one boat: being ready to set forth, they constituted an admiral among themselves, being one who had behaved himself very courageously at the taking of Puerto Bello, named Captain Hansel. This commander attempted the taking of the town of Commana, on the continent of Caraccas, nigh sixty leagues to the west of the Isle de la Trinidad. Being arrived there, they landed their men, and killed some few Indians near the coast; but approaching the town, the Spaniards having in their company many Indians, disputed the entry so briskly, that, with great loss and confusion, they were forced to retire to the ships. At last they arrived at Jamaica, where the rest of their companions, who came with Captain Morgan, mocked and jeered them for their ill success at Commana, often telling them, "Let us see what money you brought from Commana, and if it be as good silver as that which we bring from Maracaibo."

CHAPTER XIII.

Captain Morgan goes to Hispaniola to equip a new fleet, with intent to pillage again on the coast of the West Indies.

CAPTAIN MORGAN perceived now that Fortune favoured him, by giving success to all his enterprises, which occasioned him, as is usual in human affairs, to aspire to greater things, trusting she would always be constant to him.

Such was the burning of Panama, wherein Fortune failed not to assist him, as she had done before, though she had led him thereto through a thousand difficulties. The history hereof I shall now relate, being so remarkable in all its circumstances, as peradventure nothing more deserving memory will be read by future ages.

Captain Morgan arriving at Jamaica, found many of his officers and soldiers reduced to their former indigency, by their vices and debaucheries. Hence they perpetually importuned him for new exploits, thereby to get something to expend still in wine and strumpets, as they had already done what they got before.

Captain Morgan, willing to follow Fortune's call, stopped the mouths of many inhabitants of Jamaica, who were creditors to his men for large sums, with the hopes and promises of greater achievements than ever, by a new expedition. This done, he could easily levy men for any enterprise, his name being so famous through all those islands as that alone would readily bring him in more men than he could well employ. He undertook therefore to equip a new fleet, for which he assigned the south side of Tortuga as a place of rendezvous, writing letters to all the expert pirates there inhabiting, as also to the governor, and to the planters and hunters of Hispaniola, informing them of his intentions, and desiring their appearance, if they intended to go with him. These people upon this notice flocked to the place assigned, in huge numbers, with ships, canoes, and boats, being desirous to follow him. Many, who had not the convenience of coming by sea, traversed the woods of Hispaniola, and with no small difficulties arrived there by land. Thus all were present at the place assigned, and ready against October 24, 1670.

Captain Morgan was not wanting to be there punctually, coming in his ship to Port Couillon, over against the island De la Vaca, the place assigned. Having gathered the greatest part of his fleet, he called a council to deliberate about finding provisions for so many people. Here they concluded to send four ships and one boat, with four hundred men, to the continent, in order to rifle some country towns and villages for all the corn or maize they could gather. They set sail for the continent towards the river De la Hacha, designing to assault the village called La Rancheria, usually best stored with maize of all the parts thereabouts. Meanwhile Captain Morgan sent another party to hunt in the woods, who killed a huge number of beasts, and salted them: the rest remained in the ships, to clean, fit, and rig them, that, at the return of their fellows, all things might be in a readiness to weigh anchor and follow their designs.

CHAPTER XIV.

What happened in the river De la Hacha.

THESE four ships setting sail from Hispaniola, steered for the river De la Hacha, where they were suddenly overtaken with a tedious calm. Being within sight of land becalmed for some days, the Spaniards inhabiting along the coasts, who had perceived them to be enemies, had sufficient time to prepare themselves, at least to hide the best of their goods, that, without any care of preserving them, they might be ready to retire, if they proved unable to resist the pirates, by whose frequent attempts on those coasts they had already learned what to do in such cases. There was then in the river a good ship, come from Carthagena to lade with maize, and now almost ready to depart. The men of this ship endeavoured to escape; but, not being able to do it, both they and the vessel fell into their hands. This was a fit purchase for them, being good part of what they came for. Next morning, about break of day, they came with their ships ashore, and landed their men, though the Spaniards made good resistance from a battery they had raised on that side, where, of necessity, they were to land; but they were forced to retire to a village, whither the pirates followed them. Here the Spaniards rallying, fell upon them with great fury, and maintained a strong combat, which lasted till night; but then, perceiving they had lost a great number of men, which was no less on the pirates' side, they retired to secret places in the woods.

Next day the pirates seeing them all fled, and the town left empty of people, they pursued them as far as they could, and overtook a party of Spaniards, whom they made prisoners, and exercised with most cruel torments, to discover their goods. Some were forced, by intolerable tortures, to confess; but others, who would not, were used more barbarously. Thus, in fifteen days that they remained there, they took many prisoners, much plate and movables, with which booty they resolved to return to Hispaniola: yet, not content with what they had got, they dispatched some prisoners into the woods to seek for the rest of the inhabitants, and to demand a ransom for not burning the town. They answered, they had no money nor plate; but if they would be satisfied with a quantity of maize, they would give as much as they could. The pirates accepted this, it being then more useful to them than ready money, and agreed they should pay four thousand hanegs, or bushels of maize. These were brought in three days after, the Spaniards being desirous to rid themselves of that inhuman sort of people. Having laded them on board with the rest of their purchase, they returned to Hispaniola, to give account to their leader, Captain Morgan, of all they had performed.

They had now been absent five weeks on this commission, which long delay occasioned Captain Morgan almost to despair of their return, fearing lest they were fallen into the hands of the Spaniards; especially considering the place whereto they went could easily be relieved from Carthagena and Santa Maria, if the inhabitants were careful to alarm the country. On the other side, he feared lest they should have made some great fortune in that voyage, and with it have escaped to some other place. But seeing his ships return in greater numbers than they departed, he resumed new courage, this sight causing both in him and his companions infinite joy, especially when they found them full laden with maize, which they much wanted for the maintenance of so many people, from whom they expected great matters under such a commander.

Captain Morgan having divided the said maize, as also the flesh which the hunters brought, among his ships, according to the number of men, he concluded to depart; having viewed beforehand every ship, and observed their being well equipped and clean. Thus he set sail, and stood for Cape Tiburon, where he determined to resolve what enterprise he should take in hand. No sooner were they arrived, but they met some other ships newly come to join them from Jamaica; so that now their fleet consisted of thirty-seven ships, wherein were two thousand fighting men, beside mariners and boys. The admiral hereof was mounted with twenty-two great guns, and six small ones of brass; the rest carried some twenty, some sixteen, some eighteen, and the smallest vessel at least four; besides which, they had great quantities of ammunition and fire-balls, with other inventions of powder.

Captain Morgan having such a number of ships, divided the whole fleet into two squadrons, constituting a vice-admiral, and other officers of the second squadron, distinct from the former. To these he gave letters patent, or commissions to act all manner of hostilities against the Spanish nation, and take of them what ships they could, either abroad at sea, or in the harbours, as if they were open and declared enemies (as he termed it) of the king of England, his pretended master. This done, he called all his captains and other officers together, and caused them to sign some articles of agreement betwixt them, and in the name of all. Herein it was stipulated, that he should have the hundredth part of all that was gotten to himself: that every captain should draw the shares of eight men for the expenses of his ship, besides his own. To the surgeon, beside his pay, two hundred pieces of eight for his chest of medicaments. To every carpenter, above his salary, one hundred pieces of eight. The rewards were settled in this voyage much higher than before: as, for the loss of both legs, fifteen hundred pieces of eight, or fifteen slaves, the choice left to the party: for the loss of both hands, eighteen hundred pieces of eight, or eighteen slaves: for one leg, whether right or left, six hundred pieces of eight, or six slaves: for a hand, as much as for a leg; and for the loss of an eye, one hundred pieces of eight, or one slave. Lastly, to him that in any battle should signalize himself, either by entering first any castle, or taking down the Spanish colours, and setting up the English, they allotted fifty pieces of eight for a reward. All which extraordinary salaries and rewards to be paid out of the first spoil they should take, as every one should occur to be either rewarded or paid.

This contract being signed, Captain Morgan commanded his vice-admirals and captains to put all things in order, to attempt one of these three places; either Carthagena, Panama, or Vera Cruz. But the lot fell on Panama, as the richest of all three; though this city being situate at such a distance from the North Sea as they knew not well the approaches to it, they judged it necessary to go beforehand to the isle of St. Catherine, there to find some persons for guides in this enterprise; for in the garrison there are commonly many banditti and outlaws belonging to Panama and the neighbouring places, who are very expert in the knowledge of that country. But before they proceeded, they published an act through the whole fleet, promising, if they met with any Spanish vessel, the first captain who should take it should have for his reward the tenth part of what should be found in her.

CHAPTER XV.

Captain Morgan leaves Hispaniola, and goes to St. Catherine's, which he takes.

CAPTAIN MORGAN and his companions weighed anchor from the Cape of Tiburon, December 16, 1670. Four days after they arrived in sight of St. Catherine's, now in possession of the Spaniards again, as was said before, to which they commonly banish the malefactors of the Spanish dominions in the West Indies. Here are huge quantities of pigeons at certain seasons. It is watered by four rivulets, whereof two are always dry in summer. Here is no trade or commerce exercised by the inhabitants; neither do they plant more fruits than what are necessary for human life, though the country would make very good plantations of tobacco of considerable profit, were it cultivated.

As soon as Captain Morgan came near the island with his fleet, he sent one of his best sailing vessels to view the entry of the river, and see if any other ships were there, who might hinder him from landing; as also fearing lest they should give intelligence of his arrival to the inhabitants, and prevent his designs.

Next day, before sunrise, all the fleet anchored near the island, in a bay called Aguade Grande. On this bay the Spaniards had built a battery, mounted with four pieces of cannon. Captain Morgan landed about one thousand men in divers squadrons, marching through the woods, though they had no other guides than a few of his own men, who had been there before, under Mansvelt. The same day they came to a place where the governor sometimes resided: here they found a battery called the Platform, but nobody in it, the Spaniards having retired to the lesser island, which, as was said before, is so near the great one, that a short bridge only may conjoin them.

This lesser island was so well fortified with forts and batteries round it, as might seem impregnable. Hereupon, as soon as the Spaniards perceived the pirates approach, they fired on them so furiously, that they could advance nothing that day, but were content to retreat, and take up their rest in the open fields, which was not strange to these people, being sufficiently used to such kind of repose. What most afflicted them was hunger, having not eat anything that whole day. About midnight it rained so hard, that they had much ado to bear it, the greatest part of them having no other clothes than a pair of seaman's trousers or breeches, and a shirt, without shoes or stockings. In this great extremity they pulled down a few thatched houses to make fires withal; in a word, they were in such a condition, that one hundred men, indifferently well armed, might easily that night have torn them all in pieces. Next morning, about break of day, the rain ceased, and they dried their arms and marched on: but soon after it rained afresh, rather harder than before, as if the skies were melted into waters; which kept them from advancing towards the forts, whence the Spaniards continually fired at them.

The pirates were now reduced to great affliction and danger, through the hardness of the weather, their own nakedness, and great hunger; for a small relief hereof, they found in the fields an old horse, lean, and full of scabs and blotches, with galled back and sides: this they instantly killed and flayed, and divided in small pieces among themselves, as far as it would reach (for many could not get a morsel) which they roasted and devoured without salt or bread, more like ravenous wolves than men. The rain not ceasing, Captain Morgan perceived their minds to relent, hearing many of them say they would return on board. Among these fatigues of mind and body, he thought convenient to use some sudden remedy: to this effect, he commanded a canoe to be rigged in haste, and colours of truce to be hanged out. This canoe he sent to the Spanish governor, with this message: "That if within a few hours he delivered not himself and all his men into his hands, he did by that messenger swear to him, and all those that were in his company, he would most certainly put them to the sword, without granting quarter to any."

In the afternoon the canoe returned with this answer: "That the governor desired two hours' time to deliberate with his officers about it, which being past, he would give his positive answer." The time being elapsed, the governor sent two canoes with white colours, and two persons to treat with Captain Morgan; but, before they landed, they demanded of the pirates two persons as hostages. These were readily granted by Captain Morgan, who delivered them two of his captains for a pledge of the security required. With this the Spaniards propounded to Captain Morgan, that the governor, in a full assembly, had resolved to deliver up the island, not being provided with sufficient forces to defend it against such an armada. But withal, he desired Captain Morgan would be pleased to use a certain stratagem of war, for the better saving of his own credit, and the reputation of his officers both abroad and at home, which should be as follows:—That

Captain Morgan would come with his troops by night to the bridge that joined the lesser island to the great one, and there attack the fort of St. Jerome: that at the same time all his fleet would draw near the castle of Santa Teresa, and attack it by land, landing, in the meanwhile, more troops near the battery of St. Matthew: that these troops being newly landed, should by this means intercept the governor as he endeavoured to pass to St. Jerome's fort, and then take him prisoner; using the formality, as if they forced him to deliver the castle; and that he would lead the English into it, under colour of being his own troops. That on both sides there should be continual firing, but without bullets, or at least into the air, so that no side might be hurt. That thus having obtained two such considerable forts, the chiefest of the isle, he need not take care for the rest, which must fall of course into his hands.

These propositions were granted by Captain Morgan, on condition they should see them faithfully observed; otherwise they should be used with the utmost rigour: this they promised to do, and took their leave, to give account of their negotiation to the governor. Presently after, Captain Morgan commanded the whole fleet to enter the port, and his men to be ready to assault, that night, the castle of St. Jerome. Thus the false battle began, with incessant firing from both the castles, against the ships, but without bullets, as was agreed. Then the pirates landed, and assaulted by night the lesser island, which they took, as also both the fortresses; forcing the Spaniards, in appearance, to fly to the church. Before this assault, Captain Morgan sent word to the governor, that he should keep all his men together in a body; otherwise, if the pirates met any straggling Spaniards in the streets, they should certainly shoot them.

This island being taken by this unusual stratagem, and

all things put in order, the pirates made a new war against the poultry, cattle, and all sorts of victuals they could find, for some days; scarce thinking of anything else than to kill, roast, and eat, and make what good cheer they could. If wood was wanting, they pulled down the houses, and made fires with the timber, as had been done before in the field. Next day they numbered all the prisoners they had taken upon the island, which were found to be in all four hundred and fifty-nine persons, men, women, and children; viz., one hundred and ninety soldiers of the garrison; forty inhabitants, who were married: forty-three children, thirty-four slaves, belonging to the king; with eight children, eight banditti, thirty-nine negroes belonging to private persons; with twenty-seven female blacks, and thirty-four children. The pirates disarmed all the Spaniards, and sent them out immediately to the plantations to seek for provisions, leaving the women in the church to exercise their devotions.

Soon after they reviewed the whole island, and all the fortresses thereof, which they found to be nine in all, viz., the fort of St. Jerome, next the bridge, had eight great guns, of twelve, six, and eight pounds carriage; with six pipes of muskets, every pipe containing ten muskets. Here they found still sixty muskets, with sufficient powder and other ammunition. The second fortress, called St. Matthew, had three guns, of eight pounds each. The third, and chiefest, named Santa Teresa, had twenty great guns, of eighteen, twelve, eight, and six pounds; with ten pipes of muskets, like those before, and ninety muskets remaining, besides other ammunition. This castle was built with stone and mortar, with very thick walls, and a large ditch round it, twenty feet deep, which, though it was dry, yet was very hard to get over. Here was no entry, but through one door, to the middle of the castle. Within it was a mount, almost inaccessible, with four pieces of cannon at the top; whence they could shoot directly into the port. On the sea side it was impregnable, by reason of the rocks round it, and the sea beating furiously upon them. To the land it was so commodiously seated on a mountain, as there was no access to it but by a path three or four feet broad. The fourth fortress was named St. Augustine, having three guns of eight and six pounds. The fifth, named La Plattaforma de la Conception, had only two guns, of eight pounds. The sixth, by name San Salvador, had likewise no more than two guns. The seventh, called Plattaforma de los Artilleros, had also two guns. The eighth, called Santa Cruz, had three guns. The ninth, called St. Joseph's Fort, had six guns, of twelve and eight pounds, besides two pipes of muskets, and sufficient ammunition.

In the storehouses were above thirty thousand pounds of powder, with all other ammunition, which was carried by the pirates on board. All the guns were stopped and nailed, and the fortresses demolished, except that of St. Jerome, where the pirates kept guard and resistance. Captain Morgan inquired for any banditti from Panama or Puerto Bello, and three were brought him, who pretended to be very expert in the avenues of those parts. He asked them to be his guides, and show him the securest ways to Panama, which, if they performed, he promised them equal shares in the plunder of that expedition, and their liberty when they arrived in Jamaica. These propositions the banditti readily accepted, promising to serve him very faithfully, especially one of the three, who was the greatest rogue, thief, and assassin among them, who had deserved rather to be broken alive on the wheel, than punished with serving in a garrison. This wicked fellow had a great ascendant over the other two, and domineered over them as he pleased, they not daring to disobey his orders.

Captain Morgan commanded four ships and one boat to be equipped, and provided with necessaries, to go and take the castle of Chagre, on the river of that name; neither would he go himself with his whole fleet, lest the Spaniards should be jealous of his farther design on Panama. In these vessels he embarked four hundred men, to put in execution these his orders. Meanwhile, himself remained in St. Catherine's with the rest of the fleet, expecting to hear of their success.

CHAPTER XVI.

Captain Morgan takes the Castle of Chagre, with four hundred men sent to this purpose from St Catherine's.

CAPTAIN MORGAN sending this little fleet to Chagre, chose for vice-admiral thereof one Captain Brodely, who had been long in those quarters, and committed many robberies on the Spaniards, when Mansvelt took the isle of St. Catherine, as was before related; and therefore was thought a fit person for this exploit, his actions likewise having rendered him famous among the pirates, and their enemies the Spaniards. Captain Brodely being made commander, in three days after his departure arrived in sight of the said castle of Chagre, by the Spaniards called St. Lawrence. This castle is built on a high mountain, at the entry of the river, surrounded by strong palisades, or wooden walls, filled with earth, which secures them as well as the best wall of stone or brick. The top of this mountain is, in a manner, divided into two parts, between which is a ditch thirty feet deep. The castle hath but one entry, and that by a drawbridge over this ditch. To the land it has four bastions, and to the sea two more. The south part is totally inaccessible, through the cragginess of the mountain. The north is surrounded by the river, which here is very broad. At the foot of the castle, or rather mountain, is a strong fort, with eight great guns, commanding the entry of the river. Not much lower are two other batteries, each of six pieces, to defend likewise the mouth of the river. At one side of the castle are two great storehouses of all sorts of warlike ammunition and merchandise, brought thither from the island country. Near these houses is a high pair of stairs hewn out of the rock, to mount to the top of the castle. On the west is a small port, not above seven or eight fathoms deep, fit for small vessels, and of very good anchorage; besides, before the castle, at the entry of the river, is a great rock, scarce to be descried but at low tides.

No sooner had the Spaniards perceived the pirates, but they fired incessantly at them with the biggest of their guns. They came to an anchor in a small port, about a league from the castle. Next morning, very early, they went ashore, and marched through the woods, to attack the castle on that side. This march lasted till two of the clock in the afternoon, before they could reach the castle, by reason of the difficulties of the way, and its mire and dirt; and though their guides served them very exactly, yet they came so nigh the castle at first, that they lost many of their men by its shot, they being in an open place without covert. This much perplexed the pirates, not knowing what course to take; for on that side, of necessity, they must make the assault: and being uncovered from head to foot, they could not advance one step without danger: besides that, the castle, both for its situation and strength, made them much doubt of success. But to give it over they dared not, lest they should be reproached by their companions.

At last, after many doubts and disputes, resolving to hazard the assault and their lives desperately, they advanced towards the castle with their swords in one hand, and fireballs in the other. The Spaniards defended themselves very briskly, ceasing not to fire at them continually;

crying withal, "Come on, ye English dogs! enemies to God and our king; and let your other companions that are behind come on too, ye shall not go to Panama this bout." The pirates making some trial to climb the walls, were forced to retreat, resting themselves till night. This being come, they retured to the assault, to try, by the help of their fire-balls, to destroy the pales before the wall; and while they were about it, there happened a very remarkable accident, which occasioned their victory. One of the pirates being wounded with an arrow in his back, which pierced his body through, he pulled it out boldly at the side of his breast, and winding a little cotton about it, he put it into his musket, and shot it back to the castle; but the cotton being kindled by the powder, fired two or three houses in the castle, being thatched with palm-leaves, which the Spaniards perceived not so soon as was necessary: for this fire meeting with a parcel of powder, blew it up, thereby causing great ruin, and no less consternation to the Spaniards, who were not able to put a stop to it, not having seen it time enough.

The pirates perceiving the effect of the arrow, and the misfortunes of the Spaniards, were infinitely glad; and while they were busied in quenching the fire, which caused a great confusion for want of water, the pirates took this opportunity, setting fire likewise to the palisades. The fire thus seen at once in several parts about the castle, gave them great advantage against the Spaniards, many breaches being made by the fire among the pales, great heaps of earth falling into the ditch. Then the pirates climbing up, got over into the castle, though those Spaniards, who were not busy about the fire, cast down many flaming pots full of combustible matter, and odious smells, which destroyed many of the English.

The Spaniards, with all their resistance, could not

hinder the palisades from being burnt down before midnight. Meanwhile the pirates continued in their intention of taking the castle; and though the fire was very great, they would creep on the ground, as near as they could, and shoot amidst the flames against the Spaniards on the other side, and thus killed many from the walls. When day was come, they observed all the movable earth, that lay betwixt the pales, to be fallen into the ditch; so that now those within the castle lay equally exposed to them without, as had been on the contrary before; whereupon the pirates continued shooting very furiously, and killed many Spaniards; for the governor had charged them to make good those posts, answering to the heaps of earth fallen into the ditch, and caused the artillery to be transported to the breaches.

The fire within the castle still continuing, the pirates from abroad did what they could to hinder its progress, by shooting incessantly against it; one party of them was employed only for this, while another watched all the motions of the Spaniards. About noon the English gained a breach, which the governor himself defended with twenty-five soldiers. Here was made a very courageous resistance by the Spaniards, with muskets, pikes, stones, and swords; but through all these the pirates fought their way, till they gained the castle. The Spaniards, who remained alive, cast themselves down from the castle into the sea, choosing rather to die thus (few or none surviving the fall) than to ask quarter for their lives. The governor himself retreated to the corps du gard, before which were placed two pieces of cannon: here he still defended himself, not demanding any quarter, till he was killed with a musket-shot in the head.

The governor being dead, and the corps du gard surrendering, they found remaining in it alive thirty men, whereof scarce ten were not wounded: these informed the pirates that eight or nine of their soldiers had deserted, and were gone to Panama, to carry news of their arrival and invasion. These thirty men alone remained of three hundred and fourteen wherewith the castle was garrisoned, among which not one officer was found alive. These were all made prisoners, and compelled to tell whatever they knew of their designs and enterprises. Among other things, that the governor of Panama had notice sent him three weeks ago from Carthagena, that the English were equipping a fleet at Hispaniola, with a design to take Panama; and, beside, that this had been discovered by a deserter from the pirates at the river De la Hacha, where they had victualled. That upon this, the governor had sent one hundred and sixty-four men to strengthen the garrison of that castle, with much provision and ammunition; the ordinary garrison whereof was only one hundred and fifty men, but these made up two hundred and fourteen men, very well armed. Besides this, they declared that the governor of Panama had placed several ambuscades along the river of Chagre; and that he waited for them in the open fields of Panama with three thousand six hundred men.

The taking of this castle cost the pirates excessively dear, in comparison to what they were wont to lose, and their toil and labour was greater than at the conquest of the isle of St. Catherine; for, numbering their men, they had lost above a hundred, beside seventy wounded. They commanded the Spanish prisoners to cast the dead bodies of their own men from the top of the mountain to the seaside, and to bury them. The wounded were carried to the church, of which they made an hospital, and where also they shut up the women. Thus it was likewise turned into a place of prostitution, the pirates ceasing not to defile the bodies of those afflicted widows with all manner of insolent actions and threats.

Captain Morgan remained not long behind at St. Catherine's, after taking the castle of Chagre, of which he had notice presently; but before he departed, he embarked all the provisions that could be found, with much maize, or Indian wheat, and cazave, whereof also is made bread in those parts. He transported great store of provisions to the garrison of Chagre, whencesoever they could be got. At a certain place they cast into the sea all the guns belonging thereto, designing to return, and leave that island well garrisoned, to the perpetual possession of the pirates; but he ordered all the houses and forts to be fired, except the castle of St. Teresa, which he judged to be the strongest and securest wherein to fortify himself at his return from Panama.

Having completed his arrangements, he took with him all the prisoners of the island, and then sailed for Chagre, where he arrived in eight days. Here the joy of the whole fleet was so great, when they spied the English colours on the castle, that they minded not their way into the river, so that they lost four ships at the entry thereof, Captain Morgan's being one; yet they saved all the men and goods. The ships, too, had been preserved, if a strong northerly wind had not risen, which cast them on the rock at the entry of the river.

Captain Morgan was brought into the castle with great acclamations of all the pirates, both of those within, and those newly come. Having heard the manner of the conquest, he commanded all the prisoners to work, and repair what was necessary, especially to set up new palisades round the forts of the castle. There were still in the river some Spanish vessels, called chatten, serving for transportation of merchandise up and down the river, and to go to Puerto Bello and Nicaragua. These commonly carry two great guns of iron, and four small ones of brass. These vessels they seized, with four little ships they found there, and all the canoes. In the castle they left a garrison of five hundred men, and in the ships in the river one hundred and fifty more. This done, Captain Morgan departed for Panama at the head of twelve hundred men. He carried little provisions with him, hoping to provide himself sufficiently among the Spaniards, whom he knew to lie in ambuscade by the way.

CHAPTER XVII.

Captain Morgan departs from Chagre, at the head of twelve hundred men, to take the city of Panama.

CAPTAIN MORGAN set forth from the castle of Chagre, towards Panama, August 18, 1670. He had with him twelve hundred men, five boats laden with artillery, and thirty-two canoes. The first day they sailed only six leagues, and came to a place called De los Bracos. Here a party of his men went ashore, only to sleep and stretch their limbs, being almost crippled with lying too much crowded in the boats. Having rested awhile, they went abroad to seek victuals in the neighbouring plantations; but they could find none, the Spaniards being fled, and carrying with them all they had. This day, being the first of their journey, they had such scarcity of victuals, as the greatest part were forced to pass with only a pipe of tobacco, without any other refreshment.

Next day, about evening, they came to a place called Cruz de Juan Gallego. Here they were compelled to leave their boats and canoes, the river being very dry for want of rain, and many trees having fallen into it.

The guides told them, that, about two leagues farther, the country would be very good to continue the journey by land. Hereupon they left one hundred and sixty men on board the boats, to defend them, that they might serve for a refuge in necessity.

Next morning, being the third day, they all went ashore, except those who were to keep the boats. To these Captain Morgan gave order, under great penalties, that no man, on any pretext whatever, should dare to leave the boats, and go ashore; fearing lest they should be surprised by an ambuscade of Spaniards in the neighbouring woods, which appeared so thick as to seem almost impenetrable. This morning beginning their march, the ways proved so bad, that Captain Morgan thought it more convenient to transport some of the men in canoes (though with great labour) to a place farther up the river, called Cedro Bueno. Thus they re-embarked, and the canoes returned for the rest; so that about night they got altogether at the said place. The pirates much desired to meet some Spaniards or Indians, hoping to fill their bellies with their provisions, being reduced to extremity and hunger.

The fourth day the greatest part of the pirates marched by land, being led by one of the guides; the rest went by water farther up, being conducted by another guide, who always went before them, to discover, on both sides the river, the ambuscades. These had also spies, who were very dextrous to give notice of all accidents, or of the arrival of the pirates, six hours, at least, before they came. This day, about noon, they came near a post called Torna Cavallos: here the guide of the canoes cried out, that he perceived an ambuscade. His voice caused infinite joy to all the pirates, hoping to find some provisions to satiate their extreme hunger. Being come to the place, they found nobody in it, the Spaniards being fled, and leaving nothing behind but a few leathern bags, all empty, and a few crumbs of bread scattered on the ground where they had eaten. Being angry at this, they pulled down a few little huts which the Spaniards had made, and fell to eating the leathern bags, to allay the ferment of their stomachs, which was now so sharp as to gnaw their very bowels. Thus they made a huge banquet upon these bags of leather, divers quarrels arising concerning the greatest shares. By the bigness of the place, they conjectured about five hundred Spaniards had been there, whom, finding no victuals, they were now infinitely desirous to meet, intending to devour some of them rather than perish.

Having feasted themselves with those pieces of leather, they marched on, till they came about night to another post, called Torna Munni. Here they found another ambuscade, but as barren as the former. They searched the neighbouring woods, but could not find anything to eat, the Spaniards having been so provident, as not to leave anywhere the least crumb of sustenance, whereby the pirates were now brought to this extremity. Here again he was happy that had reserved since noon any bit of leather to make his supper of, drinking after it a good draught of water for his comfort. Some, who never were out of their mothers' kitchens, may ask, how these pirates could eat and digest those pieces of leather, so hard and dry? Whom I answer, that, could they once experiment what hunger, or rather famine, is, they would find the way as the pirates did. For these first sliced it in pieces, then they beat it between two stones, and rubbed it, often dipping it in water, to make it supple and tender. Lastly, they scraped off the hair, and broiled it. Being thus cooked, they cut it into small morsels, and ate it, helping it down with frequent gulps of water, which, by good fortune, they had at hand.

The fifth day, about noon, they came to a place called Barbacoa. Here they found traces of another ambuscade, but the place totally as unprovided as the former. At a small distance were several plantations, which they searched very narrowly, but could not find any person.

animal, or other thing, to relieve their extreme hunger. Finally, having ranged about, and searched a long time, they found a grot, which seemed to be but lately hewn out of a rock, where were two sacks of meal, wheat, and like things, with two great jars of wine, and certain fruits called platanoes. Captain Morgan, knowing some of his men were now almost dead with hunger, and fearing the same of the rest, caused what was found to be distributed among them who were in greatest necessity. Having refreshed themselves with these victuals, they marched anew with greater courage than ever. Such as were weak were put into the canoes, and those commanded to land that were in them before. Thus they prosecuted their journey till late at night; when coming to a plantation, they took up their rest, but without eating anything; for the Spaniards, as before, had swept away all manner of provisions.

The sixth day they continued their march, part by land and part by water. Howbeit, they were constrained to rest very frequently, both for the ruggedness of the way, and their extreme weakness, which they endeavoured to relieve by eating leaves of trees and green herbs, or grass; such was their miserable condition. This day at noon they arrived at a plantation, where was a barn full of maize. Immediately they beat down the doors and ate it dry, as much as they could devour; then they distributed a great quantity, giving every man a good allowance. Thus provided, and prosecuting their journey for about an hour, they came to another ambuscade. This they no sooner discovered, but they threw away their maize, with the sudden hopes of finding all things in abundance. But they were much deceived, meeting neither Indians nor victuals, nor anything else: but they saw, on the other side of the river, about a hundred Indians, who, all fleeing, escaped. Some few pirates leaped into the river to cross it, and try to take any of the Indians, but in vain: for, being much more nimble than the pirates, they not only baffled them, but killed two or three with their arrows; hooting at them, and crying, "Ha, perrros! a la savana, a la savana."—"Ha, ye dogs! go to the plain, go to the plain."

This day they could advance no farther, being necessitated to pass the river, to continue their march on the other side. Hereupon they reposed for that night, though their sleep was not profound; for great murmurings were made at Captain Morgan, and his conduct; some being desirous to return home, while others would rather die there than go back a step from their undertaking: others, who had greater courage, laughed and joked at their discourses. Meanwhile, they had a guide who much comforted them, saying, "It would not now be long before they met with people from whom they should reap some considerable advantage."

The seventh day, in the morning, they made clean their arms, and every one discharged his pistol, or musket, without bullet, to try their firelocks. This done, they crossed the river, leaving the post where they had rested, called Santa Cruz, and at noon they arrived at a village called Cruz. Being yet far from the place, they perceived much smoke from the chimneys: the sight hereof gave them great joy, and hopes of finding people and plenty of good cheer. Thus they went on as fast as they could, encouraging one another, saying, "There is smoke comes out of every house: they are making good fires, to roast and boil what we are to eat;" and the like.

At length they arrived there, all sweating and panting, but found no person in the town, nor anything eatable to refresh themselves, except good fires, which they wanted not; for the Spaniards, before their departure, had every one set fire to his own house, except the king's storehouses and stables.'

They had not left behind them any beast, alive or dead, which much troubled their minds, not finding anything but a few cats and dogs, which they immediately killed and devoured. At last, in the king's stables, they found, by good fortune, fifteen or sixteen jars of Peru wine, and a leathern sack full of bread. No sooner had they drank of this wine, when they fell sick, almost every man: this made them think the wine was poisoned, which caused a new consternation in the whole camp, judging themselves now to be irrecoverably lost. But the true reason was, their want of sustenance, and the manifold sorts of trash they had eaten. Their sickness was so great, as caused them to remain there till the next morning, without being able to prosecute their journey in the afternoon. This village is seated in 9 deg. 2 min. north latitude, distant from the river Chagre twenty-six Spanish leagues, and eight from Panama. This is the last place to which boats or canoes can come; for which reason they built here storehouses for all sorts of merchandise, which to and from Panama are transported on the backs of mules.

Here Captain Morgan was forced to leave his canoes, and land all his men, though never so weak; but lest the canoes should be surprised, or take up too many men for their defence, he sent them all back to the place where the boats were, except one, which he hid, that it might serve to carry intelligence. Many of the Spaniards and Indians of this village having fled to the near plantations, Captain Morgan ordered that none should go out of the village, except companies of one hundred together, fearing lest the enemy should take an advantage upon his men. Notwithstanding, one party contravened these orders, being tempted with the desire of victuals: but they were soon glad to fly into the town again, being assaulted with great fury by some Spaniards and Indians, who carried one of them away prisoner. Thus the vigilancy and care of Captain Morgan was not sufficient to prevent every accident.

The eighth day in the morning Captain Morgan sent two hundred men before the body of his army, to discover the way to Panama, and any ambuscades therein: the path being so narrow, that only ten or twelve persons could march abreast, and often not so many. After ten hours' march they came to a place called Quebrada Obscura: here, all on a sudden, three or four thousand arrows were shot at them, they not perceiving whence they came, or who shot them: though they presumed it was from a high rocky mountain, from one side to the other, whereon was a grot, capable of but one horse or other beast laded. This multitude of arrows much alarmed the pirates, especially because they could not discover whence they were discharged. At last, seeing no more arrows, they marched a little farther, and entered a wood: here they perceived some Indians to fly as fast as they could, to take the advantage of another post, thence to observe their march; yet there remained one troop of Indians on the place, resolved to fight and defend themselves, which they did with great courage till their captain fell down wounded; who, though he despaired of life, yet his valour being greater than his strength, would ask no quarter, but, endeavouring to raise himself, with undaunted mind laid hold of his azagayo, or javelin, and struck at one of the pirates; but before he could second the blow, he was shot to death. This was also the fate of many of his companions, who, like good soldiers, lost their lives with their captain, for the defence of their country.

The pirates endeavoured to take some of the Indians prisoners, but they being swifter than the pirates, every one escaped, leaving eight pirates dead, and ten wounded: yea, had the Indians been more dextrous in military affairs, they might have defended that passage, and not let one man pass. A little while after they came to a large champaign, open, and full of fine meadows; hence they could perceive at a distance before them some Indians, on the top of a mountain, near the way by which they were to pass: they sent fifty men, the nimblest they had, to try to catch any of them, and force them to discover their companions: but all in vain; for they escaped by their nimbleness, and presently showed themselves in another place, hallooing to the English, and crying, "A la savana, a la savana, cornudos, perros Ingleses!" that is, "To the plain, to the plain, ye cuckolds, ye English dogs!" Meanwhile the ten pirates that were wounded were dressed, and plastered up.

Here was a wood, and on each side a mountain. The Indians possessed themselves of one, and the pirates of the other. Captain Morgan was persuaded the Spaniards had placed an ambuscade there, it lying so conveniently: hereupon, he sent two hundred men to search it. The Spaniards and Indians perceiving the pirates descend the mountain, did so too, as if they designed to attack them; but being got into the wood, out of sight of the pirates, they were seen no more, leaving the passage open.

About night fell a great rain, which caused the pirates to march the faster, and seek for houses to preserve their arms from being wet; but the Indians had set fire to every one, and driven away all their cattle, that the pirates, finding neither houses nor victuals, might be constrained to return: but, after diligent search, they found a few shepherds' huts, but in them nothing to eat. These not holding many men, they placed in them, out of every company, a small number, who kept the arms of the rest: those who remained in the open field endured much hardship that night, the rain not ceasing till morning.

Next morning, about break of day, being the ninth of that tedious journey, Captain Morgan marched on while the fresh air of the morning lasted; for the clouds hanging yet over their heads, were much more favourable than the scorching rays of the sun, the way being now more difficult than before. After two hours' march, they discovered about twenty Spaniards, who observed their motions: they endeavoured to catch some of them, but could not, they suddenly disappearing, and absconding themselves in caves among the rocks, unknown to the pirates. At last, ascending a high mountain, they discovered the South Sea. This happy sight, as if it were the end of their labours, caused infinite joy among them: hence they could descry also one ship, and six boats, which were set forth from Panama, and sailed towards the islands of Tavoga and Tavogilla: then they came to a vale where they found much cattle, whereof they killed good store: here, while some killed and flayed cows, horses, bulls, and chiefly asses, of which there were most; others kindled fires, and got wood to roast them: then cutting the flesh into convenient pieces, or gobbets, they threw them into the fire, and, half carbonaded or roasted, they devoured them, with incredible haste and appetite; such was their hunger, as they more resembled cannibals than Europeans; the blood many times running down from their beards to their waists.

Having satisfied their hunger, Captain Morgan ordered them to continue the march. Here, again, he sent before the main body fifty men to take some prisoners, if they could; for he was much concerned, that in nine days he could not meet one person to inform him of the condition and forces of the Spaniards. About evening they discovered about two hundred Spaniards, who hallooed to the pirates, but they understood not what they said. A little while after they came in sight of the highest steeple of Panama: this they no sooner discovered but they showed signs of extreme joy, casting up their hats into the air, leaping and shouting, just as if they had already obtained the victory, and accomplished their designs. All their trumpets sounded, and drums beat, in token of this alacrity of their minds: thus they pitched their camp for that night, with general content of the whole army, waiting with impatience for the morning, when they intended to attack the city. This evening appeared fifty horse, who came out of the city, on the noise of the drums and trumpets, to observe, as it was thought, their motions: they came almost within musket-shot of the army, with a trumpet that sounded marvellously well. Those on horseback hallooed aloud to the pirates, and threatened them, saying, "Perros! nos veremos," that is, "Ye dogs! we shall meet ye." Having made this menace, they returned to the city, except only seven or eight horsemen, who hovered thereabouts to watch their motions. Immediately after the city fired, and ceased not to play their biggest guns all night long against the camp, but with little or no harm to the pirates, whom they could not easily reach. Now also the two hundred Spaniards, whom the pirates had seen in the afternoon, appeared again, making a show of blocking up the passages, that no pirates might escape their hands: but the pirates, though in a manner besieged, instead of fearing their blockades, as soon as they had placed sentinels about their camp, opened their satchels, and, without any napkins or plates, fell to eating, very heartily, the pieces of bulls' and horses' flesh which they had reserved since noon. This done, they laid themselves down to sleep on the grass, with great repose and satisfaction, expecting only, with impatience, the dawning of the next day.

The tenth day, betimes in the morning, they put all their men in order, and, with drums and trumpets sounding, marched directly towards the city; but one of the guides desired Captain Morgan not to take the common highway, lest they should find in it many ambuscades. He took his advice, and chose another way through the wood, though very irksome and difficult. The Spaniards perceiving the pirates had taken another way they scarce had thought on, were compelled to leave their stops and batteries, and come out to meet them. The governor of Panama put his forces in order, consisting of two squadrons, four regiments of foot, and a huge number of wild bulls, which were driven by a great number of Indians, with some negroes, and others, to help them.

The pirates, now upon their march, came to the top of a little hill, whence they had a large prospect of the city and champaign country underneath. Here they discovered the forces of the people of Panama, in battle array, to be so numerous, that they were surprised with fear, much doubting the fortune of the day: yea, few or none there were but wished themselves at home, or at least free from the obligation of that engagement, it so nearly concerning their lives. Having been some time wavering in their minds, they at last reflected on the straits they had brought themselves into, and that now they must either fight resolutely, or die; for no quarter could be expected from an enemy on whom they had committed so many cruelties. Hereupon they encouraged one another, resolving to conquer, or spend the last drop of blood. Then they divided themselves into three battalions, sending before two hundred bucaniers, who were very dextrous at their guns. Then descending the hill, they marched directly towards the Spaniards, who in a spacious field waited for their coming. As soon as they drew nigh, the Spaniards began to shout and cry, "Viva el rey!" "God save the king!" and immediately their horse moved against the pirates: but the fields being full of quags, and soft underfoot, they could not wheel about as they desired. The two hundred bucaniers, who went before, each putting one knee to the ground, began the battle briskly, with a full volley of shot: the Spaniards defended themselves courageously, doing all they could to disorder the pirates. Their foot endeavoured to second the horse, but were constrained by the pirates to leave them. Finding themselves baffled, they attempted to drive the bulls against them behind, to put them into disorder; but the wild cattle ran away, frighted with the noise of the battle; only some few broke through the English companies, and only tore the colours in pieces, while the bucaniers shot every one of them dead.

The battle having continued two hours, the greatest part of the Spanish horse was ruined, and almost all killed: the rest fled, which the foot seeing, and that they could not possibly prevail, they discharged the shot they had in their muskets, and throwing them down, fled away, every one as he could. The pirates could not follow them, being too much harassed and wearied with their long journey. Many, not being able to fly whither they desired, hid themselves, for that present, among the shrubs of the seaside, but very unfortunately; for most of them being found by the pirates, were instantly killed, without any quarter. Some religious men were brought prisoners before Captain Morgan; but he, being deaf to their cries, commanded them all to be pistolled, which was done. Soon after they brought a captain to him, whom he examined very strictly; particularly, wherein consisted the forces of those of Panama? He answered, their whole strength consisted in four hundred horse, twenty-four companies of foot, each of one hundred men complete; sixty Indians, and some negroes, who were to drive two thousand wild bulls upon the English, and thus, by breaking their files, put them into a total disorder: beside, that in the city they had made trenches, and raised batteries in several places, in all which they had placed many guns; and that at the entry of the highway, leading to the city, they had built a fort mounted with eight great brass guns, defended by fifty men.

Captain Morgan having heard this, gave orders instantly to march another way; but first he made a review of his men, whereof he found both killed and wounded a considerable number, and much greater than had been believed. Of the Spaniards were found six hundred dead on the place, besides the wounded and prisoners. The pirates, nothing discouraged, seeing their number so diminished, but rather filled with greater pride, perceiving what huge advantage they had obtained against their enemies, having rested some time, prepared to march courageously towards the city, plighting their oaths to one another, that they would fight till not a man was left alive. With this courage they recommenced their march, either to conquer or be conquered; carrying with them all the prisoners.

They found much difficulty in their approach to the city, for within the town the Spaniards had placed many great guns, at several quarters, some charged with small pieces of iron, and others with musket bullets; with all these they saluted the pirates at their approaching, and gave them full and frequent broadsides, firing at them incessantly; so that unavoidably they lost at every step great numbers of men. But these manifest dangers of their lives, nor the sight of so many as dropped continually at their sides, could deter them from advancing, and gaining ground every moment on the enemy; and though the Spaniards never ceased to fire, and act the best they could for their defence, yet they were forced to yield, after three hours' combat. And the pirates having possessed themselves, killed and destroyed all that attempted in the least to oppose them. The inhabitants had transported the best of their goods to more remote and occult places; howbeit, they found in the city several warehouses well stocked with merchandise, as well silks and cloths, as linen and other things of value. As soon as the first fury of their entrance was over, Captain Morgan assembled his men, and commanded them, under great penalties, not to drink or taste any wine; and the reason he gave for it was, because he had intelligence that it was all poisoned by the Spaniards. Howbeit, it was thought he gave these prudent orders to prevent the debauchery of his people, which he foresaw would be very great at the first, after so much hunger sustained by the way; fearing, withal, lest the Spaniards, seeing them in wine, should rally, and, falling on the city, use them as inhumanly as they had used the inhabitants before.

CHAPTER XVIII.

Captain Morgan sends canoes and boats to the South Sea—He fires the city of Panama—Robberies and cruelties committed there by the pirates, till their return to the Castle of Chagre.

CAPTAIN MORGAN, as soon as he had placed necessary guards at several quarters within and without the city, commanded twenty-five men to seize a great boat, which had stuck in the mud of the port, for want of water, at a low tide. The same day about noon, he caused fire privately to be set to several great edifices of the city, nobody knowing who were the authors thereof, much less on what motives Captain Morgan did it, which are unknown to this day: the fire increased so, that before night the greatest part of the city was in a flame. Captain Morgan pretended the Spaniards has done it, perceiving that his own people reflected on him for that action. Many of the Spaniards, and some of the pirates, did what they could, either to quench the flame, or, by blowing up houses with gunpowder, and pulling down others, to stop it, but in vain : for in less than half an hour it consumed a whole street. All the houses of the city were built with cedar, very curious and magnificent, and richly adorned, especially with hangings and paintings, whereof part were before removed, and another great part were consumed by fire.

There were in this city (which is the see of a bishop) eight monasteries, seven for men, and one for women ; two stately churches, and one hospital. The churches and monasteries were all richly adorned with altar-pieces and paintings, much gold and silver, and other precious things, all which the ecclesiastics had hidden. Besides which, here were two thousand houses of magnificent building, the greatest part inhabited by merchants vastly rich. For the rest of less quality, and tradesmen, this city contained five thousand more. Here were also many stables for the horses and mules that carry the plate of the king of Spain, as well as private men, towards the North Sea. The neighbouring fields are full of fertile plantations and pleasant gardens, affording delicious prospects to the inhabitants all the year.

The Genoese had in this city a stately house for their trade of negroes. This likewise was by Captain Morgan burnt to the very ground. Besides which building, there were consumed two hundred warehouses, and many slaves, who had hid themselves therein, with innumerable sacks of meal; the fire of which continued four weeks after it had begun. The greatest part of the pirates still encamped without the city, fearing and expecting the Spaniards would come and fight them anew, it being known they much outnumbered the pirates. This made them keep the field, to preserve their forces united, now much diminished by their loses. Their wounded, which were many, they put into one church, which remained standing, the rest being consumed by the fire. Besides these decreases of their men, Captain Morgan had sent a convoy of one hundred and fifty men to the castle of Chagre, to carry the news of his victory at Panama.

They saw often whole troops of Spaniards run to and fro in the fields, which made them suspect their rallying, which they never had the courage to do. In the afternoon Captain Morgan re-entered the city with his troops, that every one might take up their lodgings, which now they could hardly find, few houses having escaped the fire. Then they sought very carefully among the ruins and ashes, for utensils of plate or gold, that were not quite wasted by the flames: and of such they found no small number, especially in wells and cisterns, where the Spaniards had hid them.

Next day Captain Morgan dispatched away two troops, of one hundred and fifty men each, stout and well armed, to seek for the inhabitants who were escaped. These having made several excursions up and down the fields, woods, and mountains adjacent, returned after two days, bringing above two hundred prisoners, men, women, and slaves. The same day returned also the boat which Captain Morgan had sent to the South Sea, bringing three other boats which they had taken. But all these prizes they could willingly have given, and greater labour into the bargain, for one galleon, which miraculously escaped, richly laden with all the king's plate, jewels, and other precious goods of the best and richest merchants of Panama: on board which were also the religious women of the nunnery, who had embarked with them all the ornaments of their church, consisting in much gold, plate, and other things of great value.

The strength of this galleon was inconsiderable, having only seven guns, and ten or twelve muskets, and very ill provided with victuals, necessaries, and fresh water, having no more sails than the uppermost of the mainmast. This account the pirates received from some who had spoken with seven mariners belonging to the galleon, who came ashore in the cockboat for fresh water. Hence they concluded they might easily have taken it, had they given her chase, as they should have done; but they were impeded from following this vastly rich prize, by their lascivious exercises with women, which they had carried and forced on board their boat. To this vice were also joined those of gluttony and drunkenness, having plentifully debauched themselves with several rich wines they found ready, choosing rather to satiate their lusts and appetites than to lay hold on such huge advantage; since this only prize would have been of far greater value than all they got at Panama, and the places thereabout. Next day, repenting of their negligence, being weary of their vices and debaucheries, they set forth another boat, well armed, to pursue with all speed the said galleon; but in vain, the Spaniards who were on board having had intelligence of their own danger one or two days before, while the pirates were cruising so near them; whereupon they fled to places more remote and unknown.

The pirates found, in the ports of the island of Tavoga and Tavogilla, several boats laden with very good merchandise; all which they took, and brought to Panama, where they made an exact relation of all that had passed to Captain Morgan. The prisoners confirmed what the pirates said, adding, that they undoubtedly knew where the galleon might then be, but that it was very probable they had been relieved before now from other places. This stirred up Captain Morgan anew, to send forth all the boats in the port of Panama to seek the said galleon till they could find her. These boats, being in all four, after eight days' cruising to and fro, and searching several ports and creeks, lost all hopes of finding her : hereupon they returned to Tavoga and Tavogilla; here they found a reasonable good ship newly come from Payta, laden with cloth, soap, sugar, and biscuit, with 20,000 pieces of eight; this they instantly seized, without the least resistance; as also a boat which was not far off, on which they laded great part of the merchandises from the ship, with some slaves. With this purchase they returned to Panama, somewhat better satisfied: yet, withal, much discontented that they could not meet with the galleon.

The convoy which Captain Morgan had sent to the castle of Chagre returned much about the same time, bringing with them very good news; for while Captain Morgan was on his journey to Panama, those he had left in the castle of Chagre had sent forth two boats to cruise. These met with a Spanish ship, which they chased within sight of the castle. This being perceived by the pirates in the castle, they put forth Spanish colours, to deceive the ship that fled before the boats; and the poor Spaniards, thinking to take refuge under the castle, were caught in a snare, and made prisoners. The cargo on board the said vessel consisted in victuals and provisions, than which nothing could be more opportune for the castle, where they began already to want things of this kind.

This good luck of those of Chagre caused Captain Morgan to stay longer at Panama, ordering several new excursions into the country round about; and while the pirates at Panama were upon these expeditions, those at Chagre was busy in piracies on the North Sea. Captain Morgan sent forth, daily, parties of two hundred men, to make inroads into all the country round about; and when one party came back, another went forth, who soon gathered much riches, and many prisoners. These being brought into the city, were put to the most exquisite tortures, to make them confess both other people's goods and their own. Here it happened that one poor wretch was found in the house of a person of quality, who had put on, amidst the confusion, a pair of taffety breeches of his master's, with a little silver key hanging out; perceiving which, they asked him for the cabinet of the said key. His answer was, he knew not what was become of it, but that finding those breeches in his master's house, he had made bold to wear them. Not being able to get any other answer, they put him on the rack, and inhumanly disjointed his arms; then they twisted a cord about his forehead, which they wrung so hard that his eyes appeared as big as eggs, and were ready to fall out. But with these torments not obtaining any positive answer, they hung him up by the testicles, giving him many blows and stripes under that intolerable pain and posture of body. Afterwards they cut off his nose and ears, and singed his face with burning straw, till he could not speak, nor lament his misery any longer: then, losing all hopes of any confession, they bade a negro run him through, which put an end to his life, and to their inhuman tortures. Thus did many others of those miserable prisoners finish their days, the common sport and recreation of these pirates being such tragedies.

They spared in these their cruelties no sex nor condition: for as to religious persons, and priests, they granted them less quarter than others, unless they could produce a considerable sum, sufficient for a ransom. Women were no better used, except they submitted to their filthy lusts; for such as would not consent were treated with all the rigour imaginable. Captain Morgan gave them no good example in this point: for when any beautiful woman was brought prisoner to his presence, he used all means, both of rigour and mildness, to bend them to his lascivious pleasure. For confirmation of which, I shall give a short history of a lady, whose virtue and constancy ought to be transmitted to posterity.

Among the prisoners brought by the pirates from Tavoga and Tavogilla was a gentlewoman of good quality, and no less virtue and chastity, wife to one of the richest merchants there. She was young, and so beautiful, as perhaps few in all Europe surpassed her, either in comeliness or honesty. Her husband then was from home, being gone as far as Peru, about his commerce and trade. This virtuous lady, hearing of the pirates' coming, had fled, with other friends and relations, to preserve her life from the cruelties and tyrannies of those hard-hearted enemies: but no sooner did she appear before Captain Morgan, but she was designed for his pleasure. Hereupon, he lodged her in an apartment by herself, giving her a negro, or black woman, to wait on her, and treated her with all the respect due to her quality. The poor afflicted lady begged, with many sobs and tears, to lodge among the other prisoners; her relations fearing that unexpected kindness of the commander might be a design on her chastity. But Captain Morgan would by no means hearken to her; but commanded she should be treated with more particular care than before, and have her victuals from his own table.

This lady had formerly heard very strange reports concerning the pirates, as if they were not men, but, as they said, heretics, who did neither invoke the blessed Trinity, nor believe in Jesus Christ. But now she began to have better thoughts of them, upon these civilities of Captain Morgan; especially hearing him many times swear by God, and Jesus Christ, in whom, she thought, they did not believe. Nor did she think them to be so bad, or to have the shapes of beasts, as had been related. As to the name of robbers, or thieves, commonly given them, she wondered not much at it, seeing, among all nations of the universe, there were wicked men, covetous to possess the goods of others. Like this was the opinion of another woman of weak understanding at Panama, who used to say, before the pirates came thither, she had a great curiosity to see a pirate, her husband having often told her that they were not like other men, but rather irrational beasts. This silly woman happening to see the first of them, cried out aloud, "Jesus bless me! these thieves are like us Spaniards."

This false civility of Captain Morgan towards this lady, as is usual to such as pretend, and cannot obtain, was soon changed into barbarous cruelty; for after three or four days he came to see her, and entertained her with lascivious discourses, desiring the accomplishment of his lust. The virtuous lady constantly denied him, with much civility, and many humble and modest expressions; but Captain Morgan still persisted in his base request, presenting to her much pearl, gold, and whatever he had that was precious and valuable: but the lady, not willing to consent, or accept his presents, showing herself like Susannah for constancy, he presently changed his note, and addressed her in another tone, threatening a thousand cruelties and hard usages. To all which she gave only this resolute and positive answer: "Sir, my life is in your hands: but as to my body, in relation to that which you would persuade me to, my soul shall sooner be separated from it, through the violence of your arms, than I shall condescend to your request." Captain Morgan understanding this her heroic resolution, commanded her to be stripped of the best of her apparel, and imprisoned in a darksome stinking cellar; here she was allowed a small quantity of meat and drink, wherewith she had much ado to sustain her life.

Under this hardship the virtuous lady prayed daily to God Almighty for constancy and patience; but Captain Morgan, now thoroughly convinced of her chaste resolutions, as also desirous to conceal the cause of her hard usage—since many of his companions compassionated her condition — pretended she held intelligence with the Spaniards, and corresponded with them, abusing his lenity and kindness. I myself was an eye-witness thereof, and could never have judged such constancy and chastity to be found in the world, if my own eyes and ears had not assured me thereof. But of this incomparable lady I shall say something more hereafter.

Captain Morgan having now been at Panama full three weeks, commanded all things to be prepared for his departure. He ordered every company of men to seek so many beasts of carriage as might convey the spoil to the river where his canoes lay. About this time there was a great rumour, that a considerable number of pirates intended to to leave Captain Morgan; and that, taking a ship then in the port, they determined to go and rob on the South Sea, till they had got as much as they thought fit, and then return homewards, by way of the East Indies. For which purpose they had gathered much provisions, which they had hid in private places, with sufficient powder, bullets, and all other ammunition: likewise some great guns belonging to the town, muskets, and other things, wherewith they designed not only to equip their vessel, but to fortify themselves in some island which might serve them for a place of refuge.

This design had certainly taken effect, had not Captain Morgan had timely advice of it from one of their comrades: hereupon he commanded the mainmast of the said ship to be cut down and burnt, with all the other boats in the port: hereby the intentions of all or most of his companions were totally frustrated. Then Captain Morgan sent many of the Spaniards into the adjoining fields and country to seek for money, to ransom not only themselves, but the rest of the prisoners, as likewise the ecclesiastics. Moreover, he commanded all the artillery of the town to be nailed and stopped up. At the same time he sent out a strong company of men to seek for the governor of Panama, of whom intelligence was brought, that he had laid several ambuscades in the way by which he ought to return: but they returned soon after, saying they had not found any sign of any such ambuscades. For confirmation whereof, they brought some prisoners, who declared that the said governor had had an intention of making some opposition by the way, but that the men designed to effect it were unwilling to undertake it: so that for want of means he could not put his design in execution.

February 24, 1671, Captain Morgan departed from Panama, or rather from the place where the city of Panama stood; of the spoils whereof he carried with him one hundred and seventy-five beasts of carriage, laden with silver, gold, and other precious things, beside about six hundred prisoners, men, women, children and slaves. That day they came to a river that passes through a delicious plain, a league from Panama: here Captain Morgan put all his forces into good order, so as that the prisoners were in the middle, surrounded on all sides with pirates, where nothing else was to be heard but lamentations, cries, shrieks, and doleful sighs of so many women and children, who feared Captain Morgan designed to transport them all into his own country for slaves. Besides, all those miserable prisoners endured extreme hunger and thirst at that time, which misery Captain Morgan designedly caused them to sustain, to excite them to seek for money to ransom themselves, according to the tax he had set upon every one. Many of the women begged Captain Morgan, on their knees, with infinite sighs and tears, to let them return to Panama, there to live with their dear husbands and children in little huts of straw, which they would erect, seeing they had no houses till the rebuilding of the city. But his answer was, "He came not thither to hear lamentations and cries, but to seek money: therefore they ought first to seek out that, wherever it was to be had, and bring it to him; otherwise he would assuredly transport them all to such places whither they cared not to go."

Next day, when the march began, those lamentable cries and shrieks were renewed, so as it would have caused compassion in the hardest heart: but Captain Morgan, as a man little given to mercy, was not moved in the least. They marched in the same order as before, one party of the pirates in the van, the prisoners in the middle, and the rest of the pirates in the rear; by whom the miserable Spaniards were at every step punched and thrust in their backs and sides, with the blunt ends of their arms, to make them march faster.

That beautiful and virtuous lady, mentioned before for her unparalleled constancy and chastity, was led prisoner by herself, between two pirates. Her lamentations now pierced the skies, seeing herself carried away into captivity often crying to the pirates, and telling them, "That she had given orders to two religious persons, in whom she had relied, to go to a certain place, and fetch so much money as her ransom did amount to; that they had promised faithfully to do it, but having obtained the money, instead of bringing it to her, they had employed it another way, to ransom some of their own, and particular friends." This ill action of theirs was discovered by a slave, who brought a letter to the said lady. Her complaints, and the cause thereof, being brought to Captain Morgan, he thought fit to inquire thereinto. Having found it to be true—especially hearing it confirmed by the confession of the said religious men, though under some frivolous excuses of having diverted the money but for a day or two, in which time they expected more sums to repay it—he gave liberty to the said lady, whom otherwise he designed to transport to Jamaica. But he detained the said religious men as prisoners in her place, using them according to their deserts.

Captain Morgan arriving at the town called Cruz, on the banks of the river Chagre, he published an order among the prisoners, that within three days every one should bring in their ransom, under the penalty of being transported to Jamaica. Meanwhile he gave orders for so much rice and maize to be collected thereabouts, as was necessary for victualling his ships. Here some of the prisoners were ransomed, but many others could not bring in their money. Hereupon he continued his voyage, leaving the village on the 5th of March following, carrying with him all the spoil he could. Hence he likewise led away some new prisoners, inhabitants there, with those of Panama, who had not paid their ransoms. But the two religious men, who had diverted the lady's money, were ransomed three days after by other persons, who had more compassion for them than they had showed for her.

About the middle of the way to Chagre, Captain Morgan commanded them to be mustered, and caused every one to be sworn, that they had concealed nothing, even not to the value of sixpence. This done, Captain Morgan knowing those lewd fellows would not stick to swear falsely for interest, he commanded every one to be searched very strictly, both in their clothes and satchels, and elsewhere. Yea, that this order might not be ill taken by his companions, he permitted himself to be searched, even to his very shoes. To this effect, by common consent, one was assigned out of every company to be searchers of the rest. The French pirates that assisted on this expedition disliked this new practice of searching; but, being outnumbered by the English, they were forced to submit as well as the rest. The search being over, they re-embarked, and arrived at the castle of Chagre on the 9th of March. Here they found all things in good order, excepting the wounded men whom they had left at their departure; for of these the greatest number were dead of their wounds.

From Chagre, Captain Morgan sent, presently after his arrival, a great boat to Puerto Bello, with all the prisoners taken at the isle of St. Catherine, demanding of them a considerable ransom for the castle of Chagre, where he then was; threatening otherwise to ruin it. To this those of Puerto Bello answered, they would not give one farthing towards the ransom of the said castle, and the English might do with it as they pleased. Hereupon the dividend was made of all the spoil made in that voyage; every company, and every particular person therein, receiving their proportion, or rather what part thereof Captain Morgan pleased to give them. For the rest of his companions, even of his own nation, murmured at his proceedings, and told him to his face that he had reserved the best jewels to himself: for they judged it impossible that no greater share should belong to them than two hundred pieces of eight, per capita, of so many valuable plunders they had made; which small sum they thought too little for so much labour, and such dangers, as they had been exposed to. But Captain Morgan was deaf to all this, and many other like complaints, having designed to cheat them of what he could.

At last, finding himself obnoxious to many censures of his people, and fearing the consequence, he thought it unsafe to stay any longer at Chagre, but ordered the ordnance of the castle to be carried on board his ship; then he caused most of the walls to be demolished, the edifices to be burnt, and as many other things ruined as could be done in a short time. This done, he went secretly on board his own ship, without giving any notice to his companions, and put out to sea, being only followed by three or four vessels of the whole fleet. These were such (as the French pirates believed) as went shares with Captain Morgan in the best part of the spoil, which had been concealed from them in the dividend. The Frenchmen could willingly have revenged themselves on Captain Morgan and his followers, had they been able to encounter him at sea; but they were destitute of necessaries, and had much ado to find sufficient provisions for their voyage to Jamaica, he having left them unprovided for all things.

END OF THE BUCCANEERS.

A GENUINE ACCOUNT OF FOUR NOTORIOUS PIRATES.

Blackbeard the Pirate.

I.

CAPTAIN TEACH *alias* BLACK-BEARD.

His beginning—His confederacy with Hornygold—The confederacy broken—Takes a large Guineaman—Engages the *Scarborough* man-of-war—His alliance with Major Stede Bonnet—Deposes his new ally—His advice to the Major—His progress and success—Takes prizes in sight of Charles Town—Sends ambassadors to the Governor of Carolina upon an impudent demand—Runs his ship aground designedly—His cruelty to some of his own companions—Surrenders to the King's Proclamation—The Governor of North Carolina's exceeding generosity to him—He marries—The number of his wives then living—Makes a second excursion in the way of pirating—Some State legerdemain betwixt him and the Governor—His frolics on shore—The merchants apply for a force against him, and where—A proclamation with a reward for taking or killing of pirates—Lieutenant Maynard sent in pursuit of him—Black-beard's good intelligence—The lieutenant engages Black-beard—A most execrable health drunk by Black-beard—The fight bloody; the particulars of it—Black-beard killed—His sloop taken—The lieutenant's conduct—A reflection on the humours of seamen—Black-beard's correspondents discovered by his papers—Black-beard's desperate resolution before the fight—The lieutenant and Governor no very good friends—The prisoners hanged—Samuel Odell saved, and why—The good luck of Israel Hands—Black-beard's mischievous frolics—His beard described—Several instances of his wickedness—Some memoranda taken from his journal—The names of the pirates killed in the engagement—Of those executed—The value of the prize.

EDWARD TEACH was a Bristol man born, but had sailed some time out of Jamaica, in privateers, in the late French war; yet though he had often distinguished himself for his uncommon boldness and personal courage, he was never raised to any command, till he went a-pirating, which, I think, was at the latter end of the year 1716, when Captain Benjamin Hornygold put him into a sloop that he had made prize of, and with whom he continued in consortship till a little while before Hornygold surrendered.

In the spring of the year 1717 Teach and Hornygold sailed from Providence, for the main of America, and took in their way a billop from the Havana, with 120 barrels of flour, as also a sloop from Bermuda, Thurbar master, from whom they took only some gallons of wine, and then let him go; and a ship from Madeira to South Carolina, out of which they got plunder to a considerable value.

After cleaning on the coast of Virginia, they returned to the West Indies, and in the latitude of 24, made prize of a large French Guineaman, bound to Martinico, which, by Hornygold's consent, Teach went aboard of as captain, and took a cruise in her. Hornygold returned with his sloop to Providence, where, at the arrival of Captain Rogers, the governor, he surrendered to mercy, pursuant to the king's proclamation.

Aboard of this Guineaman Teach mounted forty guns, and named her the *Queen Ann's Revenge*; and cruising near the island of St. Vincent, took a large ship, called the *Great Allen*, Christopher Taylor, commander; the pirates plundered her of what they thought fit, put all the men ashore upon the island above mentioned, and set fire to the ship.

A few days after Teach fell in with the *Scarborough*, man-of-war, of thirty guns, who engaged him for some hours; but she, finding the pirate well-manned, and having tried her strength, gave over the engagement and returned to Barbadoes, the place of her station, and Teach sailed towards the Spanish America.

In his way he met with a pirate sloop of ten guns,

commanded by one Major Bonnet, lately a gentleman of good reputation and estate in the island of Barbadoes, whom he joined; but in a few days after, Teach, finding that Bonnet knew nothing of a maritime life, with the consent of his own men, put in another captain, one Richards, to command Bonnet's sloop, and took the Major on board his own ship, telling him, that as he had not been used to the fatigues and care of such a post, it would be better for him to decline it and live easy, at his pleasure, in such a ship as his, where he would not be obliged to perform the necessary duties of a sea-voyage.

At Turniff, ten leagues short of the Bay of Honduras, the pirates took in fresh water, and while they were at anchor there, they saw a sloop coming in, whereupon Richards, in the sloop called the *Revenge*, slipped his cable and run out to meet her; who, upon seeing the black flag hoisted, struck his sail and came to under the stern of Teach, the commodore. She was called the *Adventure*, from Jamaica, David Harriot, master. They took him and his men aboard the great ship, and sent a number of other hands with Israel Hands, master of Teach's ship, to man the sloop for the piratical account.

The 9th of April they weighed from Turniff, having lain there about a week, and sailed to the bay, where they found a ship and four sloops; three of the latter belonged to Jonathan Bernard, of Jamaica, and the other to Captain James. The ship was of Boston, called the *Protestant Cæsar*, Captain Wyar, commander. Teach hoisted his black colours and fired a gun, upon which Captain Wyar and all his men left their ship and got ashore in their boat. Teach's quartermaster and eight of his crew took possession of Wyar's ship, and Richards secured all the sloops, one of which they burnt out of spite to the owner. The *Protestant Cæsar* they also burnt, after they had plundered her, because she belonged to Boston, where some men had been hanged for piracy; and the three sloops belonging to Bernard they let go.

From hence the rovers sailed to Turkill, and then to the Grand Caimanes, a small island about thirty leagues to the westward of Jamaica, where they took a small turtler, and so to the Havana, and from thence to the Bahama Wrecks; and from the Bahama Wrecks they sailed to Carolina, taking a brigantine and two sloops in their way, where they lay off the bar of Charles Town for five or six days. They took here a ship as she was coming out, bound for London, commanded by Robert Clark, with some passengers on board for England. The next day they took another vessel coming out of Charles Town, and also two pinks coming into Charles Town; likewise a brigantine with fourteen negroes aboard; all of which, being done in the face of the town, struck a great terror to the whole province of Carolina, having just before been visited by Vane, another notorious pirate, that they abandoned themselves to despair, being in no condition to resist their force. There were eight sail in the harbour, ready for the sea, but none dared to venture out, it being almost impossible to escape their hands. The inward bound vessels were under the same unhappy dilemma, so that the trade of this place was totally interrupted. What made these misfortunes heavier to them was a long, expensive war the colony had had with the natives, which was but just ended when these robbers infested them.

Teach detained all the ships and prisoners, and, being in want of medicines, resolved to demand a chest from the government of the province. Accordingly, Richards, the captain of the *Revenge* sloop, with two or three more pirates, were sent up along with Mr. Marks, one of the prisoners whom they had taken in Clark's ship, and very insolently made their demands, threatening that if they did not send immediately the chest of medicines and let the pirate ambassadors return, without offering any violence to their persons, they would murder all their prisoners, send up their heads to the governor, and set the ships they had taken on fire.

Whilst Mr. Marks was making application to the council, Richards and the rest of the pirates walked the streets publicly in the sight of all people, who were fired with the utmost indignation, looking upon them as robbers and murderers, and particularly the authors of their wrongs and oppressions, but durst not so much as think of executing their revenge for fear of bringing more calamities upon themselves, and so they were forced to let the villains pass with impunity. The government were not long in deliberating upon the message, though it was the greatest affront that could have been put upon them, yet, for the saving so many men's lives (among them Mr. Samuel Wragg, one of the council), they complied with the necessity and sent aboard a chest, valued at between three and four hundred pounds, and the pirates went back safe to their ships.

Black-beard (for so Teach was generally called, as we shall hereafter show), as soon as he had received the medicines and his brother rogues, let go the ships and the prisoners, having first taken out of them in gold and silver about £1,500 sterling, besides provisions and other matters.

From the bar of Charles Town they sailed to North Carolina, Captain Teach in the ship, which they called the man-of-war, Captain Richards and Captain Hands in the sloops, which they termed privateers, and another sloop serving them as a tender. Teach began now to think of breaking up the company and securing the money and the best of the effects for himself and some others of his companions he had most friendship for, and to cheat the rest. Accordingly, on pretence of running into Topsail inlet to clean, he grounded his ship, and then, as if it had been done undesignedly and by accident, he orders Hands' sloop to come to his assistance and get him off again, which he, endeavouring to do, ran the sloop on shore near the other, and so were both lost. This done, Teach goes into the tender sloop, with forty hands, and leaves the *Revenge* there, then takes seventeen others and maroons them upon a small sandy island, about a league from the main, where there was neither bird, beast, or herb for their subsistence, and where they must have perished if Major Bonnet had not, two days after, taken them off.

Teach goes up to the governor of North Carolina, with about twenty of his men, and they surrender to his Majesty's proclamation, and receive certificates thereof from his Excellency; but it did not appear that their submitting to this pardon was from any reformation of manners, but only to await a more favourable opportunity to play the same game over again; which he soon after effected, with greater security to himself, and with much better prospect of success, having in this time cultivated a very good understanding with Charles Eden, Esq., the governor above mentioned.

The first piece of service this kind governor did to Black-beard was to give him a right to the vessel which he had taken when he was a-pirating in the great ship called the *Queen Ann's Revenge*, for which purpose a court of vice-admiralty was held at Bath Town, and, though Teach had never any commission in his life, and the sloop belonging to the English merchants, and taken in time of peace, yet was she condemned as a prize taken from the Spaniards by the said Teach. These proceedings show that governors are but men.

Before he sailed upon his adventures, he married a young creature of about sixteen years of age, the governor performing the ceremony. As it is a custom to marry here by a priest, so it is there by a magistrate; and this, I have been informed, made Teach's fourteenth wife whereof about a dozen might be still living.

In June, 1718, he went to sea upon another expedition, and steered his course towards Bermudas. He met with two or three English vessels in his way, but robbed them only of provisions, stores, and other necessaries, for his present expense; but near the island before mentioned, he fell in with two French ships, one of them was laden with sugar and cocoa, and the other light, both bound to Martinico. The ship that had no lading he let go, and putting all the men of the loaded ship aboard her, he brought home the other with her cargo to North Carolina, where the governor and the pirates shared the plunder.

When Teach and his prize arrived he and four of his crew went to his Excellency and made affidavit that they found the French ship at sea without a soul on board her; and then a court was called, and the ship condemned. The governor had sixty hogsheads of sugar for his dividend, and one Mr. Knight, who was his secretary and collector for the province, twenty, and the rest was shared among the other pirates.

The business was not yet done; the ship remained, and it was possible one or other might come into the river that might be acquainted with her, and so discover the roguery. But Teach thought of a contrivance to prevent this, for, upon a pretence that she was leaky, and that she might sink, and so stop up the mouth of the inlet or cove where she lay, he obtained an order from the governor to bring her out into the river and set her on fire, which was accordingly executed, and she was burnt down to the water's edge, her bottom sunk, and with it their fears of her ever rising in judgment against them.

Captain Teach, alias Black-beard, passed three or four months in the river, sometimes lying at anchor in the coves, at other times sailing from one inlet to another, trading with such sloops as he met for the plunder he had taken, and would often give them presents for stores and provisions he took from them; that is, when he happened to be in a giving humour; at other times he made bold with them, and took what he liked, without saying "By your leave," knowing well they dared not send him a bill for the payment. He often diverted himself with going ashore among the planters, where he revelled night and day. By these he was well received, but whether out of love or fear I cannot say. Sometimes he used them courteously enough, and made them presents of rum and sugar in recompense of what he took from them; but, as for liberties, which it is said he and his companions often took with the wives and daughters of the planters, I cannot take upon me to say whether he paid them *ad valorem* or no At other times he carried it in a lordly manner towards them, and would lay some of them under contribution; nay, he often proceeded to bully the governor, not that I can discover the least cause of quarrel between them, but it seemed only to be done to show he dared do it.

The sloops trading up and down this river being so frequently pillaged by Black-beard, consulted with the traders and some of the best of the planters what course to take. They saw plainly it would be in vain to make any application to the governor of North Carolina, to whom it properly belonged to find some redress; so that if they could not be relieved from some other quarter, Black-beard would be like to reign with impunity; therefore, with as much secrecy as possible, they sent a deputation to Virginia, to lay the affair before the governor of that colony, and to solicit an armed force from the men-of-war lying there to take or destroy this pirate.

This governor consulted with the captains of the two men-of-war, viz., the *Pearl* and *Lime*, who had lain in St. James's river about ten months. It was agreed that the governor should hire a couple of small sloops, and the men-of-war should man them. This was accordingly done, and the command of them given to Mr. Robert Maynard, first lieutenant of the *Pearl*, an experienced officer, and a gentleman of great bravery and resolution, as will appear by his gallant behaviour in this expedition. The sloops were well manned, and furnished with ammunition and small arms, but had no guns mounted.

About the time of their going out the governor called an assembly, in which it was resolved to publish a proclamation, offering certain rewards to any person or persons who, within a year after that time, should take or destroy any pirate. The original proclamation, being in our hands, is as follows :—

By his Majesty's Lieutenant-Governor and Commander-in-Chief of the Colony and Dominion of Virginia.

A PROCLAMATION,

Publishing the Rewards given for apprehending or killing Pirates.

WHEREAS, by an Act of Assembly, made at a Session of Assembly, begun at the capital in Williamsburg, the eleventh day of November, in the fifth year of his Majesty's reign, entitled, An Act to Encourage the Apprehending and Destroying of Pirates: It is, amongst other things, enacted, that all and every person, or persons, who, from and after the fourteenth day of November, in the Year of our Lord one thousand seven hundred and eighteen, and before the fourteenth day of November, which shall be in the Year of our Lord one thousand seven hundred and nineteen, shall take any pirate, or pirates, on the sea or land, or, in case of resistance, shall kill any such pirate, or pirates, between the degrees of thirty-four and thirty-nine of northern latitude, and within one hundred leagues of the continent of Virginia, or within the provinces of Virginia, or North Carolina, upon the conviction, or making due proof of the killing of all and every such pirate, and pirates, before the Governor and Council, shall be entitled to have, and receive out of the public money, in the hands of the Treasurer of this Colony, the several rewards following: that is to say, for Edward Teach, commonly called Captain Teach, or Black-beard, one hundred pounds; for every other commander of a pirate ship, sloop, or vessel, forty pounds; for every lieutenant, master, or quartermaster, boatswain, or carpenter, twenty pounds; for every other inferior officer, fifteen pounds; and for every private man taken on board such ship, sloop, or vessel, ten pounds; and that for every pirate which shall be taken by any ship, sloop, or vessel, belonging to this colony, or North Carolina, within the time aforesaid, in any place whatsoever, the like rewards shall be paid according to the quality and condition of such pirates. Wherefore, for the encouragement of all such persons as shall be willing to serve his Majesty, and their country, in so just and honourable an undertaking as the suppressing a sort of people who may be truly called enemies to mankind: I have thought fit, with the advice and consent of his Majesty's Council, to issue this Proclamation, hereby declaring the said rewards shall be punctually and justly paid, in current money of Virginia, according to the directions of the said Act. And I do order and appoint this proclamation to be published by the sheriffs at their respective country houses, and by all ministers and readers in the several churches and chapels throughout this colony.

  Given at our Council-Chamber at Williamsburgh, this 24th day of November, 1718, in the fifth year of his Majesty's reign.

    GOD SAVE THE KING.

           A. SPOTSWOOD.*

  The 17th of November, 1718, the lieutenant sailed from Kicquetan, in James river in Virginia, and the 31st, in the evening, came to the mouth of Okerecock inlet, where he got sight of the pirate. This expedition was made with all imaginable secrecy, and the officer managed with all the prudence that was necessary, stopping all boats and vessels he met with in the river from going up, and thereby preventing any intelligence from reaching Black-beard, and receiving at the same time an account from them all of the place where the pirate was lurking. But notwithstanding this caution, Black-beard had information of the design from his Excellency of the province; and his secretary, Mr. Knight, wrote him a letter particularly concerning it, intimating "that he had sent him four of his men, which were all he could meet with in or about town, and so bid him be upon his guard." These men belonged to Black-beard, and were sent from Bath Town to Okerecock inlet, where the sloop lay, which is about twenty leagues.

    * Spottswood.

Black-beard had heard several reports, which happened not to be true, and so gave the less credit to this advice; nor was he convinced till he saw the sloops. Then it was time to put his vessel in a posture of defence. He had no more than twenty-five men on board, though he gave out to all the vessels he spoke with that he had forty. When he had prepared for battle he sat down and spent the night in drinking with the master of a trading sloop, who, it was thought, had more business with Teach than he should have had.

Lieutenant Maynard came to an anchor, for the place being shoal, and the channel intricate, there was no getting in where Teach lay that night; but in the morning he weighed, and sent his boat ahead of the sloops to sound, and coming within gun-shot of the pirate, received his fire; whereupon Maynard hoisted the king's colours, and stood directly towards him with the best way that his sails and oars could make. Black-beard cut his cable, and endeavoured to make a running fight, keeping a continual fire at his enemies with his guns. Mr. Maynard, not having any, kept a constant fire with small arms, while some of his men laboured at their oars. In a little time Teach's sloop ran aground, and Mr. Maynard's, drawing more water than that of the pirate, he could not come near him; so he anchored within half gun-shot of the enemy, and, in order to lighten his vessel, that he might run him aboard, the lieutenant ordered all his ballast to be thrown overboard, and all the water to be staved, and then weighed and stood for him; upon which Black-beard hailed him in this rude manner: "Damn you for villains, who are you; and from whence came you?" The lieutenant made him answer, "You may see by our colours we are no pirates." Black-beard bid him send his boat on board that he might see who he was; but Mr.

Maynard replied thus: "I cannot spare my boat, but I will come aboard of you as soon as I can with my sloop." Upon this Black-beard took a glass of liquor, and drank to him with these words: "Damnation seize my soul if I give you quarter, or take any from you." In answer to which Mr. Maynard told him "that he expected no quarter from him, nor should he give him any."

By this time Black-beard's sloop fleeted as Mr. Maynard's sloops were rowing towards him, which being not above a foot high in the waist, and consequently the men all exposed, as they came near together (there being hitherto little or no execution done on either side), the pirate fired a broadside charged with all manner of small shot. A fatal stroke to them!—the sloop the lieutenant was in having twenty men killed and wounded, and the other sloop nine. This could not be helped, for there being no wind, they were obliged to keep to their oars, otherwise the pirate would have got away from him, which, it seems, the lieutenant was resolute to prevent.

After this unlucky blow Black-beard's sloop fell broadside to the shore; Mr. Maynard's other sloop, which was called the *Ranger*, fell astern, being for the present disabled. So the lieutenant, finding his own sloop had way and would soon be on board of Teach, he ordered all his men down, for fear of another broadside, which must have been their destruction and the loss of their expedition. Mr. Maynard was the only person that kept the deck, except the man at the helm, whom he directed to lie down snug, and the men in the hold were ordered to get their pistols and their swords ready for close fighting, and to come up at his command; in order to which two ladders were placed in the hatchway for the more expedition. When the lieutenant's sloop boarded the other Captain Teach's men threw in several new-fashioned sort of grenades, viz., case-bottles filled with powder and small shot, slugs, and pieces of lead or iron, with a quick-match in the mouth of it, which, being lighted without side, presently runs into the bottle to the powder, and, as it is instantly thrown on board, generally does great execution, besides putting all the crew into a confusion. But, by good Providence, they had not that effect here, the men being in the hold. Black-beard, seeing few or no hands aboard, told his men "that they were all knocked to head, except three or four; and therefore," says he, "let's jump on board and cut them to pieces."

Whereupon, under the smoke of one of the bottles just mentioned, Black-beard enters with fourteen men over the bows of Maynard's sloop, and were not seen by him until the air cleared. However, he just then gave a signal to his men, who all rose in an instant, and attacked the pirates with as much bravery as ever was done upon such an occasion. Black-beard and the lieutenant fired the first shots at each other, by which the pirate received a wound, and then engaged with swords, till the lieutenant's unluckily broke, and stepping back to cock a pistol, Black-beard, with his cutlass, was striking at that instant that one of Maynard's men gave him a terrible wound in the neck and throat, by which the lieutenant came off with only a small cut over his fingers.

They were now closely and warmly engaged, the lieutenant and twelve men against Black-beard and fourteen, till the sea was tinctured with blood round the vessel. Black-beard received a shot into his body from the pistol that Lieutenant Maynard discharged, yet he stood his ground, and fought with great fury till he received five-and-twenty wounds, and five of them by shot. At length, as he was cocking another pistol, having fired several before, he fell down dead; by which time eight more out of the fourteen dropped, and all the rest, much wounded, jumped overboard and called out for quarter, which was granted, though it was only prolonging their lives a few days. The sloop *Ranger* came up and attacked the men that remained in Black-beard's sloop with equal bravery, till they likewise cried for quarter.

Here was an end of that courageous brute, who might have passed in the world for a hero had he been employed in a good cause. His destruction, which was of such consequence to the plantations, was entirely owing to the conduct and bravery of Lieutenant Maynard and his men, who might have destroyed him with much less loss had they had a vessel with great guns; but they were obliged to use small vessels, because the holes and place she lurked in would not admit of others of greater draught. And it was no small difficulty for this gentleman to get to him, having grounded his vessel at least a hundred times in getting up the river, beside other discouragements, enough to have turned back any gentleman without dishonour had he been less resolute and bold than this lieutenant. The broadside that did so much mischief before they boarded in all probability saved the rest from destruction; for, before that, Teach had little or no hopes of escaping, and therefore had posted a resolute fellow, a negro, whom he had bred up, with a lighted match in the powder-room, with commands to blow up when he should give him orders, which was as soon as the lieutenant and his men could have entered, that so he might have destroyed his conquerors with himself. And when the negro found how it went with Black-beard, he could hardly be persuaded from the rash action by two prisoners that were then in the hold of the sloop.

What seems a little odd is that some of these men, who behaved so bravely against Black-beard, went afterwards a-pirating themselves, and one of them was taken along with Roberts; but I do not find that any of them were provided for, except one that was hanged. But this is a digression.

The lieutenant caused Black-beard's head to be severed from his body, and hung up at the boltsprit end; then he sailed to Bath Town, to get relief for his wounded men.

It must be observed that, in rummaging the pirate's sloop, they found several letters and written papers, which discovered the correspondence between Governor Eden, the secretary and collector, and also some traders at New York, and Black-beard. It is likely he had regard enough for his friends to have destroyed these papers before the action, in order to hinder them from falling into such hands, where the discovery would be of no use either to the interest or reputation of these fine gentlemen, if it had not been his fixed resolution to have blown up together, when he found no possibility of escaping.

When the lieutenant came to Bath Town, he made bold to seize in the governor's storehouse the sixty hogsheads of sugar, and from honest Mr. Knight, twenty; which it seems was their dividend of the plunder taken in the French ship. The latter did not survive this shameful discovery, for, being apprehensive that he might be called to an account for these trifles, fell sick, it is thought, with the fright, and died in a few days.

After the wounded men were pretty well recovered, the lieutenant sailed back to the men-of-war in James River, in Virginia, with Black-beard's head still hanging at the boltsprit end, and fifteen prisoners, thirteen of whom were hanged, it appearing, upon trial, that one of them, viz., Samuel Odell, was taken out of the trading sloop but the night before the engagement. This poor fellow was a little unlucky at his first entering upon his new trade, there appearing no less than seventy wounds upon him after the action; notwithstanding which he lived and was cured of them all. The other person that escaped the gallows was one Israel Hands, the master of Black-beard's sloop, and formerly captain of the same, before the *Queen Ann's Revenge* was lost in Topsail inlet.

The aforesaid Hands happened not to be in the fight, but was taken afterwards ashore at Bath Town, having been sometime before disabled by Black-beard, in one of his savage humours, after the following manner: One night, drinking in his cabin with Hands, the pilot, and another man, Black beard, without any provocation, privately draws out a small pair of pistols, and cocks them under the table, which being perceived by the man, he withdrew and went upon deck, leaving Hands, the pilot, and the captain together. When the pistols were ready he blew out the candle, and, crossing his hands, discharged them at his company; Hands, the master, was shot through the knee and lamed for life, the other pistol did no execution. Being asked the meaning of this, he only answered by damning them, that "if he did not now and then kill one of them, they would forget who he was."

Hands being taken, was tried and condemned, but just as he was about to be executed a ship arrived at Virginia with a proclamation for prolonging the time of his Majesty's pardon to such of the pirates as should surrender by a limited time therein expressed. Notwithstanding the sentence, Hands pleaded the pardon, and was allowed the benefit of it, and was alive some time ago in London, begging his bread.

Now that we have given some account of Teach's life and actions, it will not be amiss that we speak of his beard, since it did not a little contribute towards making his name so terrible in those parts.

Plutarch and other grave historians have taken notice that several great men amongst the Romans took their surnames from certain odd marks in their countenances—as Cicero, from a mark, or vetch, on his nose—so our hero, Captain Teach, assumed the cognomen of Blackbeard, from that large quantity of hair which, like a frightful meteor, covered his whole face, and frightened America more than any comet that has appeared there a long time.

This beard was black, which he suffered to grow of an extravagant length; as to breadth, it came up to his eyes. He was accustomed to twist it with ribbons, in small tails, after the manner of our Ramilie wigs, and turn them about his ears. In time of action he wore a sling over his shoulders, with three brace of pistols hanging in holsters like bandaliers, and stuck lighted matches under his hat, which, appearing on each side of his face, his eyes naturally looking fierce and wild, made him altogether such a figure that imagination cannot form an idea of a fury from hell to look more frightful.

If he had the look of a fury, his humours and passions were suitable to it. We shall relate two or three more of his extravagances which we omitted in the body of his history, by which it will appear to what a pitch of wickedness human nature may arrive if its passions are not checked.

In the commonwealth of pirates, he who goes the greatest length of wickedness is looked upon with a kind of envy amongst them as a person of a more extraordinary gallantry, and is thereby entitled to be distinguished by some post, and if such a one has but courage, he must certainly be a great man. The hero of whom we are writing was thoroughly accomplished this way, and some of his frolics of wickedness were so extravagant, as if he aimed at making his men believe he was a devil incarnate;

for being one day at sea, and a little flushed with drink, "Come," says he, "let us make a hell of our own, and try how long we can bear it." Accordingly he, with two or three others, went down into the hold, and closing up all the hatches, filled several pots full of brimstone and other combustible matter, and set it on fire, and so continued till they were almost suffocated, when some of the men cried out for air. At length he opened the hatches, not a little pleased that he held out the longest.

The night before he was killed he sat up and drank till the morning with some of his own men and the master of a merchantman; and having had intelligence of the two sloops coming to attack him, as has been before observed, one of his men asked him, in case anything should happen to him in the engagement with the sloops, whether his wife knew where he had buried his money? He answered, "That nobody but himself and the devil knew where it was, and the longest liver should take all.

Those of his crew who were taken alive told a story which may appear a little incredible; however, we think it will not be fair to omit it since we had it from their own mouths. That once upon a cruise they found out that they had a man on board more than their crew; such a one was seen several days amongst them, sometimes below and sometimes upon deck, yet no man in the ship could give an account who he was, or from whence he came, but that he disappeared a little before they were cast away in their great ship; but it seems they verily believed it was the devil.

One would think these things should induce them to reform their lives, but so many reprobates together, encouraged and spirited one another up in their wickedness, to which a continual course of drinking did not a little contribute, for in Black-beard's journal, which was taken, there were several memorandums of the following nature found writ with his own hand: Such a day rum all out; our company somewhat sober; a damned confusion amongst us; rogues a-plotting; great talk of separation; so I looked sharp for a prize; such a day took one with a great deal of liquor on board, so kept the company hot, damned hot, then all things went well again.

Thus it was these wretches passed their lives, with very little pleasure or satisfaction in the possession of what they violently take away from others, and sure to pay for it at last by an ignominious death.

The names of the pirates killed in the engagement, are as follows:—

Edward Teach, commander; Philip Morton, gunner; Garret Gibbens, boatswain; Owen Roberts, carpenter; Thomas Miller, quartermaster; John Husk, Joseph Curtice, Joseph Brooks (1), Nath. Jackson. All the rest, except the two last, were wounded, and afterwards hanged in Virginia:—John Carnes, Joseph Brooks (2), James Blake, John Gills, Thomas Gates, James White, Richard Stiles, Cæsar, Joseph Philips, James Robbins, John Martin, Edward Salter, Stephen Daniel, Richard Greensail, Israel Hands, pardoned, Samuel Odel, acquitted.

There were in the pirate sloops, and ashore in a tent near where the sloops lay, twenty-five hogsheads of sugar, eleven teirces, and one hundred and forty-five bags of cocoa, a barrel of indigo, and a bale of cotton; which, with what was taken from the governor and secretary, and the sale of the sloop, came to £2,500, besides the rewards paid by the governor of Virginia, pursuant to his proclamation; all which was divided among the companies of the two ships, *Lime* and *Pearl*, that lay in James River; the brave fellows that took them coming in for no more than their dividend amongst the rest, and were paid it not till four years afterwards.

II.

CAPTAIN WILLIAM KID.

Commanded a privateer in the West Indies—Recommended to the Government by Lord Bellamont, &c.—Not encouraged—He is sent out in a private man-of-war with the king's commission—He sails for New York—In his way takes a French banker—Arrived there—Ships more hands—Sails to Madeira, Bonavista, Cape de Verde Islands, and Madagascar—Meets three English men-of-war—Meets with nothing at Madagascar—Goes to the Malabar coast—Cruises about Mohila and Johanna—Borrows money and repairs his ship—At Mabbee he takes some corn—From thence steers for Bab's Key—He sends a boat along the coast, and gains intelligence—He falls in with a fleet, but is obliged to sheer off—Goes to the Malabar coast—Takes a Moorish vessel—Treats the men cruelly, and discharges the vessel—Touches at Carawar, and is suspected of piracy—Engages a Portuguese man-of-war sent after him and gets off—Takes a Moor ship under pretence of her being French—Keeps company with a Dutch ship—Quarrels with and kills his gunner—Plunders a Portuguese ship on the Malabar coast and lets her go—His cooper is murdered in one of the Malabar Islands—He burns and pillages several houses—Commands a native to be shot—He takes the *Queda*, and shares £200 a man amongst his crew—He cheats the Indians—Goes to Madagascar—Meets there Culliford the pirate—Shifts into the *Queda*, and shares the rest of her cargo—His men desert from him to forty—Goes to Amboyna—hears he is declared a pirate in England—Lord Bellamont prints his justification—A pardon granted to pirates—Avery and Kid excepted—Kid goes to, and is secured at, New York—Some of his crew depending on the pardon, are confined—Sent to England and condemned—Three excepted—A distinction of the lawyers—Kid found guilty of the murder of his gunner—Some plead the king's pardon to no purpose—Mullins's plea—Kid's plea useless—He and his men indicted—Executed.

WE are now going to give an account of one whose name is better known in England than most of those whose histories we have already related; the person we mean is Captain Kid, whose public trial and execution here rendered him the subject of all conversation, so that his actions have been chanted about in ballads; however, it is now a considerable time since these things passed, and though the people knew in general that Captain Kid was hanged, and that his crime was piracy, yet there were scarce any, even at that time, who were acquainted with his life or actions, or could account for his turning pirate.

In the beginning of King William's war, Captain Kid commanded a privateer in the West Indies, and by several adventurous actions acquired the reputation of a brave man, as well as an experienced seaman. About this time the pirates were very troublesome in those parts, wherefore Captain Kid was recommended by the Lord Bellamont, then governor of Barbadoes, as well as by several other persons, to the Government here, as a person very fit to be entrusted with the command of a Government ship, and to be employed in cruising upon the pirates, as knowing those seas perfectly well, and being acquainted with all their lurking places; but what reasons governed the politics of those times I cannot tell, but this proposal met with no encouragement here, though it is certain it would have been of great consequence to the subject, our merchants suffering incredible damages by those robbers.

Upon this neglect the Lord Bellamont and some others, who knew what great captures had been made by the pirates, and what a prodigious wealth must be in their possession, were tempted to fit out a ship at their own private charge, and to give the command of it to Captain Kid; and to give the thing a greater reputation, as well as to keep their seamen under the better command, they procured the King's Commission for the said Captain Kid, of which the following is an exact copy :—

"WILLIAM REX,—William the Third, by the grace of God, King of England, Scotland, France, and Ireland, Defender of the Faith, &c. To our trusty and wellbeloved Captain William Kid, Commander of the ship the *Adventure* galley, or to any other the commander of the same for the time being, greeting; Whereas we are informed, that Captain Thomas Too, John Ireland, Captain Thomas Wake, and Captain William Maze, or Mace, and other subjects, natives or inhabitants of New York, and elsewhere, in our plantations in America, have associated themselves, with divers others, wicked and ill-disposed persons, and do, against the law of nations, commit many and great piracies, robberies, and depredations on the seas upon the parts of America, and in other parts, to the great hindrance and discouragement of trade and navigation, and to the great danger and hurt of our loving subjects, our allies, and all others, navigating the seas upon their lawful occasions. Now know ye, that we being desirous to prevent the aforesaid mischiefs, and, as much as in us lies, to bring the said pirates, freebooters and sea-rovers to justice, have thought fit, and do hereby give and grant to the said William Kid (to whom our Commissioners for exercising the office of Lord High Admiral of England, have granted a commission as a private man-of-war, bearing date December 11, 1695), and unto the commander of the said ship for the time being, and unto the officers, mariners, and others, which shall be under your command, full power and authority to apprehend, seize, and take into your custody as well the said Captain Thomas Too, John Ireland, Captain

Thomas Wake, and Captain William Maze, or Mace, as all such pirates, freebooters and sea-rovers, being either our subjects, or of other nations associated with them, which you shall meet with upon the seas or coasts of America, or upon any other seas or coasts, with all their ships and vessels; and all such merchandises, money, goods, and wares as shall be found on board, or with them, in case they shall willingly yield themselves; but if they will not yield without fighting, then you are by force to compel them to yield. And we do also require you to bring, or cause to be brought, such pirates, freebooters, or sea-rovers, as you shall seize, to a legal trial, to the end they may be proceeded against according to the law in such cases. And we do hereby command all our officers, ministers, and other our loving subjects whatsoever, to be aiding and assisting to you in the premisses. And we do hereby enjoin you to keep an exact journal of your proceedings in the execution of the premisses, and set down the names of such pirates, and of their officers and company, and the names of such ships and vessels as you shall by virtue of these presents take and seize, and the quantities of arms, ammunition, provision, and lading of such ships, and the true value of the same, as near as you judge. And we do hereby strictly charge and command you as you will answer the contrary at your peril, that you do not, in any manner, offend or molest our friends or allies, their ships, or subjects, by colour or pretence of these presents, or the authority thereby granted. In witness whereof we have caused our Great Seal of England to be affixed to these presents. Given at our Court of Kensington, the 26th day of January, 1695, in the seventh year of our reign."

Captain Kid had also another commission, which was

called a Commission of Reprisals; for it being then war time, this commission was to justify him in the taking of French merchant ships, in case he should meet with any; but as this commission is nothing to our present purpose, we shall not burthen the readers with it.

With these two commissions he sailed out of Plymouth in May, 1696, in the *Adventure* galley of thirty guns and eighty men. The place he first designed for was New York; in his voyage thither he took a French banker, but this was no act of piracy, he having a commission for that purpose, as we have just observed.

When he arrived at New York he put up articles for engaging more hands, it being necessary to his ship's crew, since he proposed to deal with a desperate enemy. The terms he offered were that every man should have a share of what was taken, reserving for himself and owners forty shares. Upon which encouragement he soon increased his company to a hundred and fifty-five men.

With this company he sailed first for Madeira, where he took in wine and some other necessaries; from thence he proceeded to Bonavist, one of the Cape de Verde islands, to furnish the ship with salt, and from thence went immediately to St. Jago, another of the Cape de Verde islands, in order to stock himself with provisions. When all this was done he bent his course to Madagascar, the known rendezvous of pirates. In his way he fell in with Captain Warren, commodore of three men-of-war; he acquainted them with his design, kept them company two or three days, and then leaving them made the best way for Madagascar, where he arrived in February, 1696, just nine months from his departure from Plymouth.

It happened that at this time the pirate ships were most of them out in search of prey, so that, according to the best intelligence Captain Kid could get, there was not one of them at that time about the island, wherefore, having spent some time in watering his ship and taking in more provisions, he thought of trying his fortune on the coast of Malabar, where he arrived in the month of June following, four months from his reaching Madagascar. Hereabouts he made an unsuccessful cruise, touching sometimes at the island of Mahala, sometimes at that of Joanna, between Malabar and Madagascar. His provisions were every day wasting, and his ship began to want repair; wherefore, when he was at Joanna, he found means of borrowing a sum of money from some Frenchmen who had lost their ship, but saved their effects, and with this he purchased materials for putting his ship in good repair.

It does not appear all this while that he had the least design of turning pirate, for near Mahala and Joanna both he met with several Indian ships richly laden, to which he did not offer the least violence, though he was strong enough to have done what he pleased with them; and the first outrage or depredation I find he committed upon mankind was after his repairing his ship and leaving Joanna. He touched at a place called Mabbee, upon the Red Sea, where he took some Guinea corn from the natives, by force.

After this he sailed to Bab's Key, a place upon a little island at the entrance of the Red Sea. Here it was that he first began to open himself to his ship's company, and let them understand that he intended to change his measures; for, happening to talk of the Moca fleet which was to sail that way, he said, "We have been unsuccessful hitherto; but courage, my boys, we'll make our fortunes out of this fleet." And finding that none of them appeared averse to it he ordered a boat out, well manned, to go upon the coast to make discoveries, commanding them to take a prisoner and bring to him, or get intelligence any way they could. The boat returned in a few days, bringing him word that they saw fourteen or fifteen ships ready to sail, some with English, some with Dutch, and some with Moorish colours.

We cannot account for this sudden change in his conduct, otherwise than by supposing that he first meant well, while he had hopes of making his fortune by taking of pirates; but now, weary of ill-success, and fearing lest his owners, out of humour at their great expenses, should dismiss him, and he should want employment, and be marked out for an unlucky man—rather, I say, than run the hazard of poverty, he resolved to do his business one way, since he could not do it another.

He therefore ordered a man continually to watch at the mast-head, lest this fleet should go by them; and about four days after, towards evening, it appeared in sight, being convoyed by one English and one Dutch man-of-war. Kid soon fell in with them, and, getting into the midst of them, fired at a Moorish ship which was next him; but the men-of-war, taking the alarm, bore down upon Kid, and, firing upon him, obliged him to sheer off, he not being strong enough to contend with them. Now he had begun hostilities he resolved to go on, and therefore he went and cruised along the coast of Malabar. The first prize he met was a small vessel belonging to Aden; the vessel was Moorish, and the owners were Moorish merchants, but the master was an Englishman; his name was Parker. Kid forced him and a Portuguese that was called Don Antonio, which were all the Europeans on board, to take on with them; the first he designed as a pilot, and the last as an interpreter. He also used the men very cruelly, causing them to be hoisted up by the arms, and drubbed with a naked cutlass, to force them to discover whether they had money on board, and where it lay; but as they had neither gold nor silver on board he got nothing by his cruelty; however, he took from them a bale of pepper, and a bale of coffee, and so let them go.

A little time after he touched at Carawar, a place upon the same coast, where, before he arrived, the news of what he had done to the Moorish ship had reached them; for some of the English merchants there had received an account of it from the owners, who corresponded with them; wherefore, as soon as Kid came in, he was suspected to be the person who committed this piracy, and one Mr. Harvey and Mr. Mason, two of the English factory, came on board and asked for Parker and Antonio, the Portuguese, but Kid denied that he knew any such persons, having secured them both in a private place in the hold, where they were kept for seven or eight days, that is till Kid sailed from thence.

However, the coast was alarmed, and a Portuguese man-of-war was sent out to cruise. Kid met with her, and fought her about six hours, gallantly enough; but finding her too strong to be taken, he quitted her, for he was able to run away from her when he would. Then he went to a place called Porco, where he watered the ship, and bought a number of hogs of the natives to victual his company.

Soon after this he came up with a Moorish ship, the master whereof was a Dutchman, called Schipper Mitchel, and chased her under French colours, which, they observing, hoisted French colours too. When he came up with her he hailed her in French, and they, having a Frenchman on board, answered him in the same language; upon which he ordered them to send their boat on board.

They were obliged to do so, and having examined who they were, and from whence they came, he asked the Frenchman, who was a passenger, if he had a French pass for himself? The Frenchman gave him to understand that he had. Then he told the Frenchman he must pass for captain, and "by G—d," says he, "you are the captain." The Frenchman durst not refuse doing as he would have him. The meaning of this was, that he would seize the ship as fair prize, and as if she had belonged to French subjects, according to a commission he had for that purpose; though, one would think, after what he had already done, that he need not have recourse to a quibble to give his actions a colour.

In short, he took the cargo and sold it some time after; yet still he seemed to have some fears upon him lest these proceedings should have a bad end, for, coming up with a Dutch ship some time, when his men thought of nothing but attacking her, Kid opposed it; upon which a mutiny arose, and the majority being for taking the said ship, and arming themselves to man the boat to go and seize her, he told them, such as did, never should come on board him again, which put an end to the design, so that he kept company with the said ship some time, without offering her any violence. However, this dispute was the occasion of an accident, upon which an indictment was afterwards grounded against Kid; for Moor, the gunner, being one day upon deck, and talking with Kid about the said Dutch ship, some words arose between them, and Moor told Kid that he had ruined them all; upon which Kid, calling him dog, took up a bucket and struck him with it, which, breaking his skull, he died the next day.

But Kid's penitential fit did not last long, for, coasting along Malabar, he met with a great number of boats, all which he plundered. Upon the same coast he also lighted upon a Portuguese ship, which he kept possession of a week, and then, having taken out of her some chests of Indian goods, thirty jars of butter, with some wax, iron, and a hundred bags of rice, he let her go.

Much about the same time he went to one of the Malabar islands for wood and water, and his cooper, being ashore, was murdered by the natives; upon which Kid himself landed, and burnt and pillaged several of their houses, the people running away; but having taken one, he caused him to be tied to a tree, and commanded one of his men to shoot him; then putting to sea again he took the greatest prize which fell into his hands while he followed this trade. This was a Moorish ship of four hundred tons, richly laden, named the *Queda*, merchant, the master whereof was an Englishman—he was called Wright, for the Indians often make use of English or Dutch men to command their ships, their own mariners not being so good artists in navigation. Kid chased her under French colours, and, having come up with her, he ordered her to hoist out her boat and to send on board of him, which, being done, he told Wright he was his prisoner; and informing himself concerning the said ship, he understood there were no Europeans on board except two Dutch, and one Frenchman, all the rest being Indians or Armenians, and that the Armenians were part owners of the cargo. Kid gave the Armenians to understand that if they would offer anything that was worth his taking for their ransom, he would hearken to it; upon which they proposed to pay him twenty thousand rupees, not quite three thousand pounds sterling; but Kid judged this would be making a bad bargain, wherefore he rejected it, and setting the crew on shore at different places on the coast, he soon sold as much of the cargo as came to near ten thousand pounds. With part of it he also trafficked, receiving in exchange provisions or such other goods as he wanted. By degrees he disposed of the the whole cargo, and when the division was made it came to about two hundred pounds a man, and, having reserved forty shares to himself, his dividend amounted to about eight thousand pounds sterling.

The Indians along the coast came on board and trafficked with all freedom, and he punctually performed his bargains, till about the time he was ready to sail; and then, thinking he should have no further occasion for them, he made no scruple of taking their goods and setting them on shore without any payment in money or goods, which they little expected; for as they had been used to deal with pirates, they always found them men of honour in the way of trade—a people, enemies to deceit, and that scorned to rob but in their own way.

Kid put some of his men on board the *Queda*, merchant, and with this ship and his own sailed for Madagascar. As soon as he was arrived and had cast anchor there came on board of him a canoe, in which were several Englishmen who had formerly been well acquainted with Kid. As soon as they saw him they saluted him and told him they were informed he was come to take them, and hang them, which would be a little unkind in such an old acquaintance. Kid soon dissipated their doubts by swearing he had no such design, and that he was now in every respect their brother, and just as bad as they, and, calling for a cup of bomboo, drank their captain's health.

These men belonged to a pirate ship, called the *Resolution*, formerly the *Mocco*, merchant, whereof one Captain Culliford was commander, and which lay at an anchor not far from them. Kid went on board with them, promising them his friendship and assistance, and Culliford in his turn came on board of Kid; and Kid, to testify his sincerity in iniquity, finding Culliford in want of some necessaries, made him a present of an anchor and some guns, to fit him out for the sea again.

The *Adventure* galley was now so old and leaky that they were forced to keep two pumps continually going, wherefore Kid shifted all the guns and tackle out of her into the *Queda*, merchant, intending her for his man-of-war; and as he had divided the money before, he now made a division of the remainder of the cargo. Soon after which the greatest part of the company left him, some going on board Captain Culliford, and others absconding in the country, so that he had not above forty men left.

He put to sea and happened to touch at Amboyna, one of the Dutch spice islands, where he was told that the news of his actions had reached England, and that he was there declared a pirate.

The truth of it is, his piracies so alarmed our merchants that some motions were made in Parliament, to inquire into the commission that was given him, and the persons who fitted him out. These proceedings seemed to lean a little hard upon the Lord Bellamont, who thought himself so much touched thereby that he published a justification of himself in a pamphlet after Kid's execution. In the meantime it was thought advisable, in order to stop the course of these piracies, to publish a proclamation, offering the king's free pardon to all such pirates as should voluntarily surrender themselves, whatever piracies they had been guilty of at any time, before the last day of April, 1699. That is to say, for all piracies committed eastward of the Cape of Good Hope, to the longitude and meridian of Socatora and Cape Camorin. In which proclamation Avery and Kid were excepted by name.

When Kid left Amboyna he knew nothing of this proclamation, for certainly had he had notice of his being excepted in it he would not have been so infatuated to run himself into the very jaws of danger; but relying upon his interest with the Lord Bellamont, and fancying that a French pass or two he found on board some of the ships he took would serve to countenance the matter, and that part of the booty he got would gain him new friends—I say, all these things made him flatter himself that all would be hushed, and that justice would but wink at him. Wherefore he sailed directly for New York, where he was no sooner arrived but by the Lord Bellamont's orders he was secured with all his papers and effects. Many of his fellow-adventurers who had forsook him at Madagascar, came over from thence passengers, some to New England, and some to Jersey, where, hearing of the king's proclamation for pardoning of pirates, they surrendered themselves to the governor of those places. At first they were admitted to bail, but soon after were laid in strict confinement, where they were kept for some time, till an opportunity happened of sending them with their captain over to England to be tried.

Accordingly, a Sessions of Admiralty being held at the Old Bailey, in May, 1701, Captain Kid, Nicholas Churchill, James How, Robert Lumley, William Jenkins, Gabriel Loff, Hugh Parrot, Richard Barlicorn, Abel Owens, and Darby Mullins, were arraigned for piracy and robbery on the high seas, and all found guilty except three: these were Robert Lumley, William Jenkins, and Richard Barlicorn, who, proving themselves to be apprentices to some of the officers of the ship, and producing their indentures in court, were acquitted.

The three above mentioned, though they were proved to be concerned in taking and sharing the ship and goods mentioned in the indictment, yet, as the gentlemen of the long robe rightly distinguished, there was a great difference between their circumstances and the rest; for there must go an intention of the mind and a freedom of the will to the committing an act of felony or piracy. A pirate is not to be understood to be under constraint, but a free agent; for, in this case, the bare act will not make a man guilty, unless the will make it so.

Now a servant, it is true, if he go voluntarily and have his proportion, he must be accounted a pirate, for then he acts upon his own account, and not by compulsion. And these persons, according to the evidence, received their part, but whether they accounted to their masters for their shares afterwards is the matter in question, and what distinguishes them as free agents or men, that did go under the compulsion of their masters, which being left to the consideration of the jury, they found them "Not Guilty."

Kid was tried upon an indictment of murder also—viz., for killing Moor, the gunner—and found guilty of the same. Nicholas Churchill and James How pleaded the king's pardon, as having surrendered themselves within the time limited in the proclamation, and Colonel Bass, governor of West Jersey, to whom they surrendered, being in court, and called upon, proved the same; however, this plea was overruled by the court, because there being four commissioners named in the proclamation, viz., Captain Thomas Warren, Israel Hayes, Peter Delannoye, and Christopher Pollard, Esqs., who were appointed commissioners, and sent over on purpose to receive the submissions of such pirates as should surrender, it was adjudged no other person was qualified to receive their surrender, and that they could not be entitled to the benefit of the said proclamation because they had not in all circumstances complied with the conditions of it.

Darby Mullins urged in his defence that he served under the king's commission, and therefore could not disobey his commander without incurring great punishments; that whenever a ship or ships went out upon any expedition under the king's commissioners, the men were never allowed to call their officers to an account, why they did this, or why they did that, because such a liberty would destroy all discipline; that if anything was done which was unlawful, the officers were to answer it, for the men did no more than their duty in obeying orders. He was told by the court that acting under the commission justified in what was lawful but not in what was unlawful. He answered, he stood in need of nothing to justify him in what was lawful, but that the case of seamen must be very hard, if they must be brought into such danger for obeying the commands of their officers, and punished for not obeying them; and if they were allowed to dispute the orders, there could be no such thing as command kept up at sea.

This seemed to be the best defence the thing could bear. But his taking a share of the plunder, the seamen mutinying on board several times, and taking upon them to control the captain, showed there was no obedience paid to the commission, and that they acted in all things according to the custom of pirates and freebooters, which weighing with the jury they brought him in guilty with the rest.

As to Captain Kid's defence, he insisted much upon his own innocence, and the villainy of his men. He said he went out in a laudable employment, and had no occasion, being then in good circumstances, to go a-pirating; that the men often mutinied against him, and did as they pleased; that he was threatened to be shot in his cabin, and that ninety-five left him at one time, and set fire to his boat, so that he was disabled from bringing his ship home, or the prizes he took, to have them regularly condemned, which he said were taken by virtue of a commission under the broad seal, they having French passes. The captain called one Colonel Hewson to his reputation, who gave him an extraordinary character, and declared to the court that he had served under his command, and been in two engagements with him against the French, in which he fought as well as any man he ever saw; that there were only Kid's ship and his own against Monsieur du Cass, who commanded a squadron of six sail, and they got the better of him. But this being several years before the facts mentioned in the indictment were committed, proved of no manner of service to the prisoner on his trial.

As to the friendship shown to Culliford, a notorious pirate, Kid denied, and said he intended to have taken him, but his men, being a parcel of rogues and villains, refused to stand by him, and several of them ran away from his ship to the said pirate. But the evidence being full and particular against him, he was found guilty as before mentioned.

When Kid was asked what he had to say why sentence should not pass against him, he answered that "he had nothing to say, but that he had been sworn against by perjured, wicked people." And when sentence was pronounced, he said, "My lord, it is a very hard sentence. For my part I am the innocentest person of them all, only I have been sworn against by perjured persons."

Wherefore, about a week after, Captain Kid, Nicholas Churchill, James How, Gabriel Loff, Hugh Parrot, Abel Owen, and Darby Mullins, were executed at Execution Dock, and afterwards hung up in chains, at some distance from each other down the river, where their bodies hung exposed for many years.

III.

CAPTAIN BARTHOLOMEW ROBERTS AND HIS CREW.

His beginning—Elected captain in the room of Davis—The speech of Lord Dennis at the election—Lord Sympson objects against a papist—The death of Davis revenged—Roberts sails southward in quest of adventures—The names of the prizes taken by them—Brazil described—Roberts falls into a fleet of Portuguese—Boards and takes the richest ship amongst them—Mako the Devil's Islands—An unfortunate adventure of Roberts—Kennedy's treachery—Irishmen excluded by Roberts and his crew—Articles sworn to by them—A copy of them—Some account of the laws and customs of the pirates—An instance of Roberts's cunning—He proceeds again upon business, and takes prizes—Narrowly escapes being taken—Sails for the Island Dominico—Another escape—Sails for Newfoundland—Plunders, sinks, and burns twenty-two sail in the harbour of Trepassi—Plunders ten sail of Frenchmen—The mad behaviour of the crew—A correspondence hinted at—The pirates caressed at the island of St. Bartholomew—In extreme distress—Sail for Martinico—A stratagem of Roberts—The insolent device in his colours—Odd compliment paid to Roberts—Three men desert the pirates, and are taken by them—Their trial—Two executed and one saved—the brigantine deserts them—Great divisions in the company—A description of Sierra Leone River—The names of English settled there, and way of life—The *Onslow* belonging to the African Company taken—The pirates' contempt of soldiers—They are for entertaining a chaplain—Their skirmish with the Calabar negroes—The *King Solomon*, belonging to the African Company taken—The frolics of the pirates—Take eleven sail in Whydah Road—A comical receipt given by the pirates—A cruel action of Roberts—Sails for Anna Bona—The progress of the *Swallow* man-of-war, in pursuit of Roberts—Roberts's consort taken—The bravery of Skyrme, a

Welsh pirate—The surly humour of some of the prisoners—The *Swallow* comes up with Roberts—Roberts's dress described—Is killed—His character—His ship taken—The behaviour of the pirates when prisoners—A conspiracy of theirs discovered—Reflections on the manner of trying them—The form of the commission for trying the pirates—The oath taken by the commissioners—The names of those arraigned taken in the ship *Ranger*—The form of the indictment—The sum of the evidence against them—Their defence—The names of the prisoners of the *Royal Fortune*—Proceedings against them—Harry Glasby acquitted—The particular trial of Captain James Skyrme—Of John Walden—Of Peter Scudamore—Of Robert Johnson—Of George Wilson—Of Benjamin Jeffries—Of John Mansfield—Of William Davis—The names of those executed at Cape Corso—The petition of some condemned—The court's resolution—The form of an indenture of a pardoned pirate—The names of those pardoned upon indenture to serve seven years—The pirates how disposed of—The dying behaviour of those executed.

BARTHOLOMEW ROBERTS sailed in an honest employ from London, aboard of the *Princess*, Captain Plumb, commander, of which ship he was second mate. He left England November, 1719, and arrived at Guinea about February following, and being at Anamaboe, taking in slaves for the West Indies, was taken in the said ship by Captain Howel Davis. In the beginning he was very averse to this sort of life, and would certainly have escaped from them had a fair opportunity presented itself; yet afterwards he changed his principles, as many besides him have done upon another element, and perhaps for the same reason too, viz., preferment; and what he did not like as a private man he could reconcile to his conscience as a commander.

Davis having been killed in the Island of Princes whilst planning to capture it with all its inhabitants, the company found themselves under the necessity of filling up his post, for which there appeared two or three candidates among the select part of them that were distinguished by the title of Lords—such were Sympson, Ashplant, Anstis, &c.—and on canvassing this matter, how shattered and weak a condition their government must be without a head, since Davis had been removed in the manner before mentioned, my Lord Dennis proposed, it is said, over a bowl, to this purpose:

"That it was not of any great signification who was dignified with title, for really and in good truth all good governments had, like theirs, the supreme power lodged with the community, who might doubtless depute and revoke as suited interest or humour. We are the original of this claim," says he, "and should a captain be so saucy as to exceed prescription at any time, why, down with him! It will be a caution after he is dead to his successors of what fatal consequence any sort of assuming may be. However, it is my advice that while we are sober we pitch upon a man of courage and skilled in navigation, one who by his council and bravery seems best able to defend this commonwealth, and ward us from the dangers and tempests of an unstable element, and the fatal consequences of anarchy; and such a one I take Roberts to be —a fellow, I think, in all respects worthy your esteem and favour."

This speech was loudly applauded by all but Lord Sympson, who had secret expectations himself, but on this disappointment grew sullen and left them, swearing "he did not care who they chose captain so it was not a papist, for against them he had conceived an irreconcilable hatred, for that his father had been a sufferer in Monmouth's rebellion."

Roberts was accordingly elected, though he had not been above six weeks among them. The choice was confirmed both by the Lords and Commoners, and he accepted of the honour, saying that, since he had dipped his hands in muddy water and must be a pirate, it was better being a commander than a common man.

As soon as the government was settled, by promoting other officers in the room of those that were killed by the Portuguese, the company resolved to avenge Captain Davis's death, he being more than ordinarily respected by the crew for his affability and good nature, as well as his conduct and bravery upon all occasions; and, pursuant to this resolution, about thirty men were landed, in order to make an attack upon the fort, which must be ascended to by a steep hill against the mouth of the cannon. These men were headed by one Kennedy, a bold, daring fellow, but very wicked and profligate; they marched directly up under the fire of their ship guns, and as soon as they were discovered, the Portuguese quitted their post and fled to the town, and the pirates marched in without opposition, set fire to the fort, and threw all the guns off the hill into the sea, which after they had done they retreated quietly to their ship.

But this was not looked upon as a sufficient satisfaction for the injury they received, therefore most of the company were for burning the town, which Roberts said he would yield to if any means could be proposed of doing it without their own destruction, for the town had a securer situation than the fort, a thick wood coming almost close to it, affording cover to the defendants, who, under such an advantage, he told them, it was to be feared, would fire and stand better to their arms; besides, that bare houses would be but a slender reward for their trouble and loss. This prudent advice prevailed; however, they mounted the French ship they seized at this place with twelve guns, and lightened her, in order to come up to the town, the water being shoal, and battered down several houses; after which they all returned on board, gave back the French ship to those that had most right to her, and sailed out of the harbour by the light of two

Portuguese ships, which they were pleased to set on fire there.

Roberts stood away to the southward, and met with a Dutch Guineaman, which he made prize of, but, after having plundered her, the skipper had his ship again. Two days after he took an English ship, called the *Experiment*, Captain Cornet, at Cape Lopez; the men went all into the pirate service, and having no occasion for the ship they burnt her and then steered for St. Thome, but meeting with nothing in their way, they sailed for Annabona, and there watered, took in provisions, and put it to a vote of the company whether their next voyage should be to the East Indies or to Brazil. The latter being resolved on, they sailed accordingly, and in twenty-eight days arrived at Ferdinando, an uninhabited island on that coast. Here they watered, boot-topped their ship, and made ready for the designed cruise.

Upon this coast our rovers cruised for about nine weeks, keeping generally out of sight of land, but without seeing a sail, which discouraged them so that they determined to leave the station and steer for the West Indies; and, in order thereto, stood in to make the land for the taking of their departure; and thereby they fell in unexpectedly with a fleet of forty-two sail of Portuguese ships off the bay of Los Todos Santos, with all their lading in, for Lisbon, several of them of good force, who lay-to waiting for two men-of-war of seventy guns each, their convoy. However, Roberts thought it should go hard with him, but he would make up his market among them, and thereupon mixed with the fleet, and kept his men hid till proper resolutions could be formed. That done, they came close up to one of the deepest, and ordered her to send the master on board quietly, threatening to give them no quarter if any resistance or signal of distress was made. The Portuguese, being surprised at these threats, and the sudden flourish of cutlasses from the pirates, submitted without a word, and the captain came on board. Roberts saluted him after a friendly manner, telling him that they were gentlemen of fortune, but that their business with him was only to be informed which was the richest ship in that fleet; and if he directed them right he should be restored to his ship without molestation, otherwise he must expect immediate death.

Whereupon this Portuguese master pointed to one of forty guns and a hundred and fifty men, a ship of greater force than the *Rover*; but this no ways dismayed them; they were Portuguese, they said, and so immediately steered away for him. When they came within hail, the master whom they had prisoner was ordered to ask "how Seignior Captain did?" and to invite him on board, "for that he had a matter of consequence to impart to him;" which being done, he returned for answer that "he would wait upon him presently," but by the bustle that immediately followed, the pirates perceived that they were discovered, and that this was only a deceitful answer to gain time to put their ship in a posture of defence; so without further delay they poured in a broadside, boarded, and grappled her. The dispute was short and warm, wherein many of the Portuguese fell, and two only of the pirates. By this time the fleet was alarmed: signals of top-gallant sheets flying and guns fired to give notice to the men-of-war, who rid still at an anchor, and made but scurvy haste out to their assistance; and if what the pirates themselves related be true, the commanders of those ships were blameable to the highest degree, and unworthy the title, or so much as the name, of men. For Roberts, finding the prize to sail heavy, and yet resolving not to lose her, lay by for the headmost of them, which much outsailed the other, and prepared for battle, which was ignominiously declined, though of such superior force; for, not daring to venture on the pirate alone, he tarried so long for his consort as gave them both time leisurely to make off.

They found this ship exceeding rich, being laden chiefly with sugar, skins, and tobacco, and in gold forty thousand moidores, besides chains and trinkets of considerable value; particularly a cross set with diamonds designed for the king of Portugal, which they afterwards presented to the governor of Caiana, by whom they were obliged.

Elated with this booty, they had nothing now to think of but some safe retreat where they might give themselves up to all the pleasures that luxury and wantonness could bestow; and for the present pitched upon a place called the Devil's Islands in the river of Surinam, on the coast of Caiana, where they arrived, and found the civilest reception imaginable, not only from the governor and factory, but their wives, who exchanged wares, and drove a considerable trade with them.

They seized in this river a sloop, and by her gained intelligence that a brigantine had also sailed in company with her from Rhode Island, laden with provisions for the coast—a welcome cargo! They growing short in the sea store, and, as Sancho says, "No adventures to be made without belly-timber." One evening, as they were rummaging their mine of treasure, the Portuguese prize, this expected vessel was descried at the masthead, and Roberts, imagining nobody could do the business so well as himself, takes forty men in the sloop, and goes in pursuit of her; but a fatal accident followed this rash, though inconsiderable adventure, for Roberts, thinking of nothing less than bringing in the brigantine that afternoon, never troubled his head about the sloop's provision, nor inquired what there was on board to subsist such a number of men:

but out he sails after his expected prize, which he not only lost further sight of, but after eight days' contending with contrary winds and currents, found themselves thirty leagues to leeward. The current still opposing their endeavours, and perceiving no hopes of beating up to their ship, they came to an anchor, and inconsiderately sent away the boat to give the rest of the company notice of their condition, and to order the ship to them; but too soon—even the next day—their wants made them sensible of their infatuation, for their water was all expended, and they had taken no thought how they should be supplied till either the ship came or the boat returned, which was not likely to be under five or six days. Here, like Tantalus, they almost famished in sight of the fresh streams and lakes, being drove to such extremity at last that they were forced to tear up the floor of the cabin and patch up a sort of tub or tray with ropeyarns to paddle ashore and fetch off immediate supplies of water to preserve life.

After some days the long-wished-for boat came back, but with the most unwelcome news in the world; for Kennedy, who was lieutenant, and left, in absence of Roberts, to command the privateer and prize, was gone off with both. This was mortification with a vengeance, and you may imagine they did not depart without some hard speeches from those that were left and had suffered by their treachery. And that there need be no further mention of this Kennedy, I shall leave Captain Roberts for a page or two with the remains of his crew, to vent their wrath in a few oaths and execrations, and follow the other, whom we may reckon from that time as steering his course towards Execution Dock.

Kennedy was now chosen captain of the revolted crew, but could not bring his company to any determined resolution. Some of them were for pursuing the old game, but the greater part of them seemed to have inclinations to turn from those evil courses, and get home privately, for there was no act of pardon in force; therefore they agreed to break up, and every man to shift for himself, as he should see occasion. The first thing they did was to part with the great Portuguese prize, and having the master of the sloop (whose name, I think, was Cane) aboard, who, they said, was a very honest fellow—for he had humoured them upon every occasion—told them of the brigantine that Roberts went after; and when the pirates first took him he complimented them at an odd rate, telling them they were welcome to his sloop and cargo, and wished that the vessel had been larger and the loading richer for their sakes. To this good-natured man they gave the Portuguese ship, which was then above half loaded, three or four negroes, and all his own men, who returned thanks to his kind benefactors, and departed.

Captain Kennedy, in the *Rover*, sailed to Barbadoes, near which island they took a very peaceable ship belonging to Virginia. The commander was a Quaker, whose name was Knot; he had neither pistol, sword, nor cutlass on board; and Mr. Knot appearing so very passive to all they said to him, some of them thought this a good opportunity to go off; and accordingly eight of the pirates went aboard, and he carried them safe to Virginia. They made the Quaker a present of ten chests of sugar, ten rolls of Brazil tobacco, thirty moidores, and some gold dust, in all to the value of about £250. They also made presents to the sailors, some more, some less, and lived a jovial life all the while they were upon their voyage, Captain Knot giving them their way; nor, indeed, could he help himself, unless he had taken an opportunity to surprise them when they were either drunk or asleep, for awake they wore arms aboard the ship and put him in a continual terror, it not being his principle (or the sect's) to fight, unless with art and collusion. He managed these weapons well till he arrived at the Capes; and afterwards four of the pirates went off in a boat, which they had taken with them for the more easily making their escapes, and made up the bay towards Maryland, but were forced back by a storm into an obscure place of the country, where, meeting with good entertainment among the planters, they continued several days without being discovered to be pirates. In the meantime Captain Knot, leaving four others on board his ship who intended to go to North Carolina, made what haste he could to discover to Mr. Spotswood, the governor, what sort of passengers he had been forced to bring with him, who, by good fortune, got them seized; and search being made after the others, who were revelling about the country, they were also taken, and all tried, convicted, and hanged, two Portuguese Jews, who were taken on the coast of Brazil and whom they brought with them to Virginia, being the principal evidences. The latter had found means to lodge part of their wealth with the planters, who never brought it to account. But Captain Knot surrendered up everything that belonged to them that were taken aboard, even what they presented to him, in lieu of such things as they had plundered him of in their passage, and obliged his men to do the like.

Some days after the taking of the Virginiaman last mentioned, in cruising in the latitude of Jamaica, Kennedy took a sloop bound thither from Boston, loaded with bread and flour; aboard of this sloop went all the hands who were for breaking the gang, and left those behind that had a mind to pursue further adventures. Among the former was Kennedy, their captain, of whose honour they had such a despicable notion that they were about to throw him overboard when they found him in the sloop, as fearing he might betray them all at their return to England; he having in his childhood been bred a pickpocket, and before he became a pirate a house-breaker; both professions that these gentlemen have a very mean opinion of. However, Captain Kennedy, by taking solemn oaths of fidelity to his companions, was suffered to proceed with them.

In this company there was but one that pretended to any skill in navigation (for Kennedy could neither write nor read, he being preferred to the command merely for his courage, which indeed he had often signalized, particularly in taking the Portuguese ship), and he proved to be a pretender only; for, shaping their course to Ireland, where they agreed to land, they ran away to the northwest coast of Scotland, and there were tossed about by hard storms of wind for several days without knowing where they were, and in great danger of perishing. At length they pushed the vessel into a little creek and went all ashore, leaving the sloop at an anchor for the next comers.

The whole company refreshed themselves at a little village about five miles from the place where they left the sloop, and passed there for shipwrecked sailors, and no doubt might have travelled on without suspicion, but the mad and riotous manner of their living on the road occasioned their journey to be cut short, as we shall observe presently.

Kennedy and another left them here, and, travelling to one of the seaports, shipped themselves for Ireland, and arrived there in safety. Six or seven wisely withdrew from the rest, travelled at their leisure, and got to their much-desired port of London without being disturbed or suspected, but the main gang alarmed the country wherever they came, drinking and roaring at such a rate that the people shut themselves up in their houses, in some places not daring to venture out among so many mad fellows. In other villages they treated the whole town, squandering their money away as if, like Æsop, they wanted to lighten their burthens. This expensive manner of living procured two of their drunken stragglers to be knocked on the head, they being found murdered in the road and their money taken from them. All the rest, to the number of seventeen, as they drew nigh to Edinburgh, were arrested and thrown into gaol upon suspicion of they knew not what; however, the magistrates were not long at a loss for proper accusations, for two of the gang offering themselves for evidences were accepted of, and the others were brought to a speedy trial, whereof nine were convicted and executed.

Kennedy having spent all his money, came over from Ireland and kept a common B——y-house on Deptford-Road, and now and then it was thought, made an excursion abroad in the way of his former profession, till one of his household w——s gave information against him for a robbery, for which he was committed to Bridewell; but because she would not do the business by halves she found out a mate of a ship that Kennedy had committed piracy upon, as he foolishly confessed to her. This mate, whose name was Grant, paid Kennedy a visit in Bridewell, and knowing him to be the man, procured a warrant, and had him committed to the Marshalsea prison.

The game that Kennedy had now to play was to turn evidence himself; accordingly he gave a list of eight or ten of his comrades, but, not being acquainted with their habitations, one only was taken, who, though condemned, appeared to be a man of a fair character, was forced into their service, and took the first opportunity to get from them, and therefore received a pardon; but Walter Kennedy, being a notorious offender, was executed July 19, 1721, at Execution Dock.

The rest of the pirates who were left in the ship *Rover* stayed not long behind, for they went ashore to one of the West India islands. What became of them afterwards I cannot tell, but the ship was found at sea by a sloop belonging to *St. Christophers*, and carried into that island with only nine negroes aboard.

Thus we see what a disastrous fate ever attends the wicked, and how rarely they escape the punishment due to their crimes, who, abandoned to such a profligate life, rob, spoil, and prey upon mankind, contrary to the light and law of nature, as well as the law of God. It might have been hoped that the examples of these deaths would have been as marks to the remainder of this gang, how to shun the rocks their companions had split on; that they would have surrendered to mercy, or divided themselves for ever from such pursuits, as in the end they might be sure would subject them to the same law and punishment, which they must be conscious they now equally deserved; impending law, which never let them sleep well unless when drunk. But all the use that was made of it here, was to commend the justice of the court that condemned Kennedy, for he was a sad dog, they said, and deserved the fate he met with.

But to go back to Roberts, whom we left on the coast of Caiana, in a grievous passion at what Kennedy and the crew had done, and who was now projecting new adventures with his small company in the sloop; but finding hitherto they had been but as a rope of sand, they formed a set of articles to be signed and sworn to for the better conservation of their society, and doing justice to one another, excluding all Irishmen from the benefit of it, to whom they had an implacable aversion upon the account of Kennedy. How, indeed, Roberts could think that an oath would be obligatory where defiance had been given to the laws of God and man, I cannot tell, but he thought their greatest security lay in this—" that it was every one's interest to observe them, if they minded to keep up so abominable a combination."

The following is the substance of articles as taken from the pirates own informations :—

I.

Every man has a vote in affairs of moment, has equal title to the fresh provisions or strong liquors at any time seized, and may use them at pleasure, unless a scarcity (no uncommon thing among them) make it necessary for the good of all to vote a retrenchment.

II.

Every man to be called fairly in turn by list, on board of prizes, because, over and above their proper share, they were on these occasions allowed a shift of clothes. But if they defrauded the company to the value of a dollar, in plate, jewels, or money, marooning was their punishment. (This was a barbarous custom of putting the offender on shore, on some desolate or uninhabited cape or island, with a gun, a few shot, a bottle of water, a bottle of powder, to subsist with or starve.) If the robbery was only between one another, they contented themselves with slitting the ears and nose of him that was guilty, and set him on shore, not in an uninhabited place, but somewhere where he was sure to encounter hardships.

III.

No person to game at cards or dice for money.

IV.

The lights and candles to be put out at eight o'clock at night. If any of the crew after that hour still remained inclined for drinking, they were to do it on the open deck. (Which Roberts believed would give a check to their debauches, for he was a sober man himself, but found at length that all his endeavours to put an end to this debauch proved ineffectual.)

V.

To keep their piece, pistols, and cutlass clean, and fit for service. (In this they were extravagantly nice, endeavouring to outdo one another in the beauty and richness of their arms, giving sometimes at an auction—at the the mast—£30 or £40 a pair for pistols. These were slung in time of service, with different coloured ribbons, over their shoulders, in a way peculiar to these fellows, in which they took great delight.)

VI.

No boy or woman to be allowed amongst them. If any man were found seducing any of the latter sex, and carried her to sea disguised, he was to suffer death. (So that when any fell into their hands, as it chanced in the *Onslow*, they put a sentinel immediately over her to prevent ill consequences from so dangerous an instrument of division and quarrel; but then here lies the roguery—they contend who shall be sentinel, which happens generally to one of the greatest bullies, who, to secure the lady's virtue, will let none lie with her but himself.)

VII.

To desert the ship or their quarters in battle, was punished with death or marooning.

VIII.

No striking one another on board, but every man's quarrels to be ended on shore, at sword and pistol. Thus the quartermaster of the ship, when the parties will not come to any reconciliation, accompanies them on shore with what assistance he thinks proper, and turns the disputants back to back at so many paces distance. At the word of command they turn and fire immediately, or else the piece is knocked out of their hands. If both miss, they come to their cutlasses, and then he is declared victor who draws the first blood.

IX.

No man to talk of breaking up their way of living till each had shared £1,000. If, in order to this, any man should lose a limb, or become a cripple in their service, he was to have 800 dollars out of the public stock, and for lesser hurts proportionably.

X.

The captain and quartermaster to receive two shares of a prize; the master, boatswain, and gunner, one share and a half, and other officers one and a quarter.

XI.

The musicians to have rest on the Sabbath-day, but the other six days and nights none without special favour.

These, we are assured, were some of Roberts's articles, but as they had taken care to throw overboard the original they had signed and sworn to, there is a great deal of room to suspect the remainder contained something too horrid to be disclosed to any, except such as were willing to be sharers in the iniquity of them. Let them be what they will, they were together the test of all new-comers, who were initiated by an oath taken on a Bible, reserved for that purpose only, and were subscribed to in presence of the worshipful Mr. Roberts. And in case any doubt should arise concerning the construction of these laws, and it should remain a dispute whether the party had infringed them or no, a jury was appointed to explain them, and bring in a verdict upon the case in doubt.

Since we are now speaking of the laws of this company, I shall go on, and, in as brief a manner as I can, relate the principal customs and government of this roguish commonwealth, which are pretty near the same with all pirates.

For the punishment of small offences which are not provided for by the articles, and which are not of consequence enough to be left to a jury, there is a principal officer among the pirates, called the quartermaster, of the men's own choosing, who claims all authority this way, excepting in time of battle. If they disobey his command, are quarrelsome and mutinous with one another, misuse prisoners, plunder beyond his order, and in particular, if they be negligent of their arms, which he musters at discretion, he punishes at his own arbitrement, with drubbing or whipping, which no one else dare do without incurring the lash from all the ship's company. In short, this officer is trustee for the whole, is the first on board any prize, separating for the company's use what he pleases, and returning what he thinks fit to the owners, excepting gold and silver, which they have voted not returnable.

After a description of the quartermaster and his duty, who acts as a sort of a civil magistrate on board a pirate ship, I shall consider their military officer, the captain: what privileges he exerts in such anarchy and unruliness of the members. Why, truly very little—they only permit him to be captain, on condition that they may be captain over him; they separate to his use the great cabin, and sometimes vote him small parcels of plate and china (for it may be noted that Roberts drank his tea constantly), but then every man, as the humour takes him, will use the plate and china, intrude into his apartment, swear at him, seize a part of his victuals and drink, if they like it, without his offering to find fault or contest it. Yet Roberts, by a better management than usual, became the chief director in everything of moment; and it happened thus:—The rank of captain being obtained by the suffrage of the majority, it falls on one superior for knowledge and boldness—pistol proof, as they call it—and can make those fear who do not love him. Roberts is said to have exceeded his fellows in these respects, and when advanced, enlarged the respect that followed it by making a sort of privy council of half a dozen of the greatest bullies, such as were his competitors, and had interest enough to make his government easy; yet even those, in the latter part of his reign, he had run counter to in every project that opposed his own opinion; for which, and because he grew reserved and would not drink and roar at their rate, a cabal was formed to take away his captainship, which death did more effectually.

The captain's power is uncontrollable in chase or in battle, drubbing, cutting, or even shooting any one who dares deny his command. The same privilege he takes over prisoners, who receive good or ill usage mostly as he approves of their behaviour, for though the meanest would take upon them to misuse a master of a ship, yet he would control herein when he sees it, and merrily over a bottle give his prisoners this double reason for it: first, that it preserved his precedence; and secondly, that it took the punishment out of the hands of a much more rash and mad set of fellows that himself. When he found that rigour was not expected from his people (for he often practised it to appease them), then he would give strangers to understand that it was pure inclination that induced him to a good treatment of them, and not any love or partiality to their persons; for, says he, " there is none of you but will hang me, I know, whenever you can clinch me within your power."

And now, seeing the disadvantages they were under for pursuing the account, viz., a small vessel ill repaired, and without provisions or stores, they resolved, one and all, with the little supplies they could get, to proceed for the West Indies, not doubting to find a remedy for all these evils and to retrieve their loss.

In the latitude of Deseada, one of the islands, they took two sloops, which supplied them with provisions and other necessaries, and a few days afterwards took a brigantine belonging to Rhode Island, and then proceeded to Barbadoes, off of which island they fell in with a Bristol ship of ten guns, in her voyage out, from whom they took abundance of clothes, some money, twenty-five bales of goods, five barrels of powder, a cable, hawser, ten casks of oatmeal, six casks of beef, and several other goods, besides five of their men; and after they had detained her three days let her go, who, being bound for the abovesaid island, she acquainted the governor with what had happened as soon as she arrived.

Whereupon a Bristol galley that lay in the harbour was ordered to be fitted out with all imaginable expedition of 20 guns and 80 men, there being then no man-of-war upon that station, and also a sloop with 10 guns and 40 men.

The galley was commanded by one Captain Rogers, of Bristol, and the sloop by Captain Graves, of that island, and Captain Rogers, by a commission from the governor, was appointed commodore.

The second day after Rogers sailed out of the harbour he was discovered by Roberts, who, knowing nothing of their design, gave them chase. The Barbadoes ships kept an easy sail till the pirates came up with them, and then Roberts gave them a gun, expecting they would have immediately struck to his piratical flag; but instead thereof, he was forced to receive the fire of a broadside, with three huzzas at the same time, so that an engagement ensued; but Roberts, being hardly put to it, was obliged to crowd all the sail the sloop would bear to get off. The galley, sailing pretty well, kept company for a long while, keeping a constant fire, which galled the pirate; however, at length, by throwing over their guns and other heavy goods, and thereby lightening the vessel, they, with much ado, got clear; but Roberts could never endure a Barbadoes man afterwards, and when any ships belonging to that island fell in his way, he was more particularly severe to them than others.

Captain Roberts sailed in the sloop to the island of Dominico, where he watered and got provisions of the inhabitants, to whom he gave goods in exchange. At this place he met with thirteen Englishmen, who had been set ashore by a French Guard de la Coste, belonging to Martinico, taken out of two New England ships that had been seized as prizes by the said French sloop. The men willingly entered with the pirates, and it proved a seasonable recruit.

They stayed not long here, though they had immediate occasion for cleaning their sloop, but did not think this a proper place; and herein they judged right, for the touching at this island had like to have been their destruction, because they, having resolved to go away to the Granada Islands for the aforesaid purpose, by some accident it came to be known to the French colony, who, sending word to the governor of Martinico, he equipped and manned two sloops to go in quest of them. The pirates sailed directly for the Granadilloes, and hall'd into a lagoon at Corvocoo, where they cleaned with unusual dispatch, staying but a little above a week, by which expedition they missed of the Martinico sloops only a few hours, Roberts sailing overnight that the French arrived the next morning. This was a fortunate escape, especially considering that it was not from any fears of their being discovered that they made so much haste from the island, but, as they had the impudence themselves to own, for the want of wine and women.

Thus narrowly escaped, they sailed for Newfoundland, and arrived upon the banks the latter end of June, 1720. They entered the harbour of Trepassi with their black colours flying, drums beating, and trumpets sounding. There were two-and-twenty vessels in the harbour, which the men all quitted upon the sight of the pirate, and fled ashore. It is impossible particularly to recount the destruction and havoc they made here, burning and sinking all the shipping except a Bristol galley, and destroying the fisheries and stages of the poor planters without remorse or compunction; for nothing is so deplorable as power in mean and ignorant hands—it makes men wanton and giddy, unconcerned at the misfortunes they are imposing on their fellow-creatures, and keeps them smiling at the mischiefs that bring themselves no advantage. They are like madmen that cast fire-brands, arrows, and death, and say, Are not we in sport?

Roberts manned the Bristol galley he took in the

harbour, and mounted 16 guns on board her, and cruising out upon the banks, he met with nine or ten sail of French ships, all which he destroyed except one of 26 guns, which they seized and carried off for their own use. This ship they christened the *Fortune*, and leaving the Bristol galley to the Frenchmen, they sailed away in company with the sloop on another cruise, and took several prizes, viz., the *Richard*, of Biddiford, Jonathan Whitfield, master; the *Willing Mind*, of Pool; the *Expectation*, of Topsham; and the *Samuel*, Captain Cary, of London; out of these ships they increased their company by entering all the men they could well spare in their own service. The *Samuel* was a rich ship, and had several passengers on board, who were used very roughly in order to make them discover their money, threatening them every moment with death if they did not resign everything up to them. They tore up the hatches and entered the hold like a parcel of furies, and with axes and cutlasses cut and broke open all the bales, cases, and boxes they could lay their hands on; and when any goods came upon deck that they did not like to carry abroad, instead of tossing them into the hold again, threw them overboard into the sea. All this was done with incessant cursing and swearing, more like fiends than men. They carried with them sails, guns, powder, cordage, and £8,000 or £9,000 worth of the choicest goods, and told Captain Cary "that they should accept of no Act of Grace, that the K—— and P——t might be damned with their Acts of G—— for them; neither would they go to Hope Point to be hanged up a-sundrying, as Kid's and Braddish's company were; but that if they should ever be overpowered, they would set fire to the powder with a pistol, and go all merrily to hell together."

After they had brought all the booty aboard a consultation was held whether they should sink or burn the ship, but whilst they were debating the matter they spied a sail, and so left the *Samuel*, to give her chase; at midnight they came up with the same, which proved to be a snow from Bristol, bound for Boston, Captain Bowles, master. They used him barbarously, because of his countryman, Captain Rogers, who attacked them off Barbadoes, was of the city of Bristol.

July 16th, which was two days afterwards, they took a Virginiaman called the *Little York*, James Philips, master, and the *Love*, of Liverpool, which they plundered and let go. The next day a snow from Bristol, called the *Phœnix*, John Richards, master, met with the same fate from them, as also a brigantine, Captain Thomas, and a sloop called the *Sudbury*; they took all the men out of the brigantine and sunk the vessel.

When they left the banks of Newfoundland they sailed for the West Indies, and the provisions growing short, they went for the latitude of the island Deseada, to cruise, it being esteemed the likeliest place to meet with such ships as (they used in their mirth to say) were consigned to them, with supplies. And it has been very much suspected that ships have loaded with provisions at the English colonies, on pretence of trading on the coast of Africa, when they have in reality been consigned to them, and though a show of violence is offered to them when they meet, yet they are pretty sure of bringing their cargo to a good market.

However, at this time they missed their usual luck, and provisions and necessaries becoming more scarce every day, they retired towards St. Christophers, where, being denied all succour or assistance from the Government, they fired in revenge on the town, and burnt two ships in the road, one of them commanded by Captain Cox, of Bristol; and then retreated farther to the island of St. Bartholomew, where they met with much handsomer treatment, the governor not only supplying them with refreshments, but he and the chiefs caressing them in the most friendly manner; and the women, from so good an example, endeavoured to outvie each other in dress and behaviour to attract the good graces of such generous lovers, that paid well for their favours.

Sated at length with these pleasures, and having taken on board a good supply of fresh provisions, they voted unanimously for the coast of Guinea, and in the latitude of 22 N. in their voyage thither, met with a French ship from Martinico, richly laden, and, which was unlucky for the master, had a property of being fitter for their purpose than the banker. "Exchange was no robbery," they said, and so after a little mock complaisance to monsieur for the favour he had done them, they shifted their men and took leave. This was their first royal fortune.

In this ship Roberts proceeded on his designed voyage; but before they reached Guinea, he proposed to touch at Brava, the southernmost of Cape Verde Islands, and clean. But here again, by an intolerable stupidity and want of judgment, they got so far to leeward of their port, that, despairing to regain it, or any of the windward parts of Africa, they were obliged to go back again with the trade-wind, for the West Indies, which had very near been the destruction of them all. Surinam was the place now designed for, which was at no less than 700 leagues distance, and they had but one hogshead of water left to supply 124 souls for that passage—a sad circumstance that eminently exposes the folly and madness among pirates, and he must be an inconsiderate wretch indeed, who, if he could separate the wickedness and punishment from the fact, would yet hazard his life amidst such dangers as their want of skill and forecast made them liable to.

Their sins, we may presume, were never so troublesome to their memories as now that inevitable destruction seemed to threaten them, without the least glimpse of comfort or alleviation to their misery; for, with what face could wretches who had ravaged and made so many necessitous, look up for relief; they had to that moment lived in defiance of the Power that now alone they must trust for their preservation, and indeed without the miraculous intervention of Providence there appeared only this miserable choice, viz., a present death by their own hands, or a lingering one by famine.

They continued their course, and came to an allowance of one single mouthful of water for twenty-four hours; many of them drank their urine, or sea-water, which, instead of allaying, gave them an inextinguishable thirst, that killed them. Others pined and wasted a little more time in fluxes and apyrexies, so that they dropped away daily. Those that sustained the misery best were such as almost starved themselves, forbearing all sorts of food, unless a mouthful or two of bread the whole day, so that those who survived were as weak as was possible for men to be and alive.

But if the dismal prospect they set out with gave them anxiety, trouble, or pain, what must their fears and apprehensions be when they had not one drop of water left, or any other liquor to moisten or animate? This was their case, when (by the working of Divine Providence, no doubt) they were brought into soundings, and at night anchored in seven fathom water. This was an inexpressible joy to them, and, as it were, fed the expiring lamp of life with fresh spirits; but this could not hold long. When the morning came they saw land from the mast-head, but it was at so great distance that it afforded but an indifferent prospect to men who had drank nothing for the last two days; however, they dispatched their boat away, and late the same night it returned, to their no small comfort, with a load of water, informing them that they had got off the mouth of Meriwinga River on the coast of Surinam.

One would have thought so miraculous an escape should have wrought some reformation, but, alas! they had on sooner quenched their thirst, but they had forgot the miracle, till scarcity of provisions awakened their senses and bid them guard against starving. Their allowance was very small, and yet they would profanely say, "that Providence which gave them drink, would, no doubt, bring them meat also, if they would use but an honest endeavour."

In pursuance of these honest endeavours, they were steering for the latitude of Barbadoes, with what little they had left, to look out for more, or starve; and, in their way, met a ship that answered their necessities, and after that a brigantine; the former was called the *Greyhound*, belonging to St. Christophers, and bound to Philadelphia, the mate of which signed the pirates' articles, and was afterwards captain of the *Ranger*, consort to the *Royal Fortune*.

Out of the ship and brigantine the pirates got a good supply of provisions and liquor, so that they gave over the designed cruise, and watered at Tobago, and hearing of the two sloops that had been fitted and sent after them at Corvocoo, they sailed to the island of Martinico, to make the governor some sort of an equivalent, for the care and expedition he had shown in that affair

It is the custom at Martinico for the Dutch interlopers that have a mind to trade with the people of the island to hoist their jacks when they came before the town. Roberts knew the signal, and being an utter enemy to them, he

Captain Bartho. Roberts with two Ships, Viz. the Royal Fortune and Ranger, takes 11 Sail in Whydah Road on the Coast of Guiney, January 11th 1721/2.

bent his thoughts on mischief; and accordingly came in with his jack flying, which, as he expected, they mistook for a good market, and thought themselves happiest that could soonest dispatch off their sloops and vessels for trade. When Roberts had got them within his power, one after another, he told them he would not have it said that they came off for nothing, and therefore ordered them to leave their money behind, for that they were a parcel of rogues, and hoped they would always meet with such a Dutch trade as this was; he reserved one vessel to set the passengers on shore again, and fired the rest, to the number of twenty.

Roberts was so enraged at the attempts that had been made for taking of him by the governors of Barbadoes and Martinico that he ordered a new jack to be made, which they ever after hoisted, with his own figure portrayed, standing upon two skulls, and under them the letters A. B. H. and A. M. H., signifying a Barbadian's and a Martinican's head, as may be seen in the plate of Captain Roberts.

At Dominico, the next island they touched at, they took a Dutch interloper of twenty-two guns and seventy-five men, and a brigantine belonging to Rhode Island, one Norton, master. The former made some defence, till some of his men being killed, the rest were discouraged and struck their colours. With these two prizes they went down to Guadalupe, and brought out a sloop and a French fly-boat laden with sugar; the sloop they burnt, and went on to Moonay, another island, thinking to clean, but finding the sea ran too high there to undertake it with safety, they bent their course for the north part of Hispaniola, where, at Bonnet's Key, in the Gulf of Saminah, they cleaned both the ship and the brigantine. For though Hispaniola be settled by the Spaniards and French, and is the residence of a President from Spain, who receives, and finally determines appeals from all the other Spanish West India Islands, yet are its people by no means proportioned to its magnitude, so that there are many harbours in it to which pirates may securely resort without fear of discovery from the inhabitants.

Whilst they were here two sloops came in, as they pretended, to pay Roberts a visit. The masters, whose names were Porter and Tuckerman, addressed the pirate, as the Queen of Sheba did Solomon, to wit, "that having heard of his fame and achievements," they had put in there to learn his art and wisdom in the business of pirating, being vessels on the same honourable design with himself; and hoped with the communication of his knowledge they should also receive his charity, being in want of necessaries for such adventures. Roberts was won upon by the peculiarity and bluntness of these two men, and gave them powder, arms, and whatever else they had occasion for, spent two or three merry nights with them, and at parting, said, "he hoped the L—— would prosper their handy works."

They passed some time here, after they had got their vessel ready, in their usual debaucheries. They had taken a considerable quantity of rum and sugar, so that liquor was as plenty as water, and few there were who denied themselves the immoderate use of it; nay, sobriety brought a man under a suspicion of being in a plot against the commonwealth, and in their sense he was looked upon to be a villain that would not be drunk. This was evident in the affair of Harry Glasby, chosen master of the *Royal Fortune*, who, with two others, laid hold of the opportunity at the last island they were at to move off without bidding farewell to his friends. Glasby was a reserved, sober man, and therefore gave occasion to be suspected, so that he was soon missed after he went away, and a detachment being sent in quest of the deserters, they were all three brought back again next day. This was a capital offence, and for which they were ordered to be brought to an immediate trial.

Here was the form of justice kept up, which is as much as can be said of several other courts that have more lawful commissions for what they do. Here was no feeing of council, and bribing of witnesses was a custom not known among them, no packing of juries, no torturing and wresting the sense of the law, for bye ends and purposes, no puzzling or perplexing the cause with unintelligible canting terms and useless distinctions, nor was their sessions burthened with numberless officers, the ministers of rapine and extortion, with ill-boding aspects enough to fright Astrea from the court.

The place appointed for their trials was the steerage of the ship, in order to which a large bowl of rum punch was made and placed upon the table, the pipes and tobacco being ready, the judicial proceedings began. The prisoners were brought forth, and articles of indictment against them read. They were arraigned upon a statute of their own making, and the letter of the law being strong against them, and the fact plainly proved, they were about to pronounce sentence, when one of the judges moved that they should first smoke the other pipe, which was accordingly done.

All the prisoners pleaded for arrest of judgment very movingly, but the court had such an abhorrence of their crime that they could not be prevailed upon to show mercy, till one of the judges, whose name was Valentine Ashplant, stood up, and taking his pipe out of his mouth, said he had something to offer to the court in behalf of one of the prisoners, and spoke to this effect: " By G——, Glasby shall not die, d——n me if he shall." After this learned speech he sat down in his place and resumed his pipe. This motion was loudly opposed by all the rest of the judges in equivalent terms, but Ashplant, who was resolute in his opinion, made another pathetical speech in the following manner: "G—— d——n ye gentlemen, I am as good a man as the best of you; d——n my s——l if ever I turned my back to any man in my life, or ever will, by G——. Glasby is an honest fellow, notwithstanding this misfortune, and I love him, d——l d——n me if I don't. I hope he'll live and repent of what he has done, but d——n me if he must die, I will die along with him." And thereupon he pulled out a pair of pistols and presented them to some of the learned judges upon the bench, who, perceiving his argument so well supported, thought it reasonable that Glasby should be acquitted; and so they all came over to his opinion, and allowed it to be law.

But all the mitigation that could be obtained for the other prisoners was that they should have the liberty of choosing any four of the whole company to be their executioners. The poor wretches were tied immediately to the mast, and there shot dead, pursuant to their villainous sentence.

When they put to sea again, the prizes which had been detained only for fear of spreading any rumour concerning them, which had like to have been so fatal at Corvocoo, were thus disposed of: they burnt their own sloop and manned Norton's brigantine, sending the master away in the Dutch interloper, not dissatisfied.

With the *Royal Fortune* and the brigantine, which they christened the *Good Fortune*, they pushed towards the latitude of Descada, to look out for provisions, being very short again, and, just to their wish, Captain Hingstone's ill fortune brought him in their way, richly laden for

Jamaica; him they carried to Bermudas and plundered, and stretching back again to the West Indies, they continually met with some consignment or other (chiefly French) which stored them with plenty of provisions and recruited their starving condition, so that, stocked with this sort of ammunition, they began to think of something worthier their aim, for these robberies that only supplied what was in constant expenditure by no means answered their intentions, and accordingly they proceeded again for the coast of Guinea, where they thought to buy gold dust very cheap. In their passage thither they took numbers of ships of all nations, some of which they burnt or sunk, as the carriage or characters of the masters displeased them.

Notwithstanding the successful adventures of this crew, yet it was with great difficulty they could be kept together under any kind of regulation, for, being almost always mad or drunk, their behaviour produced infinite disorders, every man being in his own imagination a captain, a prince, or a king. When Roberts saw there was no managing of such a company of wild, ungovernable brutes by gentle means, nor to keep them from drinking to excess, the cause of all their disturbances, he put on a rougher deportment and a more magisterial carriage towards them, correcting whom he thought fit, and if any seemed to resent his usage he told them "they might go ashore and take satisfaction of him, it they thought fit, at sword and pistol, for he neither valued or feared any of them."

About four hundred leagues from the coast of Africa, the brigantine, who had hitherto lived with them in all amicable correspondence, thought fit to take the opportunity of a dark night and leave the commodore, which leads me back to the relation of an accident that happened at one of the islands of the West Indies, where they watered before they undertook this voyage, which had like to have thrown their government (such as it was) off the hinges, and was partly the occasion of the separation. The story is as follows :—

Captain Roberts having been insulted by one of the drunken crew (whose name I have forgot), he, in the heat of his passion, killed the fellow on the spot, which was resented by a great many others, but particularly one Jones, a brisk, active young man, who died lately in the Marshalsea, and was his messmate. This Jones was at that time ashore a-watering the ship, but as soon as he came on board was told that Captain Roberts had killed his comrade, upon which he cursed Roberts, and said he ought to be served so himself. Roberts hearing Jones's invective, ran to him with a sword, and ran him into the body, who, notwithstanding his wound, seized the captain, threw him over a gun, and beat him handsomely. This adventure put the whole company in an uproar, and some taking part with the captain and others against him, there had like to have ensued a general battle with one another, like my Lord Thomont's cocks. However, the tumult was at length appeased by the mediation of the quartermaster, and as the majority of the company were of opinion that the dignity of the captain ought to be supported on board, that it was a post of honour, and therefore the person whom they thought fit to confer it on, should not be violated by any single member; wherefore they sentenced Jones to undergo two lashes from every one of the company for his misdemeanour, which was executed upon him as soon as he was well of his wound.

This severe punishment did not at all convince Jones that he was in the wrong, but rather animated him to some sort of a revenge, but not being able to do it upon Roberts's person on board the ship, he and several of his comrades correspond with Anstis, captain of the brigantine, and conspire with him and some of the principal pirates on board that vessel to go off from the company. What made Anstis a malecontent was the inferiority he stood in with respect to Roberts, who carried himself with a haughty and magisterial air to him and his crew, he regarding the brigantine only as a tender, and, as such, left them no more than the refuse of their plunder. In short, Jones and his consort go on board of Captain Anstis on pretence of a visit, and there, consulting with their brethren, they find a majority for leaving of Roberts, and so came to a resolution to bid a soft farewell, as they call it, that night, and to throw overboard whosoever should stick out; but they proved to be unanimous, and effected their design as above mentioned.

I shall have no more to say of Captain Anstis till the story of Roberts is concluded, therefore I return to him in the pursuit of his voyage to Guinea. The loss of the brigantine was a sensible shock to the crew, she being an excellent sailor and had seventy hands aboard; however, Roberts, who was the occasion of it, put on a face of unconcern at this his ill conduct and mismanagement, and resolved not to alter his purposes upon that account.

Roberts fell in to windward nigh the Senegal, a river of great trade for gum on this part of the coast, monopolized by the French, who constantly keep cruisers to hinder the interloping trade. At this time they had two small ships on that service, one of 10 guns and 65 men, and the other of 16 guns and 75 men, who having got a sight of Mr. Roberts, and supposing him to be one of these prohibited traders, chased with all the sail they could make to come up with him; but their hopes which had brought them very nigh, too late deceived them, for on the hoisting of Jolly Roger (the name they give their black flag) their

French hearts failed, and they both surrendered without any, or at least very little, resistance. With these prizes they went into Sierra Leone, and made one of them their consort by the name of the *Ranger*, and the other a store-ship, to clean by.

Sierra Leone river disgorges with a large mouth, the starboard side of which draughts into little bays, safe and convenient for cleaning and watering; what still made it preferable to the pirates is that the traders settled here are naturally their friends. There are about thirty Englishmen in all, men who in some part of their lives have been either privateering, buccaneering, or pirating, and still retain and love the riots and humours common to that sort of life. They live very friendly with the natives, and have many of them of both sexes to be their gromettas, or servants. The men are faithful and the women so obedient that they are very ready to prostitute themselves to whomsoever their masters shall command them. The Royal African Company has a fort on a small island called Bence Island, but it is of little use, besides keeping their slaves, the distance making it incapable of giving any molestation to their starboard shore. Here lives at this place an old fellow who goes by the name of Crackers, who was formerly a noted buccaneer, and while he followed the calling robbed and plundered many a man; he keeps the best house in the place, has two or three guns before his door, with which he salutes his friends, the pirates, when they put in, and lives a jovial life with them all the while they are there.

Here follows a list of the rest of those lawless merchants and their servants who carry on a private trade with the interlopers, to the great prejudice of the Royal African Company, who, with extraordinary industry and expense, have made and maintain settlements without any consideration from those who, without such settlements and forts, would soon be under an incapacity of pursuing any such private trade. Wherefore it is to be hoped proper means will be taken to root out a pernicious set of people who have all their lives supported themselves by the labours of other men.

Two of these fellows entered with Roberts's crew, and continued with them till the destruction of the company.

A List of the White Men now living on the high land of Sierra Leone, and the craft they occupy:—

John Leadstone, three boats and a periagoe; his man, Tom; his man, John Brown. Alexander Middleton, one long-boat; his man, Charles Hawkins. John Pierce, William Mead, partners, one long-boat; their man, John Vernon. David Chatmers, one long-boat. John Chatmers, one long-boat. Richard Richardson, one long-boat. Norton, Richard Warren, Robert Glynn, partners, two long-boats and two small boats; his man, John Franks. William Waits, and one young man. John Bonnerman. John England, one long-boat. Robert Samples, one long-boat. William Presgrove, Harry Presgrove, Davis Presgrove, Mitchel Presgrove, Richard Lamb, one sloop, two long-boats, a small boat, and periagoe. With Roquis Rodrigus, a Portuguese. George Bishop. Peter Brown. John Jones, one long-boat; his Irish young man. At Rio Pungo, Benjamin Gun. At Kidham, George Yeats. At Gallyneas, Richard Lemmons.

The harbour is so convenient for wooding and watering that it occasions many of our trading ships, especially those of Bristol, to call in there with large cargoes of beer, cider, and strong liquors, which they exchange with these private traders for slaves and teeth, purchased by them at the Rio Nune's and other places to the northward, so that here was what they call good living.

Hither Roberts came the end of June, 1721, and had intelligence that the *Swallow* and *Weymouth*, two men-of-war, of fifty guns each, had left that river about a month before and designed to return about Christmas; so that the pirates could indulge themselves with all the satisfaction in the world, in that they knew they were not only secure whilst there, but that in going down the coast after the men-of-war they should always be able to get such intelligence of their rendezvous as would serve to make their expedition safe. So after six weeks' stay, the ships being cleaned and fitted, and the men weary of whoring and drinking, they bethought themselves of business, and went to sea the beginning of August, taking their progress down the whole coast as low as Jaquin, plundering every ship they met of what was valuable in her, and sometimes to be more mischievously wicked, would throw what they did not want overboard, accumulating cruelty to theft.

In this range they exchanged their old French ship for a fine frigate-built ship called the *Onslow*, belonging to the Royal African Company, Captain Gee, commander, which happened to lie at Sestos, to get water and necessaries for the company. A great many of Captain Gee's men were ashore when Roberts's bore down, and so the ship consequently surprised into his hands, though had they been all on board it was not likely the case would have been otherwise, the sailors, most of them, voluntarily joining the pirates, and encouraging the same disposition in the soldiers (who were going passengers with them to Cape Corso Castle), whose ears being constantly tickled with the feats and gallantry of those fellows, made them fancy that to go was only being bound on a voyage of knight errantry (to relieve the distressed and gather up fame) and so they likewise offered themselves. But here the pirates were at a stand; they entertained so contemptible a notion of landmen that they put them off with refusals for some time, till at length, being wearied with solicitations and pitying a parcel of stout fellows, which they said were going to starve upon a little canky and plantane, they accepted of them, and allowed them a quarter share, as it was then termed, out of charity.

There was a clergyman on board the *Onslow*, sent from England to be chaplain of Cape Corso Castle. Some of the pirates were for keeping him, alleging merrily that their ship wanted a chaplain. Accordingly they offered him a share to take on with them, promising he should do nothing for his money but make punch and say prayers; yet, however brutish they might be in other things, they bore so great a respect to his order that they resolved not to force him against his inclinations; and the parson, having no relish for this sort of life, excused himself from accepting the honour they designed him; they were satisfied, and generous enough to deliver him back everything he owned to be his. The parson laid hold of this favourable disposition of the pirates, and laid claim to several things belonging to others, which were also given up, to his great satisfaction; in fine, they kept nothing which belonged to the Church except three Prayer-books and a bottle-screw.

The pirates kept the *Onslow* for their own use, and gave Captain Gee the French ship, and then fell to making such alterations as might fit her for a sea-rover, pulling down her bulkheads and making her flush, so that she became, in all respects, as complete a ship for their purpose as any they could have found; they continued to her the name of the *Royal Fortune* and mounted her with forty guns.

She and the *Ranger* proceeded (as I said before) to

Jaquin, and from thence to Old Calabar, where they arrived about October, in order to clean their ships—a place the most suitable along the whole coast, for there is a bar with not above fifteen foot water upon it, and the channel intricate, so that had the men-of-war been sure of their being harboured here, they might still have bid defiance to their strength, for the depth of water at the bar, as well as the want of a pilot, was a sufficient security to the rovers and invincible impediments to them. Here, therefore, they sat easy and divided the fruits of their dishonest industry, and drank and drove care away. The pilot who brought them into this harbour was Captain L——e, who for this and other services was extremely well paid, according to the journal of their own accounts, which do not run in the ordinary and common way of debtor *contra* creditor, but much more concise, lumping it to their friends, and so carrying the debt in their heads against the next honest trader they meet.

They took at Calabar, Captain Loane and two or three Bristol ships, the particulars of which would be an unnecessary prolixity, therefore I come now to give an account of the usage they received from the natives of this place. The Calabar negroes did not prove so civil as they expected, for they refused to have any commerce or trade with them when they understood they were pirates. An indication that these poor creatures, in the narrow circumstances they were in, and without the light of the Gospel or the advantage of an education, have, notwithstanding, such a moral innate honesty as would upbraid and shame the most knowing Christian. But this did but exasperate these lawless fellows, and so a party of forty men were detached to force a correspondence or drive the negroes to extremities, and they accordingly landed under the fire of their own cannon. The negroes drew up in a body of two thousand men, as if they intended to dispute the matter with them, and stayed till the pirates advanced within pistol-shot; but finding the loss of two or three made no impression on the rest, the negroes thought fit to retreat, which they did with some loss. The pirates set fire to the town and then returned to their ships. This terrified the natives and put an entire stop to all the intercourse between them, so that they could get no supplies, which obliged them, as soon as they had finished the cleaning and trimming of their ships, to lose no time, but went for Cape Lopez and watered, and at Anna Bona took aboard a stock of fresh provisions, and then sailed for the coast again.

This was their last and fatal expedition, which we shall be more particular in, because it cannot be imagined that they could have had assurance to have undertaken it, but upon a presumption that the men-of-war (whom they knew were upon the coast) were unable to attack them, or else pursuant to the rumour that had indiscretionally obtained at Sierra Leone, were gone thither again.

It is impossible at this time to think they could know of the weak and sickly condition they were in, and therefore founded the success of this second attempt upon the coast on the latter presumption, and this seems to be confirmed by their falling in with the coast as low as Cape Lahou (and even that was higher than they designed), in the beginning of January, and took the ship called the *King Solomon*, with twenty men in their boat, and a trading vessel, both belonging to the Company. The pirate ship happened to fall about a league to leeward of the *King Solomon*, at Cape Appollonia, and the current and wind opposing their working up with the ship, they agreed to send the long-boat with sufficient men to take her. The pirates are all volunteers on these occasions, the word being always given, Who will go? And presently the staunch and firm men offer themselves, because, by such readiness, they recommend their courage, and have an allowance also of a shift of clothes, from head to foot, out of the prize.

They rowed towards the *King Solomon* with a great deal of alacrity, and being hailed by the commander of her, answered defiance. Captain Trahern, before this, observing a great number of men in the boat, began not to like his visitors, and prepared to receive them, firing a musket as they come under his stern, which they returned with a volley, and made greater speed to get on board. Upon this he applied to his men, and asked them whether they would stand by him to defend the ship, it being a shame they should be taken by half their number without any repulse? But his boatswain, Philips, took upon him to be the mouth of the people, and put an end to the dispute; he said plainly, he would not, laid down his his arms in the King's name, as he was pleased to term it, and called out to the boat for quarters, so that the rest, by his example, were misled to the losing of the ship.

When they came on board, they brought her under sail by an expeditious method of cutting the cable; Walden, one of the pirates, telling the master this hope of heaving up the anchor was a needless trouble when they designed to burn the ship. They brought her under Commodore Roberts's stern, and not only rifled her of what sails, cordage, &c., they wanted for themselves, but wantonly threw the goods of the Company overboard, like spendthrifts, that neither expected or designed any account.

On the same day also they took the *Flushing*, a Dutch ship, robbed her of her masts, yards, and stores, and then cut down her foremast; but what sat as heavily as anything with the skipper was, their taking some fine sausages he had on board, of his wife's making, and stringing them in a ludicrous manner round their necks, till they had sufficiently showed their contempt of them, and then threw them into the sea. Others chopped the heads of his fowls off, to be dressed for their supper, and courteously invited the landlord, provided he would find liquor. It was a melancholy request to the man, but it must be complied with, and he was obliged, as they grew drunk, to sit quietly and hear them sing French and Spanish songs out of his Dutch prayer-books, with other profaneness, that he, though a Dutchman, stood amazed at.

In chasing too near in they alarmed the coast, and expresses were sent to the English and Dutch factories, giving an account of it. They were sensible of this error immediately, and, because they would make the best of a bad market, resolved to keep out of sight of land, and lose the prizes they might expect between that and Whydah, to make the more sure of that port, where commonly is the best booty, all nations trading thither, especially Portuguese, who purchase chiefly with gold, the idol their hearts were bent upon. And notwithstanding this unlikely course, they met and took several ships between Axim and that place; the circumstantial stories of which, and the panic terrors they struck into his Majesty's subjects, being tedious and unnecessary to relate, I shall pass by, and come to their arrival in that road.

They came to Whydah with a St. George's ensign, a black silk flag flying at their mizzen-peak, and a jack and pendant of the same. The flag had a death's-head on it, with an hour-glass in one hand and cross-bones in the other, a dart by it, and underneath a heart dropping three drops of blood. The jack had a man portrayed on it with a flaming sword in his hand, and standing on two skulls, subscribed A. B. H. and A. M. H. *i.e.*, a Barbadian's and a Martinican's head, as has been before taken notice of. Here they found eleven sail in the road, English, French, and Portuguese; the French were three stout ships of thirty guns, and upwards of one hundred men each, yet, when Roberts came to fire, they, with the other ships, immediately struck their colours and surrendered to his mercy. One reason, it must be confessed, of his early victory, was, the commanders and a good part of the men being ashore, according to the custom of the place, to receive the cargoes, and return the slaves, they being obliged to watch the seasons for it, which otherwise, in so dangerous a sea as here, would be impracticable. These all, except the *Porcupine*, ransomed with him for eight pounds of gold dust, a ship, not without the trouble of some letters passing and repassing from the shore before they could settle it; and, notwithstanding the agreement and payment, they took away one of the French ships, though with a promise to return her if they found she did not sail well, taking with them several of her men for that end.

Some of the foreigners, who never had dealing this way before, desired, for satisfaction to their owners, that they might have receipts for their money, which were accordingly given, a copy of one of them I have here subjoined, viz. :—

"This is to certify whom it may or doth concern, that we GENTLEMEN OF FORTUNE have received eight pounds of gold-dust for the ransom of the *Hardy*, Captain Dittwitt Commander, so that we discharge the said ship.

"Witness our hands, *Jan.* 13, 1721-2,

"BATT. ROBERTS.
"HARRY GLASBY."

Others were given to the Portuguese captains which were in the same form, but being signed by two waggish fellows, viz., Sutton and Simpson, they subscribed by the names of—

       Aaron Whifflingpin.
       Sim. Tugmutton.

But there was something so singularly cruel and barbarous done here to the *Porcupine*, Captain Fletcher, as must not be passed over without special remark.

This ship lay in the road, almost slaved, when the pirates came in, and the commander, being on shore settling his accounts, was sent to for the ransom, but he excused it, as having no orders from the owners; though the true reason might be that he thought it dishonourable to treat with robbers, and that the ship, separate from the slaves, towards whom he could mistrust no cruelty, was not worth the sum demanded; hereupon Roberts sends the boat to transport the negroes, in order to set her on fire, but, being in haste, and finding that unshackling them cost much time and labour, they actually set her on fire, with eighty of those poor wretches on board chained two and two together, under the miserable choice of perishing by fire or water. Those who jumped overboard from the flames were seized by sharks, a voracious fish, in plenty in this road, and, in their sight, tore limb from limb alive: a cruelty unparalleled, and for which had every individual been hanged, few, I imagine, would think that Justice had been rigorous.

The pirates, indeed, were obliged to dispatch their business here in haste, because they had intercepted a letter from General Phips to Mr. Baldwin, the Royal African Company's agents at Whydah, giving an account that Roberts had been seen to windward of Cape Three

Points, that he might the better guard against the damages to the Company's ships, if he should arrive at that road before the *Swallow*, man-of-war, which he assured him, at the time of that letter, was pursuing them to that place. Roberts called up his company, and desired they would hear Phips's speech, for so he was pleased to call the letter, and, notwithstanding their vapouring, persuaded them of the necessity of moving; for, says he, "such brave fellows cannot be supposed to be frightened at this news, yet that it were better to avoid dry blows, which is the best that can be expected if overtaken."

This advice weighed with them and they got under sail, having stayed only from Thursday to Saturday night; and at sea voted for the island of Anna Bona, but the wind hanging out of the way, crossed their purpose, and brought them to Cape Lopez, where I shall leave them for their approaching fate, and relate some further particulars of his Majesty's ship the *Swallow*, viz., where it was she had spent her time during the mischief that was done, and by what means unable to prevent it; what also was the intelligence she received, and the measures thereon formed, that at last brought two such strangers as Mr. Roberts and Captain Ogle to meet in so remote a corner of the world.

The *Swallow* and *Weymouth* left Sierra Leone, May 28, where, I have already taken notice, Roberts arrived a month after, and doubtless learned the intent of their voyage, and cleaning on the coast, which made him set down with more security to his diversion, and furnish him with such intimations as made his first range down the coast in August following more prosperous; the *Swallow* and *Weymouth* being then at the port of Princes a-cleaning.

Their stay at Princes was from July 28 to September 20, 1721 where, by a fatality, common to the irregularities of seamen, who cannot in such cases be kept under due restraint, they buried one hundred men in three weeks' time, and reduced the remainder of the ships' companies into so sickly a state, that it was with difficulty they brought them to sail; and this misfortune was probably the ruin of Roberts, for it prevented the men-of-war's going back to Sierra Leone as it was intended, there being a necessity of leaving his Majesty's ship *Weymouth*—in much the worse condition of the two—under the guns of Cape Corso, to impress men, being unable at this time, either to hand the sails or weigh her anchor; and Roberts, being ignorant of the occasion or alteration of the first design, fell into the mouth of danger when he thought himself the farthest from it; for the men-of-war, not endeavouring to attain further to windward, when they came from Princes, then to secure Cape Corso road under their lee, they luckily hovered in the track he had took.

The *Swallow* and *Weymouth* fell in with the continent at Cape Appollonia, October 20th, and there received the ungrateful news from one Captain Bird—a notice that awakened and put them on their guard; but they were far from expecting any temerity should ever bring him a second time on the coast while they were there. Therefore the *Swallow* having seen the *Weymouth* into Cape Corso road, November 10th, she plied to windward as far as Bassam, rather as an airing to recover a sickly ship's company and show herself to the trade, which was found everywhere undisturbed, and were, for that reason, returning to her consort, when accidentally meeting a Portuguese ship, she told her that the day before she saw two ships chase into Junk an English vessel, which she believed must have fallen into their hands. On this story the *Swallow* clung her wind and endeavoured to gain that place, but receiving soon after (October 14th) a contrary report from Captain Plummer, an intelligent man, in the *Jason*, of Bristol, who had come further to windward and neither saw or heard anything of this, she turned her head down the second time, anchored at Cape Appollonia the 23rd, at Cape Tres Puntas the 27th, and in Corso road, January 7, 1721-2.

They learned that their consort, the *Weymouth*, was, by the assistance of some soldiers from the castle, gone to windward to demand restitution of some goods or men belonging to the African Company that were illegally detained by the Dutch at Des Minas; and while they were regretting so long a separation, an express came to General Phips from Axim, the 9th, and followed by another from Dixcove (an English factory) with information that three ships had chased and taken a galley nigh Axim Castle, and a trading boat belonging to the Company. No doubt was made concerning what they were, it being taken for granted they were pirates, and supposed to be the same that had the August before infested the coast. The natural result, therefore, from these two advices, was to hasten for Whydah, for it was concluded the prizes they had taken had informed them how nigh the *Swallow* was, and withal how much better in health than she had been for some months past; so that unless they were very mad indeed they would, after being discovered, make the best of their way for Whydah and secure the booty there, without which their time and industry had been entirely lost; most of the gold lying in that corner.

The *Swallow* weighed from Cape Corso, January 10th, but was retarded by waiting some hours on the *Margaret*, a Company's ship, at Accra, again on the *Portugal*, and a whole day at Apong on a person they used to style Miss Betty: a conduct that Mr. Phips blamed when he heard the pirates were missed at Whydah, although he had given it as his opinion they could not bo passed by, and intimated that to stay a few hours would prove no prejudice.

This, however, hindered the *Swallow's* catching them at Whydah, for the pirates came into that road with a fresh gale of wind the same day the *Swallow* was at Apong, and sailed the 13th of January from thence, that she arrived the 17th. She gained notice of them by a French shallop from Grand Papa, the 14th, at night, and from Little Papa next morning by a Dutch ship; so that the man-of-war was on all sides, as she thought, sure of her purchase, particularly when she made the ships, and discovered three of them to get under sail immediately at sight of her, making signals to one another as though they designed a defence; but they were found to be three French ships, and those at anchor Portuguese and English, all honest traders, who had been ransacked and ransomed.

This disappointment chagrined the ship's company, who were very intent upon their market, which was reported to be an arm-chest full of gold, and kept with three keys; though in all likelihood, had they met with them in that open road, one or both would have made their escapes, or if they had thought fit to have fought, an emulation in their defence would probably have made it desperate.

While they were contemplating on the matter, a letter was received from Mr. Baldwin (governor here for the Company) signifying that the pirates were at Jaquin, seven leagues lower. The *Swallow* weighed at two next morning, January 16th, and got to Jaquin by daylight, but to no other end than frightening the crews of two Portuguese ships on shore, who took her for the pirate that had struck such terror at Whydah. She returned therefore that night, and having been strengthened with thirty volunteers, English and French, the discarded crews of the *Porcupine* and the French ship they had carried from hence, she put to sea again January 19th, conjecturing that either Calabar, Princes, the river Gabone, Cape Lopez, or Anna Bona, must be touched at for water and refreshment, though they should resolve to leave the coast. As to the former of those places, I have before observed it was hazardous to think of, or rather impracticable; Princes had been a sour grape to them, but, being the first in the way, she came before the harbour the 29th, where, learning no news, without losing time, steered for the river Gabone, and anchored at the mouth of it February 1st.

This river is navigable by two channels, and has an island about five leagues up, called Popaguays, or Parrots, where the Dutch cruisers for this coast generally clean, and where sometimes pirates come in to look for prey, or to refit, it being very convenient by reason of a soft mud about it that admits a ship's lying on shore with all her guns and stores in without damage. Hither Captain Ogle sent his boat and a lieutenant, who spoke with a Dutch ship above the island, from whom he had this account, viz.: That he had been four days from Cape Lopez and had left no ship there. However, they beat up for the Cape, without regard to this story, and on the 5th, at dawning, was surprised with the noise of a gun, which, as the day brightened, they found was from Cape Lopez Bay, where they discovered three ships at anchor, the largest with the king's colours and pendant flying, which was soon after concluded to be Mr. Roberts and his consorts; but the *Swallow* being to windward and unexpectedly deep in the bay, was obliged to steer off for avoiding a sand called the Frenchman's Bank, which the pirates observed for some time, and rashly interpreting it to be fear in her, righted the French *Ranger*, which was then on the heel, and ordered her to chase out in all haste, bending several of their sails in the pursuit. The man-of-war, finding they had foolishly mistaken her design, humoured the deceit and kept off to sea, as if she had been really afraid, and managed her steerage so, under the direction of Lieutenant Sun, an experienced officer, as to let the *Ranger* come up with her when they thought they had got so far as not to have their guns heard by her consort at the Cape. The pirates had such an opinion of their own courage that they could never dream anybody would use a stratagem to speak with them, and so was the more easily drawn into the snare.

The pirates now drew nigh enough to fire their chase guns; they hoisted the black flag that was worn in Whydah road, and got their spritsail yard alongships with intent to board, no one having ever asked all this while what country ship they took the chase to be; they would have her to be a Portuguese (sugar being then a commodity wanting among them), and were swearing every minute at the wind or sail to expedite so sweet a chase; but, alas! all turned sour in an instant. It was with the utmost consternation they saw her suddenly bring-to and haul up her lower ports, now within pistol-shot, and struck their black flag upon it directly. After the first surprise was over they kept firing at a distance, hoisted it again, and vapoured with their cutlasses on the poop, though wisely endeavouring at the same time to get away. Being now at their wits' end, boarding was proposed by the heads of them, and so to make one desperate push; but the motion not being well seconded, and their maintop-mast coming down by a shot, after two hours' firing, it was declined. They grew sick, struck their colours, and called out for quarter, having had 10 men killed outright, and

20 wounded, without the loss or hurt of one of the king's men. She had 32 guns, manned with 16 Frenchmen, 20 negroes, and 77 English. The colours were thrown overboard that they might not rise in judgment nor be displayed in triumph over them.

While the *Swallow* was sending their boat to fetch the prisoners, a blast and smoke was seen to pour out of the great cabin, and they thought they were blowing up; but upon inquiry afterwards found that half a dozen of the most desperate, when they saw all hopes fled, had drawn themselves round what powder they had left in the steerage and fired a pistol into it, but it was too small a quantity to effect anything more than burning them in a frightful manner.

The ship was commanded by one Skyrme, a Welshman, who, though he had lost his leg in the action, would not suffer himself to be dressed or carried off the deck, but, like Widrington, fought upon his stump. The rest appeared gay and brisk, most of them with white shirts, watches, and a deal of silk vests, but the gold-dust belonging to them was most of it left in the *Little Ranger* in the bay (this company's proper ship) with the *Royal Fortune*.

I cannot but take notice of two among the crowd of those disfigured from the blast of powder just before mentioned, viz., William Main and Roger Ball. An officer of the ship seeing a silver call hang at the waist of the former, said to him, "I presume you are boatswain of this ship." "Then you presume wrong," answered he, "for I am boatswain of the *Royal Fortune*, Captain Roberts, commander." "Then, Mr. Boatswain, you will be hanged, I believe," replies the officer. "That is as your honour pleases," answered he again, and was for turning away; but the officer desired to know of him how the powder

which had made them in that condition came to take fire.
" By G——," says he, " they are all mad and bewitched,
for I have lost a good hat by it "—the hat and he being
both blown out of the cabin gallery into the sea. " But
what signifies a hat, friend ? " says the officer. " Not
much," answered he ; the men being busy in stripping him
of his shoes and stockings. The officer then inquired of
him whether Roberts's company were as likely fellows as
these. " There are 120 of them," answered he, " as
clever fellows as ever trod shoe-leather. Would I were
with them!" "No doubt of it," says the officer. "By
G——, it is naked truth," answered he, looking down and
seeing himself by this time quite stripped.

The officer then approached Roger Ball, who was seated in
a private corner, with a look as sullen as winter, and asked
him, how he came blown up in that frightful manner.
"Why," says he, "John Morris fired a pistol into the powder,
and if he had not done it I would " (bearing his pain without
the least complaint). The officer gave him to understand
he was surgeon, and if he desired it, he would dress him ;
but he swore it should not be done, and that if anything
was applied to him he would tear it off. Nevertheless the
surgeon had good nature enough to dress him, though with
much trouble. At night he was in a kind of delirium, and
raved on the bravery of Roberts, saying he should shortly
be released, as soon as they should meet him, which procured him a lashing down upon the forecastle, which he
resisting with all his force, caused him to be used with the
more violence, so that he was tied down with so much
severity that, his flesh being sore and tender with the blowing up, he died next day of a mortification.

They secured the prisoners with pinions and shackles,
but the ship was so much disabled in the engagement that
they had once thoughts to set her on fire ; but this would

have given them the trouble of taking the pirate's wounded men on board themselves, and that they were certain the *Royal Fortune* would wait for their consort's return, they lay by her two days, repairing her rigging and other damages, and sent her into Princes with the Frenchmen and four of their own hands.

On the 9th, in the evening, the *Swallow* gained the Cape again, and saw the *Royal Fortune* standing into the bay with the *Neptune*, Captain Hill, of London—a good presage of the next day's success, for they did not doubt but the temptation of liquor and plunder they might find in this their new prize would make the pirates very confused; and so it happened.

On the 10th, in the morning, the man-of-war bore away to round the Cape. Roberts's crew discerning their masts over the land, went down into the cabin to acquaint him of it, he being then at breakfast with his new guest, Captain Hill, on a savoury dish of solomongundy, and some of his own beer. He took no notice of it, and his men almost as little, some saying she was a Portuguese ship, others a French slave ship, but the major part swore it was the French *Ranger* returning, and were merrily debating for some time on the manner of reception, whether they should salute or not; but as the *Swallow* approached nigher things appeared plainer, and though they were stigmatized with the name of cowards who showed any apprehension of danger, yet some of them, now undeceived, declared it to Roberts, especially one Armstrong, who had deserted from that ship and knew her well. Those Roberts swore at as cowards, who meant to dishearten the men, asking them if it were so, whether they were afraid to fight, or no? and hardly restrained from blows. What his own apprehensions were till she hauled up her ports and hoisted their proper colours is uncertain; but then being perfectly convinced, he slipped his cable, got under sail, and ordered his men to arms without any show of timidity, dropping a first-rate oath, "that it was a bite," but at the same time resolved, like a gallant rogue, to get clear or die.

There was one Armstrong, as I just mentioned, a deserter from the *Swallow*, whom they inquired of concerning the trim and sailing of that ship; he told them she sailed best upon a wind, and therefore, if they designed to leave her, they should go before it.

The danger was imminent, and time very short to consult of means to extricate himself. His resolution in this strait was as follows: To pass close to the *Swallow*, with all their sails and, receive her broadside, before they returned a shot; if disabled by this, or that they could not depend on sailing, then to run on shore at the point (which is steep to) and every one to shift for himself among the negroes; or failing in these, to board, and blow up together, for he saw that the greatest part of his men were drunk, passively courageous, unfit for service.

Roberts himself made a gallant figure at the time of the engagement, being dressed in a rich crimson damask waistcoat and breeches, a red feather in his hat, a gold chain round his neck, with a diamond cross hanging to it, a sword in his hand, and two pair of pistols hanging at the end of a silk sling, flung over his shoulders (according to the fashion of the pirates), and is said to have given his orders with boldness and spirit; coming, according to what he had purposed, close to the man-of-war, received her fire, and then hoisted his black flag, and returned it, shooting away from her with all the sail he could pack; and had he took Armstrong's advice, to have gone before the wind, he had probably escaped; but keeping his tacks down, either by the winds shifting, or ill steerage, or both, he was taken a-back with his sails, and the *Swallow* came a second time very nigh to him. He had now perhaps finished the fight very desperately, if Death, who took a swift passage in a grape-shot, had not interposed, and struck him directly on the throat. He settled himself on the tackles of a gun, which one Stephenson, from the helm, observing, ran to his assistance, and not perceiving him wounded, swore at him and bid him stand up and fight like a man; but when he found his mistake, and that his captain was certainly dead, he gushed into tears and wished the next shot might be his lot. They presently threw him overboard, with his arms and ornaments on, according to the repeated requests he made in his lifetime.

Roberts was a tall black man, near forty years of age, born at Newey-bagh, nigh Haverford-West, in Pembrokeshire, of good natural parts and personal bravery, though he applied them to such wicked purposes as to make them of no commendation, frequently drinking " D——n to him who ever lived to wear a halter." He was forced himself at first among this company out of the *Prince*, Captain Plumb, at Anamaboe, about three years before, where he served as second mate, and shed, as he used to tell the fresh men, as many crocodile tears then as they did now, but time and good company had wore it off. He could not plead want of employment, nor incapacity of getting his bread in an honest way, to favour so vile a change, nor was he so much a coward as to pretend it, but frankly owned it was to get rid of the disagreeable superiority of some masters he was acquainted with, and the love of novelty and change maritime peregrinations had accustomed him to. "In an honest service," says he, "there is thin commons, low wages, and hard labour; in this, plenty and satiety, pleasure and ease, liberty and power; and who would not balance creditor on this side when all the hazard that is run for it, at worst, is only a fore-look or two at choking. No, 'a merry life and a short one' shall be my motto." Thus he preached himself into an approbation of what he at first abhorred, and being daily regaled with music, drinking, and the gaiety and diversions of his companions, these depraved propensities were quickly edged and strengthened, to the extinguishing of fear and conscience. Yet among all the vile and ignominious acts he had perpetrated he is said to have had an aversion towards forcing men into that service, and had procured some their discharge, notwithstanding so many had made force their plea.

When Roberts was gone, as though he had been the life and soul of the gang, their spirits sunk; many deserted their quarters, and all stupidly neglected any means for defence or escape; and their main-mast soon after being shot by the board, they had no way left but to surrender and call for quarter. The *Swallow* kept aloof, while her boat passed and repassed for the prisoners, because they understood they were under an oath to blow up; and some of the desperadoes showed a willingness that way, matches being lighted, and scuffles happening between those who would and those who opposed it. But I cannot easily account for this humour, which can be termed no more than a false courage, since any of them had power to destroy his own life, either by pistol or drowning, without involving others in the same fate who are in no temper of mind for it. And at best, it had been only dying for fear of death.

She had 40 guns, and 157 men, 45 whereof were negroes; three only were killed in the action, without any loss to the *Swallow*. There was found upwards of £2,000 in gold-dust in her. The flag could not be got easily from under the fallen mast, and was therefore recovered by the *Swallow*; it had the figure of a skeleton in it, and a man portrayed with a flaming sword in his hand, intimating a defiance of death itself.

The *Swallow* returned back into Cape Lopez Bay, and found the little *Ranger*, whom the pirates had deserted in haste, for the better defence of the ship. She had been plundered, according to what I could learn, of £2,000 in gold-dust (the shares of those pirates who belonged to her), and Captain Hill, in the *Neptune*, not unjustly suspected, for he would not wait the man-of-war's returning into the bay again, but sailed away immediately, making no scruple afterwards to own the seizure of other goods out of her, and surrendered, as a confirmation of all, fifty ounces at Barbadoes, for which, see the article at the end of this book: "All persons who after the 29th of September, 1690," &c.

To sum up the whole, if it be considered, first, that the sickly state of the men-of-war when they sailed from Princes was the misfortune that hindered their being as far as Sierra Leone, and consequently out of the track the pirates then took; that those pirates, directly contrary to their design, in the second expedition, should get above Cape Corso, and that nigh Axim a chase should offer that inevitably must discover them and be soon communicated to the men-of-war; that the satiating their evil and malicious tempers at Whydah in burning the *Porcupine* and running off with the French ship had strengthened the *Swallow* with thirty men; that the *Swallow* should miss them in that road, where probably she had not, or at least so effectually, obtained her end; that they should be so far infatuated at Cape Lopez as to divide their strength which, when collected, might have been so formidable; and lastly, that the conquest should be without bloodshed— I say, considering all these circumstances, it shows that the hand of Providence was concerned in their destruction.

As to their behaviour after they were taken, it was found that they had great inclinations to rebel if they could have laid hold of any opportunity, for they were very uneasy under restraint, having been lately all commanders themselves, nor could they brook their diet or quarters without cursing and swearing and upbraiding each other with the folly that had brought them to it.

So that, to secure themselves against any mad, desperate undertaking of theirs, the *Swallow* strongly barricaded the gun-room, and made another prison before it, an officer with pistols and cutlasses doing duty night and day, and the prisoners within manacled and shackled.

They would yet in these circumstances be impudently merry, saying, when they viewed their nakedness, "That they had not left them a halfpenny, to give old Charon, to ferry them over Styx;" and at their thin commons they would observe that they fell away so fast that they should not have weight left to hang them. Sutton used to be very profane, he happening to be in the same irons with another prisoner who was more serious than ordinary and read and prayed often, as became his condition; this man Sutton used to swear at and ask him, "what he proposed by so much noise and devotion?" "Heaven," says the other, "I hope." "Heaven, you fool," says Sutton, "did you ever hear of any pirates going thither? Give me h—ll, it's a merrier place; I'll give Roberts a salute of thirteen guns at entrance." And when he found such ludicrous expressions had no effect on him he made a formal complaint, and requested that the officer would either remove this man or take his Prayer Book away, as a common disturber.

A combination and conspiracy was formed betwixt Moody, Ashplant, Magnes, Mare, and others, to rise and kill the officers and run away with the ship. This they had carried on by means of a mulatto boy, who was allowed to attend them, and proved very trusty in his messages between the principals, but the evening of that night they were to have made the struggle, two of the prisoners that sat next Ashplant heard the boy whisper them upon the project and naming to him the hour they should be ready, presently gave notice of it to the captain, which put the ship in an alarm for a little time; and on examination several of them had made shift to break off or lose their shackles, no doubt for such purpose; but it tended only to procure to themselves worse usage and confinement.

In the same passage to Cape Corso, the prize, *Royal Fortune*, was in the same danger. She was left at the Island of St. Thomas's in the possession of an officer and a few men to take in some fresh provisions (which were scarce at Cape Corso), with orders to follow the ship. There were only some of the pirate's negroes, three or four wounded prisoners, and Scudamore, their surgeon, from whom they seemed to be under no apprehension especially from the last, who might have hoped for favour on account of his employ, and had stood so much indebted for his liberty, eating and drinking constantly with the officers; yet this fellow, regardless of the favour, and lost to all sense of reformation, endeavoured to bring over the negroes to his design of murdering the people and running away with the ship. He easily prevailed with the negroes to come into the design, but when he came to communicate it to his fellow-prisoners, and would have drawn them into the same measures, by telling them he understood navigation, that the negroes were stout fellows, and by a smattering he had in the Angolan language he had found willing to undertake such an enterprise, and that it was better venturing to do this, run down the coast and raise a new company, than to proceed to Cape Corso and be hanged like dogs and sun-dried. One of them abhorring the cruelty, or fearing the success, discovered it to the officer, who made him immediately a prisoner and brought the ship safe.

When they came to be lodged in Cape Corso Castle, their hopes of this kind all cut off, and that they were assured they must there soon receive a final sentence, the note was changed among most of them, and from vain insolent jesting they became serious and devout, begging for good books; and joining in public prayers, and singing of psalms, twice at least every day.

As to their trials, if we should give them at length it may appear tedious to the reader, for which reason I have, for the avoiding tautology and repetition, put as many of them together as were tried for the same fact, reserving the circumstances which are most material, with observations on the dying behaviour of such of them as came to my knowledge.

And first, it may be observed from the list that a great part of these pirate ships' crews were men entered on the coast of Africa not many months before they were taken; from whence, it may be concluded, that the pretended constraint of Roberts on them was very often a complotment between parties equally willing. And this Roberts several times openly declared, particularly to the *Onslow's* people, whom he called aft, and asked of them "who was willing to go, for he would force nobody?" As was deposed of some of his best hands, after acquittal; nor is it reasonable to think he should reject Irish volunteers, only from a pique against Kennedy, and force others, that might hazard, and, in time destroy, his government. But their behaviour soon put him out of this fear and convinced him that the plea of force was only the best artifice they had to shelter themselves under in case they should be taken, and that they were less rogues than others only in point of time.

It may likewise be taken notice of that the country

wherein they happened to be tried is, among other happinesses, exempted from lawyers and law-books, so that the office of registrar of necessity fell on one not versed in those affairs, which might justify the court in want of form, more essentially supplied with integrity and impartiality.

But perhaps if there was less law there might be more justice than in some other courts; for if the civil law be a law of universal reason, judging of the rectitude, or obliquity of men's actions, every man of common sense is endued with a portion of it, at least sufficient to make him distinguish right from wrong, or what the civilians call *malum in se.*

Therefore, here, if two persons were equally guilty of the same fact, there was no convicting one and bringing the other off by any quirk or turn of law; for they formed their judgments upon the constraint, or willingness, the aim and intention of the parties, and all other circumstances, which make a material difference. Besides, in crimes of this nature men bred up to the sea must be more knowing and much abler than others more learned in the law; for before a man can have a right idea of a thing he must know the terms standing for that thing. The sea-terms being a language by itself, which no lawyer can be supposed to understand, he must of consequence want that discriminating faculty which should direct him to judge right of the facts meant by those terms.

The court well knew it was not possible to get the evidence of every sufferer by this crew, and therefore first of all considered how that deficiency should be supplied; whether or no they could pardon one Jo. Dennis, who had early offered himself as King's evidence, and was the best read in their lives and conversations; here indeed they were at a loss for law, and concluded in the negative because it looked like compounding with a man to swear falsely, losing by it those great helps he could have afforded.

Another great difficulty in their proceedings was how to understand those words in the Act of Parliament of " particularly specifying in the charge the circumstances of time, place,' &c., i.e., so to understand them as to be able to hold a court; for if they had been indicted on particular robberies the evidence had happened mostly from the Royal African Company's ships, on which these gentlemen of Cape Corso Castle were not qualified to sit, their oath running " That they have no interest, directly or indirectly, in the ship or goods, for the robbery of which the party stands accused." And this they thought they had, commissions being paid them on such goods; and on the other side, if they were incapacitated, no court could be formed, the commission absolutely required three of them by name.

To reconcile all things, therefore, the court resolved to bottom the whole of their proceedings on the *Swallow's* depositions, which were clear and plain and had the circumstances of time when, place where, manner how, and the like, particularly specified according to the statute in that case made and provided. But this admitted only a general intimation of robbery in the indictment; therefore, " to approve their clemency," it looking arbitrary on the lives of men to lump them to the gallows in such a summary way as must have been done had they solely adhered to the *Swallow's* charge, they resolved to come to particular trials.

Secondly, " that the prisoners might not be ignorant whereon to answer," and so have all fair advantages to excuse and defend themselves, the court farther agreed with justice and equanimity to hear any evidence that could be brought to weaken or corroborate the three circumstances that complete a pirate: first, being a volunteer amongst them at the beginning; secondly, being a volunteer at the taking or robbing of any ship; or, lastly, voluntarily accepting a share in the booty of those that did; for by a parity of reason where these actions were of their own disposing, and yet committed by them, it must be believed their hearts and hands joined together in what they acted against his Majesty's ship the *Swallow*.

THE TRIALS OF THE PIRATES.

Taken by his Majesty's ship the Swallow, *begun at Cape Corso Castle, on the coast of Africa, March* 28*th*, 1722.

The Commission empowered any three named therein to all to their assistance such a number of qualified persons as might make the court always consist of seven; and accordingly summonses were signed to Lieut. Jo. Barnsley, Lieut. Ch. Fanshaw, Capt. Samuel Hartsease, and Capt. William Menzies viz.:—

"By virtue of a Power and Authority, to us given, by a Commission from the King under the Seal of Admiralty, you are hereby required to attend and make one of the Court for the trying and adjudging of the Pirates lately taken on this coast by his Majesty's ship the *Swallow*.

"Given under our hands this 28th of March, 1722, at Cape Corso Castle.

"Mungo Heardman,	Francis Boy,
James Phips,	Edward Hide.
Henry Dodson,	

The commissioners being met in the hall of the castle, the Commission was first read; after which the president, and then the other members, took the oath prescribed in the Act of Parliament, and having directed the form of that for witnesses, as follows, the court was opened:—

I, *A. B.*, solemnly promise and swear on the Holy Evangelists to bear true and faithful witness between the King and prisoner, or prisoners, in relation to the fact or facts of piracy and robbery, he or they do now stand accused of. So help me God."

The court consisted of Captain Mungo Heardman, President; James Phipps, Esq., General of the Coast; Mr. H. Dodson, Mr. F. Boye, Merchants; Mr. Edward Hyde, Secretary to the Company; Lieut. John Barnsley; Lieut. Ch. Fanshaw. The following prisoners, out of the pirate ship *Ranger*, having been commanded before them, the charge, or indictment, was exhibited:—

PRISONERS TAKEN IN THE "RANGER."

MEN'S NAMES.	SHIPS FROM.	TIME WHEN.
*James Skyrm	*Greyhound* sloop	Oct., 1720
*Rich. Hardy	Pirate with Davis	1718
*Wm. Main	Brigantine, Capt. Peet	June, 1720
*Henry Dennis	⎫	1718
*Val. Ashplant	⎬ Pirates with Capt. Davis	1719
*Rob. Birdson	⎭	1719
*Rich. Harris	⎫ *Phœnix* of Bristol, Capt.	⎫
*D. Littlejohn	⎬ Richards	⎬ June, 1720
*Thomas How	at Newfoundland	⎭
†Her. Hunkins	*Success* sloop	
*Hugh Harris	*Willing Mind*	⎫
*W. Mackintosh		⎪
Thomas Willis	*Richard* of Bideford	⎪
†John Wilden	*Mary* and *Martha*	⎬ July, 1720
*Ja. Greenham	*Little York*, Phillips, Mr.	⎪
*John Jaynson	*Love* of Lancaster	⎭
†Chri. Lang	*Thomas* brigantine	Sept., 1720
*John Mitchel	⎫ *Norman* galley	Oct., 1720
T. Withstandenot	⎭	

MEN'S NAMES.	SHIPS FROM.	TIME WHEN.
Peter la Fever	} *Jeremiah* and *Anne*	Ap., 1720
*Wm. Shurin		
*Wm. Wats	} *Sirraleon* } of Mr. Glin of Seig. Joffeé	July, 1721
*Wm. Davis		
†James Barrow	} *Martha* snow, Capt. Lady	
*Joshua Lee		
Rob. Hartley (1)	} *Robinson* of Liverpool, Capt. Kanning	Aug., 1721
†James Crane		
George Smithson		
Roger Pye	} *Stanwich* galley, Captain Tarlton	Aug., 1721
†Rob. Fletcher		
*Ro. Hartley (2)		
†Andrew Rance	A Dutch ship	
*Cuthbert Goss	} *Mercy* galley of Bristol, at Callibar	Oct., 1721
*Tho. Giles		
*Israel Hynde		
William Church	*Gertruycht* of Holland	
Philip Haak	*Flushingham* of ditto	
William Smith	} *Elizabeth*, Capt. Sharp	
Adam Comry		
William Graves	} *King Solomon*, Capt. Trehern, off Cape Appollonia	
*Peter de Vine		
John Johnson		
John Stodgill		
Henry Dawson	} *Whydah* sloop, at Jaquix	Jan., 1721-2
William Glass		
Josiah Robinson		
John Arnaught		
John Davis		
†Henry Graves	} *Tarton*, Capt. Tho. Tarlton	
Tho. Howard		
†John Rimer		
Thomas Clephen		
Wm. Guineys	*Porcupine*, Capt. Fletcher	
†James Cosins		

MEN'S NAMES.	SHIPS FROM.	TIME WHEN.
Tho. Stretton		
*William Petty		
Mic. Lemmon	Onslow, Capt. Gee, at Cestos	Jan., 1721-2
*Wm. Wood		
*Ed. Watts		
*John Horn		
Pierre Ravon	Peter Grossey	
John Dugan	Renee Frogier	
James Ardeon	Lewis Arnaus	From the
Etrion Gilliot	Renee Thoby	French ship
Ren. Marraud	Meth Roulac	in Whydah
John Gittin	John Gumar	road, Feb.,
Jo. Richardeau	John Paquete	1721-2.
John Lavogue	Allan Pigan	
John Duplaissey	Pierce Shillot	

"You, James Skyrm, Michael Lemmon, Robert Hartley, &c.

"Ye, and every one of you, are, in the name and by the authority of our dread sovereign lord, George, King of Great Britain, indicted as follows :—

"Forasmuch as, in an open contempt of the laws of your country, ye have all of you been wickedly united and articled together for the annoyance and disturbance of his Majesty's trading subjects at sea; and have, in conformity to the most evil and mischievous intentions, been twice down the coast of Africa with two ships—once in the beginning of August, and a second time in January last—sinking, burning, or robbing such ships and vessels as then happened in your way.

"Particularly ye stand charged at the instance and information of Captain Chaloner Ogle, as traitors and pirates, for the unlawful opposition ye made to his Majesty's ship, the *Swallow*, under his command.

"For that on the 5th of February last past, upon sight of the aforesaid King's ship, ye did immediately weigh anchor from under Cape Lopez, on the southern coast of Africa, in a French-built ship of thirty-two guns called the *Ranger*, and did pursue and chase the aforesaid King's ship with such dispatch and precipitancy as declared ye common robbers and pirates.

"That about ten o'clock of the same morning, drawing within gunshot of his Majesty's aforesaid ship, the *Swallow*, ye hoisted a piratical black flag, and fired several chase-guns, to deter, as much as you were able, his Majesty's servants from their duty.

"That an hour after this, being very nigh to the aforesaid King's ship, you did audaciously continue in a hostile defence and assault for about two hours more, in open violation of the laws and in defiance to the King's colours and Commission.

"And lastly, that in the acting and compassing of all this, you were all, and every one of you, in a wicked combination, voluntarily to exert, and actually did, in your several stations, use your utmost endeavours to distress the said King's ship, and murder his Majesty's good subjects."

To which they severally pleaded "Not Guilty."

Then the court called for the officers of the *Swallow*, Mr. Isaac Sun, lieutenant, Ralph Baldrick, boatswain, Daniel Maclaughlin, mate, desiring them to view the prisoners, whether they knew them, and to give an account in what manner they had attacked and fought the King's ship; and they agreed as follows:—

That they had viewed all the prisoners as they stood now before the court, and were assured they were the same taken out of one or other of the pirate ships, *Royal Fortune* or *Ranger*; but verily believe them to be taken out of the *Ranger*.

That they did, in the King's ship, at break of day, on Monday, the 5th of February, 1721-2, discover three ships at anchor, under Cape Lopez, on the southern coast of Africa, the Cape bearing then W.S.W. about three leagues, and perceiving one of them to have a pendant flying, and having heard their morning-gun before, they immediately suspected them to be Roberts the pirate, his consort, and a French ship they knew had been lately carried out of Whydah road.

The King's ship was obliged to haul off N.W. and W.N.W. to avoid a sand called the French Man's Bank, the wind then at S.S.E. and found, in half an hour's time, one of the three had got under sail from the careen, and was bending her sails in a chase towards them. To encourage this rashness and precipitancy, they kept away before the wind, as though afraid, but with their tacks on board, their main-yard braced, and making, at the same time, very bad steerage.

About half an hour after ten in the morning, the pirate ship came within gunshot, and fired four chase-guns, hoisted a black flag at the mizen-peak and got their sprit-sail yard under their bowsprit for boarding. In half an hour more, approaching still nigher, they starboarded their helm and gave her a broadside, the pirate bringing-to and returning the same.

After this, the deponents say, their fire grew slack for some time, because the pirate was shot so far ahead on the weather-bow, that few of their guns could point to her; yet in this interval their black flag was either shot away or hauled down a little space and hoisted again.

At length, by their ill-steerage and favour of the wind, they came near a second time; and about two in the afternoon shot away their maintopmast.

The colours they fought under, besides a black flag, were

a red English ensign, a King's jack, and a Dutch pendant, which they struck at, or about, three in the afternoon, and called for quarter; it proving to be a French-built ship of 32 guns, called the *Ranger*.

Isaac Sun.
Ralph Baldrick.
Daniel Maclauglin.

When the evidence had been heard the prisoners were called upon to answer how they came on board this pirate ship, and their reason for so audacious a resistance as had been made against the King's ship.

To this each, in his reply, owned himself to be one of those taken out of the *Ranger*; that he had signed their piratical articles, and shared in their plunder, some few only excepted who had been there too short a time, but that neither in this signing or sharing, nor in the resistance that had been made against his Majesty's ship, had they been volunteers, but had acted in these several parts from a terror of death, which, by a law amongst them, was to be the portion of those who refused. The court then asked, Who made those laws? How those guns came to be fired? Or why they had not deserted their stations and mutinied when so fair a prospect of redemption offered? They replied still with the same answers, and could extenuate their crimes with no other plea than being forced men. Wherefore the court were of opinion that the indictment, as it charged them with unlawful attack and resistance of the King's ship, was sufficiently proved; but then it being undeniably evident that many of these prisoners had been forced, and some of them of very short standing, they did, on mature deliberation, come to this merciful resolution :—

That they would hear further evidence for or against

each person singly, in relation to those parts of the indictment which declared them volunteers or charged them with aiding and assisting at the burning, sinking, or robbing of other ships; for if they acted, or assisted, in any robberies or devastations it would be a conviction they were volunteers; here such evidence, though it might want the form, still carried the reason of the law with it.

The charge was exhibited also against the following pirates taken out of the *Royal Fortune* :—

MEN'S NAMES.	SHIPS FROM.	TIME WHEN.
*Mich. Mare	in the *Rover* 5 years ago	
*Chris. Moody	under Davis	1718
*Mar. Johnson	a Dutch ship	1718
*James Philips	the *Revenge*, pirate sloop	1717
*David Symson	} Pirates with Davis	
*Tho. Sutton		
*Hag. Jacobson	a Dutch ship	1719
*W. Williams (1)		
*Wm. Fernon	*Sudbury*, Captain Thomas, Newfoundland	June, 1720
*W. Williams (2)		
*Roger Scot		
*Tho. Owen	} *York* of Bristol	
*Wm. Taylor		
*Joseph Nositer	*Expedition* of Topsham	May, 1720
*John Parker	*Willing Mind* of Pool	
*Robert Crow	*Happy Return* sloop	
*George Smith	*Mary* and *Martha*	July, 1720
*Ja. Clements	*Success* sloop	
*John Walden	*Blessing* of Lymington	
*Jo. Mansfield	from Martinico	
┆James Harris	*Richard* Pink	

MEN'S NAMES.	SHIPS FROM.	TIME WHEN.
*John Philips	a fishing boat	
Harry Glasby	} *Samuel*, Capt. Cary	July, 1720
Hugh Menzies		
*Wm. Magnus		
*Joseph Moor	*May Flower* sloop	Feb., 1720
†John du Frock	} *Lloyd* galley, Captain Hyngston	May, 1721
Wm. Champnies		
George Danson		
†Isaac Russel		
Robert Lilbourn	} *Jeremiah* and *Ann*, Capt. Turner	April, 1721
*Robert Johnson		
Wm. Darling		
†Wm. Mead		
Thomas Diggles	*Christopher* snow	} April, 1721
*Ben. Jeffreys	*Norman* galley	
John Francia	a sloop at St. Nicholas	
*D. Harding	a Dutch ship	
*John Coleman	*Adventure* sloop	
*Charles Bunce	a Dutch galley	
*R. Armstrong	ditto run from the *Swallow*	
*Abra. Harper		} *Onslow*, Capt. Gee at Sestos May, 1721
*Peter Lesly		
*John Jessup (1)		
Tho. Watkins		
*Philip Bill		
*Jo. Stephenson		
*James Cromby		
Thomas Garrat		
†George Ogle		
Roger Gorsuch	} *Martha* snow	Aug., 1721
John Watson		
William Child	} *Mercy* galley at Callabar	Oct., 1721
*John Griffin		
*Pet. Scudamore		

MEN'S NAMES.	SHIPS FROM.	TIME WHEN.
Christ. Granger Nicho. Brattle James White Tho. Davis Tho. Sever *Rob. Bevins *T. Oughterlauey *David Rice	*Cornwall* galley at Callabar	Oct., 1721
*Rob. Haws	*Joceline*, Capt. Loane	ditto
Hugh Riddle Stephen Thomas	*Diligence* boat	Jan., 1721
*John Lane *Sam. Fletcher *Wm. Philips Jacob Johnson *John King	*King Solomon*	ditto.
Benjamin Par	*Robinson*, Capt. Kanning	ditto.
William May Ed. Thornden	*Elizabeth*, Capt. Sharp	
*George Wilson Edward Tarlton *Robert Hays	*Tarlton* of Liverpool at Cape La Hou	ditto.
Thomas Roberts John Richards John Cane	*Charlton*, Capt. Allwright	Feb., 1721
Richard Wood Richard Scot Wm. Davison Sam. Morwell Edward Evans	*Porcupine*, Capt. Fletcher Whydah road	Feb., 1721
*John Jessup (2)	surrendered up at Princes	

"You, Harry Glasby William Davison, William Champnies. Samuel Morwell, &c.

"Ye, and every one of you, are, in the name and by the authority of our most dread sovereign lord, George, King of Great Britain, indicted as follows :—

"Forasmuch as, in open contempt and violation of the laws of your country, to which ye ought to have been subject, ye have all of you been wickedly united and articled together for the annoyance and destruction of his Majesty's trading subjects by sea; and, in conformity to so wicked an agreement and association, ye have been twice lately down this coast of Africa—once in August, and a second time in January last—spoiling and destroying many goods and vessels of his Majesty's subjects, and other trading nations.

"Particularly ye stand indicted at the information and instance of Captain Chaloner Ogle, as traitors, robbers, pirates, and common enemies to mankind.

"For that on the 10th of February last, in a ship ye were possessed of, called the *Royal Fortune*, of forty guns, ye did maintain a hostile defence and resistance for some hours against his Majesty's ship the *Swallow*, nigh Cape Lopez Bay, on the southern coast of Africa.

"That this fight and insolent resistance against the King's ship was made not only without any pretence of authority, more than that of your own private depraved will, but was done also under a black flag, flagrantly by that denoting yourselves common robbers and traitors, opposers and violaters of the laws.

"And lastly, that in this resistance, ye were all of you volunteers, and did, as such, contribute your utmost efforts, and disabling and distressing the aforesaid King's ship, and deterring his Majesty's servants therein from their duty."

To which they severally pleaded, Not Guilty.

Whereupon the officers of his Majesty's ship the *Swallow*, were called again and testified as follows:—

That they had seen all the prisoners now before the court, and knew them to be the same which were taken out of one or other of the pirate ships, *Royal Fortune* or *Ranger*, and verily believe them to be those taken out of the *Royal Fortune*.

That the prisoners were possessed of a ship of forty guns, called the *Royal Fortune*, and were at anchor under Cape Lopez, on the coast of Africa, with two others, when his Majesty's ship the *Swallow* (to which the deponents belonged, and were officers), stood in for the place on Saturday, the 10th of February, 1721-2. The largest had a jack ensign and pendant flying (being this *Royal Fortune*), who, on sight of them, had their boats passing and repassing from the other two, which they supposed to be with men. The wind not favouring the aforesaid King's ship she was obliged to make two trips to gain nigh enough the wind to fetch in with the pirates; and being at length little more than cannon-shot from them, they found she slipped her cable and got under sail.

At eleven, the pirate was within pistol-shot, abreast of them, with a black flag and pendant hoisted at their main-topmast head. The deponents say they then struck the French ensign that had continued hoisted at their staff all the morning till then, and displayed the King's colours, giving her at the same time their broadside, which was immediately returned.

The pirate's mizen-topmast fell and some of her rigging was torn, yet she still outsailed the man-of-war, and slid half gun-shot from them, while they continued to fire without intermission, and the other to return such guns as could be brought to bear, till, by favour of the winds, they were advanced very nigh again; and after exchanging a few more shot, about half an hour past one, his main-mast came down, having received a shot below the parrel.

At two, she struck her colours, and called for quarter, proving to be a ship, formerly called the *Onslow*, but by them the *Royal Fortune*; and the prisoners from her assured them, that the smallest ship of the two, then remaining in the road, belonged to them, by the name of the *Little Ranger*, which they had deserted on this occasion.

ISAAC SUN,
RALPH BALDRICK,
DANIEL MACLAUGHLIN.

The prisoners were asked by the court, to the same purpose the others had been in the morning—What exception they had to make against what had been sworn, and what they had to say in their defence? And their replies were much the same with the other prisoners: that they were forced men, had not fired a gun in this resistance against the *Swallow*, and that what little assistance they did give on this occasion was to the sails and rigging, to comply with the arbitrary commands of Roberts, who had threatened, and, they were persuaded would, have shot them on refusal.

The court, to dispense equal justice, mercifully resolved for these, as they had done for the other pirate crew—that further evidence should be heard against each man singly, to the two points, of being a volunteer at first, and to their particular acts of piracy and robbery since; that so men, who had been lately received amongst them, and as yet had not been at the taking or plundering of any ship, might have the opportunity and benefit of clearing their innocence and not fall promiscuously with the guilty.

By order of the court,
JOHN ATKINS, Registrar.

Wm. Magnes, Tho. Oughterlauney, Wm. Main, Wm. Mackintosh, Val. Ashplant, John Walden, Israel Hind, Marcus Johnson, Wm. Petty, Wm. Fernon, Abraham Harvey, Wm. Wood, Tho. How, John Stephenson, Ch. Bunce, and John Griffin.

Against these it was deposed by Captain Joseph Trahern, and George Fenn, his mate, that they were all of them, either at the attacking and taking of the ship *King Solomon*, or afterwards at the robbing and plundering of her, and in this manner :—

That on the 6th of January last, their ship riding at anchor near Cape Appollonia, in Africa, discovered a boat rowing towards them, against wind and stream, from a ship that lay about three miles to leeward. They judged from the number of men in her, as she nearer advanced, to be a pirate, and made some preparation for receiving her, believing, on a nigher view, they would think fit to withdraw from an attack that must be on their side with great disadvantage in an open boat, and against double the number of men; yet by the rashness and pusillanimity of his own people, who laid down their arms and immediately called for quarter, the ship was taken, and afterwards robbed by them.

President: Can you charge your memory with any particulars in the seizure and robbery?

Evidence: We know that Magnes, quartermaster of the pirate ship, commanded the men in this boat that took us, and assumed the authority of ordering her provisions and stores out, which, being of different kinds, we soon found were seized and sent away under more particular directions; for Main, as boatswain of the pirate ship, carried away two cables and several coils of rope, as what belonged to his province, beating some of our own men for not being brisk enough at working in the robbery. Petty, as sail maker, saw to the sails and canvas; Harper, as cooper, to the cask and tools; Griffin, to the carpenter's stores, and Oughterlauney, as pilot, having shifted himself with a suit of my clothes, a new tye wig, and called for a bottle of wine, ordered the ship, very arrogantly, to be steered under Commodore Roberts's stern (I suppose to know what orders there were concerning her). So far particularly. In the general, sir, they were very outrageous and emulous in mischief.

President: Mr. Castel, acquaint the court of what you know in relation to this robbery of the *King Solomon;* after what manner the pirate boat was dispatched for this attempt.

Tho. Castel: I was a prisoner, sir, with the pirates when their boat was ordered upon that service, and found, upon a resolution of going, word was passed through the company, Who would go? And I saw all that did, did it voluntarily; no compulsion, but rather pressing who should be foremost. The prisoners yielded to what had been sworn about the attack and robbery, but denied the latter evidence, saying Roberts hectored and upbraided them of cowardice on this very occasion, and told some they were very ready to step on board of a prize when within command of the ship, but now there seemed to be a trial of their valour, backward and fearful.

President: So that Roberts forced ye upon this attack.

Prisoners: Roberts commanded us into the boat, and the quartermaster to rob the ship, neither of whose commands we dared to have refused.

President: And granting it so, those are still your own acts, since done by orders from officers of your own election. Why would men, honestly disposed, give their votes for such a captain and such a quartermaster as were every day commanding them on distasteful services?

Here succeeded a silence among the prisoners, but at length Fernon very honestly owned that he did not give his vote to Magnes, but to David Sympson (the old quartermaster), "for in truth," says he, "I took Magnes for too honest a man, and unfit for the business."

The evidence was plain and home, and the court, without any hesitation, brought them in "Guilty."

William Church, Phil. Haak, James White, Nich. Brattle, Hugh Riddle, William Thomas, Tho. Roberts, Jo. Richards, Jo. Cane, R. Wood, R. Scot, Wm. Davison, Sam. Morwell, Edward Evans, Wm. Guineys, and eighteen Frenchmen.

The four first of these prisoners, it was evident to the court, served as music on board the pirate, were forced lately from the several merchant ships they belonged to; and that they had, during this confinement, an uneasy life of it, having sometimes their fiddles, and often their heads broke, only for excusing themselves, or saying they were tired when any fellow took it in his head to demand a tune.

The other English had been a very few days on board the pirate, only from Whydah to Cape Lopez, and no capture or robbery done by them in that time. And the Frenchmen were brought with a design to reconduct their own ship (or the *Little Ranger* in exchange) to Whydah road again, and were used like prisoners; neither quartered nor suffered to carry arms. So that the court immediately acquiesced in acquitting them.

Tho. Sutton, David Simpson, Christopher Moody, Phil. Bill, R. Hardy, Hen. Dennis, David Rice, Wm. Williams, R. Harris, George Smith, Ed. Watts, Jo. Mitchell, and James Barrow.

The evidence against these prisoners were Grata de

Haen, master of the *Flushingham*, taken nigh Axim, the beginning of January last.

Benj. Kreft, master, and James Groet, mate of the *Gertruycht*, taken nigh Gabone in December last, and Mr. Castel, Wingfield, and others that had been prisoners with the pirates.

The former deposed that all these prisoners (excepting Hardy) were on board at the robbery and plunder of their ships, behaving in a vile, outrageous manner, putting them in bodily fears, sometimes for the ship, and sometimes for themselves; and in particular Kreft charged it on Sutton that he had ordered all their gunner's stores out; on which that prisoner presently interrupted and said he was perjured—" That he had not taken half." A reply, I believe, not designed as any saucy way of jesting, but to give their behaviour an appearance of more humanity than the Dutch would allow.

From Mr. Castel, Wingfield, and others, they were proved to be distinguished men—men who were consulted as chiefs in all enterprizes; belonged most of them to the House of Lords (as they called it), and could carry an authority over others. The former said, particularly of Hardy (quartermaster of the *Ranger*), that when the *Diligence* sloop was taken (whereto he belonged) none was busier in the plunder, and was the very man who scuttled and sunk that vessel.

From some of the prisoners acquitted it was farther demanded whether the acceptance or refusal of any office was not in their own option? And it was declared that every officer was chosen by a majority of votes, and might refuse, if he pleased, since others gladly embraced what brought with it an additional share of prize. Guilty.

The court on the 31st of March remanded the following

six before them for sentence, viz., *Dav. Simpson*, *Wm. Magnes*, *R. Hardy*, *Thomas Sutton*, *Christopher Moody*, and *Valentine Ashplant*.

To whom the President spoke to the following purpose: "The crime of piracy, of which all of ye have been justly convicted, is of all other robberies the most aggravating and inhumane, in that being removed from the fears of surprise in remote and distant parts, ye do in wantonness of power often add cruelty to theft.

"Pirates, unmoved at distress or poverty, not only spoil and rob, but do it from men needy, and who are purchasing their livelihoods through hazards and difficulties, which ought rather to move compassion; and what is still worse, do often, by persuasion or force, engage the inconsiderate part of them, to their own and families' ruin, removing them from their wives and children, and by that, from the means that should support them from misery and want.

"To a trading nation nothing can be so destructive as piracy, or call for more exemplary punishment; besides the national reflection it infers, it cuts off the returns of industry, and those plentiful importations that alone can make an island flourishing; and it is your aggravation, that ye have been the chiefs and rulers in these licentious and lawless practices.

"However, contrary to the measures ye have dealt, ye have been heard with patience, and though little has, or possibly could, have been said in excuse or extenuation of your crimes, yet charity make us hope that a true and sincere repentance (which we heartily recommend) may entitle ye to mercy and forgiveness after the sentence of the law has taken place, which now remains upon me to pronounce:—

"You, Dav. Simpson, William Magnes, R. Hardy, Tho. Sutton, Christopher Moody, and Val. Ashplant.

"Ye, and each of you, are adjudged and sentenced to be carried back to the place from whence ye came, from thence to the place of execution, without the gates of this castle, and there, within the flood-marks, to be hanged by the neck till ye are dead.

"After this ye, and each of you, shall be taken down, and your bodies hanged in chains."

Warrant for Execution.

"Pursuant to the sentence given on Saturday by the Court of Admiralty at Cape Corso Castle, against Dav. Simpson, Wm. Magnes, R. Hardy, Tho. Sutton, Christopher Moody, and Valentine Ashplant.

"You are hereby directed to carry the aforesaid malefactors to the place of execution, without the gates of this castle, to-morrow morning at nine of the clock, and there, within the flood-marks, cause them to be hanged by the neck till they are dead, for which this shall be your warrant. Given under my hand, this 2nd day of April, 1722. MUNGO HEARDMAN.

"To Joseph Gordyn, provost-marshal.

"The bodies remove in chains to the gibbets already erected on the adjacent hillocks.—M. H."

William Phillips.

It appeared by the evidence of Captain Jo. Trahern and George Fenn, mate of the *King Solomon*, that this prisoner was boatswain of the same ship, when she was attacked and taken off Cape Appollonia, the 6th of January last, by the pirate's boat.

When the boat drew nigh (they say) it was judged from

the number of men in her that they were pirates, and being hailed, answered, "Defiance"; at which the commander snatched a musket from one of his men and fired, asking them at the same time whether they would stand by him to defend the ship? But the pirates returning a volley, and crying out they would give no quarter if any resistance was made, this prisoner took upon him to call out for quarter without the master's consent, and mislead the rest to the laying down their arms, and giving up the ship to half the number of men, and in an open boat. It was further evident he became after this a volunteer amongst them. First, because he was presently very forward and brisk in robbing the ship *King Solomon* of her provisions and stores; secondly, because he endeavoured to have his captain ill-used; and lastly, because he had confessed to Fenn that he had been obliged to sign their Articles that night (a pistol being laid on the table to signify he must do it or be shot), when the whole appeared to be an untruth from other evidence, who also asserted his being armed in the action against the *Swallow*.

In answer to this he first observed upon the unhappiness of being friendless in this part of the world, which, elsewhere, by witnessing to the honesty of his former life, would, he believed, in a great measure have invalidated the wrong evidence had been given of his being a volunteer with the pirates. He owns, indeed, he made no application to his captain to intercede for a discharge, but excuses it with saying he had a dislike to him, and therefore was sure that such application would have availed him nothing.

The court observed the pretences of this and other of the pirates, of a pistol and their Articles being served up in a dish together, or of their being misused and forced from an honest service, was often a complotment of the parties to render them less suspected of those they came from, and was to answer the end of being put in a newspaper or affidavit. And the pirates were so generous as not to refuse a compliment to a brother that cost them nothing, and at the same time secured them the best hands; the best I call them, because such a dependence made them act more boldly. Guilty.

Harry Glasby, master.

There appearing several persons in court, who had been taken by Roberts's ship, whereof the prisoner was master, their evidence was accepted as follows:—

Jo. Trahern, commander of the *King Solomon*, deposed, the prisoner, indeed, to act as master of the pirate ship (while he was under restraint there), but was observed like no master, every one obeying at discretion, of which he had taken notice, and complained to him how hard a condition it was to be a chief among brutes; and that he was weary of his life, and such other expressions (now out of his memory), as showed in him a great disinclination to that course of living.

Jo. Wingfield, a prisoner with them at Calabar, says the same as to the quality he acted in, but that he was civil beyond any of them, and verily believes that when the brigantine he served on board of, as a factor for the African Company, was voted to be burnt, this man was the instrument of preventing it, expressing himself with a great deal of sorrow for this and the like malicious rogueries of the company he was in, that to him showed he had acted with reluctancy, as one who could not avoid what he did. He adds further, that when one Hamilton, a surgeon, was taken by them, and the Articles about to be imposed on him, he opposed and prevented it; and that Hunter, another surgeon among them, was cleared at the prisoner's instance and persuasion, from which last this deponent had it assured to him that Glasby had once been under sentence of death on board of them, with two more, for endeavouring an escape in the West Indies, and that the other two were really shot for it.

Elizabeth Trengrove, who was taken a passenger in the African Company's ship *Onslow*, strengthened the evidence of the last witness; for having heard a good character of this Glasby, she inquired of the quartermaster, who was then on board a-robbing, whether or no she could see him? and he told her "No"; they never ventured him from the ship, for he had once endeavoured his escape, and they had ever since continued jealous of him.

Edward Crisp, Captain Trengrove, and Captain Sharp, who had all been taken in their turns, acknowledge for themselves and others, who had unluckily fallen into those pirates' hands, that the good usage they had met with was chiefly through the prisoner's means, who often interposed for leaving sufficient stores and instruments on board the ships they had robbed, alleging they were superfluous and unnecessary there.

James White, whose business was music, and was on the poop of the pirate ship in time of action with the *Swallow*, deposed that during the engagement and defence she made he never saw the prisoner busied about the guns, or giving orders, either to the loading or firing of them; but that he wholly attended to the setting, or trimming, of the sails as Roberts commanded; and that in the conclusion he verily believed him to be the man who prevented the ship's being blown up by setting trusty sentinels below and opposing himself against such hot-headed fellows as had procured lighted matches and were going down for that purpose.

Isaac Sun, lieutenant of the man-of-war, deposed, that when he came to take possession of the prize in the King's boat he found the pirates in a very distracted and divided condition, some being for blowing up, and others (who perhaps supposed themselves least culpable) opposing it. That in this confusion he inquired for the prisoner, of whom he had before heard a good character, and thinks he rendered all the service in his power for preventing it; in particular, he understood by all hands that he had seized and taken from one James Philips a lighted match, at the instant he was going down to the magazine, swearing that he should send them all to h——l together. He had heard also that after Roberts was killed the prisoner ordered the colours to be struck, and had since shown how opposite his practice and principles had been, by discovering who were the greatest rogues among them.

The prisoner in his own defence says when he had the misfortune of falling into the pirates' hands he was chief mate of the *Samuel*, of London, Captain Cary; and when he had hid himself to prevent the design of carrying him away, they found him and beat and threw him overboard. Seven days afterwards, upon his objecting against, and refusing to sign, their Articles, he was cut and abused again; that though after this he ingratiated himself by a more humble carriage it was only to make life easy; the shares they had given him having been from time to time returned again to such prisoners as fell in his way, till of late, indeed, he had made a small reservation, and had desired Captain Loan to take two or three moidores from him to carry to his wife. He was once taken, he says, at making his escape in the West Indies, and, with two more, sentenced to be shot for it by a drunken jury; the latter actually suffered, and he was preserved only by one of the chief pirates taking a sudden liking to him and bullying the others. A second time he ran away at Hispaniola, carrying a pocket compass for conducting him through the woods; but that being a most desolate and wild part of the island he fell upon, and he ignorant how to direct his course, was obliged, after two or three days' wandering, to return towards the ship again, denying with egregious oaths the design he was charged with for fear they should shoot him. From this time he hopes it will be some extenuation of his fault, that most of the acquitted prisoners can witness, they entertained jealousies of him, and Roberts would not admit him into his secrets; and withal that Captain Cary (and four other passengers with him) had made affidavit of his having been forced from his employ, which though he could not produce, yet he humbly hoped the court would think highly probable from the circumstances offered.

On the whole the court was of opinion artists had the best pretension to the plea of force, from the necessity pirates are sometimes under of engaging such, and that many parts of his own defence had been confirmed by the evidence, who had asserted he acted with reluctance, and had expressed a concern and trouble for the little hopes remained to him of extricating himself. That he had used all prisoners (as they were called) well, at the hazard of ill usage to himself; that he had not in any military capacity assisted their robberies; that he had twice endeavoured his escape with the utmost danger. Acquitted him.

Captain *James Skyrm*.

It appeared from the evidence of several prisoners acquitted that this Skyrm commanded the *Ranger* in that defence she made against the King's ship; that he ordered the men to their quarters, and the guns to be loaded and fired, having a sword in his hand to enforce those commands, and beat such to their duty whom he espied any way negligent or backward. That although he had lost a leg in the action his temper was so warm as to refuse going off the deck till he found all was lost.

In his defence he says he was forced from a mate's employ on board a sloop called the *Greyhound*, of St. Christopher's, October, 1720. The pirate having drubbed him and broke his head only for offering to go away when that sloop was dismissed. Custom and success had since indeed blunted, and in some measure worn out, the sense of shame, but that he had really for several months passed been sick and disqualified for any duty; and though Roberts had forced him on this expedition, much against his will, yet the evidence must be sensible the title of captain gave him no pre-eminence, for he could not be obeyed, though he had often called to them to leave off their fire when he perceived it to be the King's ship.

The sickness, he alleged, but more especially the circumstance of losing his leg, were aggravations of his fault, showing him more alert on such occasions than he was now willing to be thought. As to the name of captain, if it were allowed to give him no precedence out of battle, yet here it was proved a title of authority, such an authority as could direct an engagement against the King's colours, and therefore he was in the highest degree guilty.

John Walden.

Captain John Trahern and George Fenn deposed the prisoner to be one of the number who, in an open boat, piratically assailed and took their ship, and was remarkably busy at mischief, having a pole-axe in his hand, which served him instead of a key to all the locked doors and boxes he came nigh. Also in particular he cut the cable of our ship, when the other pirates were willing and busied at heaving up the anchor, saying,

"Captain, what signifies this trouble of hope and straining in hot weather; there are more anchors at London, and besides, your ship is to be burnt."

William Smith (a prisoner acquitted), says Walden was known amongst the pirates mostly by the nick-name of Miss Nanny (ironically it is presumed from the haridness of his temper). That he was one of the twenty who voluntarily came on board the *Ranger* in the chase she made out after the *Swallow*, and by a shot from that ship lost his leg, his behaviour in the fight till then being bold and daring.

The President called for Harry Glasby, and bid him relate a character of the prisoner, and what custom was among them in relation to these voluntary expeditions out of their proper ship, and this of going on board the *Ranger* in particular.

And he gave in for evidence that the prisoner was looked on as a brisk hand (*i.e.*, as he farther explained it, a staunch pirate, a great rogue); that when the *Swallow* first appeared in sight every one was willing to believe her a Portuguese, because sugar was very much in demand, and had made some jarring and dissention between the two companies (the *Fortune's* people drinking punch when the *Ranger's* could not); that Roberts, on sight of the *Swallow*, hailed the new *Ranger* and bid him right-ship and get under sail. "There is," says he, "sugar in the offing, bring it in that we may have no more mumbling;" ordering, at the same time, the word to be passed among the crew, Who would go to their assistance? and immediately the boat was fu'l of men, to transport themselves.

President: Then every one that goes on board of any prize does it voluntarily? Or were there here any other reasons for it?

H. Glasby: Every man is commonly called by list, and insists on his turn to go on board of a prize, because they then are allowed a shift of clothes (the best they can find) over and above the dividend from the robbery; and this they are so far from being compelled to that it often becomes the occasion of contest and quarrel amongst them. But in the present or such like cases, where there appears a prospect of trouble, the lazy and the timorous are often willing to decline this turn and yield to their betters, who thereby establish a greater reputation. The prisoner, and those men who went from the *Fortune* on board the *Ranger* to assist in this expedition were volunteers, and the trustiest men among us.

President: Were there no jealousies of the *Ranger's* leaving you in this chase, or at any other time, in order to surrender?

H. Glasby: Most of the *Ranger's* crew were fresh men, men who had been entered only since their being on the coast of Guinea, and therefore had not so liberal a share in fresh provisions or wine as the *Fortune's* people, who thought they had borne the burthen and heat of the day, which had given occasion indeed to some grumblings and whispers, as though they would take an opportunity to leave us, but we never supposed, if they did, it would be with any other design then setting up for themselves, they having, many of them, behaved with greater severity than the old standers.

The prisoner appeared undaunted, and rather solicitous about resting his stump than giving any answer to the court, or making any defence for himself till called upon; then he related in a careless, or rather hopeless, manner, the circumstances of his first entrance, being forced, he said, out of the *Blessing*, of Lemmington, at Newfoundland, about twelve months past; this, he is sure, most of the old pirates knew, and that he was for some time as sick of the change as any man, but custom and ill company had altered him, owning very frankly that he was at the attack and taking of the *King Solomon*, that he did cut her cable, and that none were forced on those occasions.

As to the last expedition in the *Ranger*, he confesses he went on board of her, but that it was by Roberts's order, and in the chase loaded one gun to bring her to, but when he saw it was a bite he declared to his comrades that it was not worth while to resist, forebore firing, and assisted to reeve the braces in order, if they could, to get away, in which sort of service he was busied when a shot from the man-of-war took off his leg. And being asked that supposing the chase had proved a Portuguese? "Why then," says he, "I don't know what I might have done," intimating withal that everybody then would have been ready enough at plundering. Guilty.

Peter Scudamore.

Harry Glasby, Jo. Wingfield, and Nicholas Brattle, depose thus much as to his being a volunteer with the pirates from Captain Rolls at Calabar. First, that he quarrelled with Moody (one of the heads of the gang), and fought with him because he opposed his going, asking Rolls in a leering manner whether he would not be so kind as to put him into the *Gazette* when he came home. And, at another time, when he was going from the pirate ship in his boat a tornado arose. "I wish," says he, "the rascal may be drowned, for he is a great rogue, and has endeavoured to do me all the ill offices he could among these gentlemen" (*i.e.*, pirates).

And secondly, that he had signed the pirates' Articles with a great deal of alacrity, and gloried in having been the first surgeon that had done so (for before this it was their custom to change their surgeons when they desired it, after having served a time, and never obliged them to sign, but he was resolved to break through this for the good of those who were to follow), swearing immediately upon it, he was now, he hoped, as great a rogue as any of them.

Captain Jo. Trahern and George Fenn, his mate, deposed the prisoner to have taken out of the *King Solomon* their surgeon's capital instruments, some medicines, and a backgammon table, which latter became the means of a quarrel between one Wincon, and he, whose property they should be, and were yielded to the prisoner.

Jo. Sharp, master of the *Elizabeth*, heard the prisoner ask Roberts' leave to force Comry, his surgeon, from him, which was accordingly done, and with him carried also some of the ship's medicines ; but what gave a fuller proof of the dishonesty of his principles was the treacherous design he had formed of running away with the prize in her passage to Cape Corso, though he had been treated with all humanity and very unlike a prisoner on account of his employ and better education, which had rendered him less to be suspected.

Mr. Child (acquitted) deposed that in their passage from the Island of St. Thomas in the *Fortune* prize, this prisoner was several times tempting him into measures of rising with the negroes, and killing the *Swallow's* people, showing him how easily the white men might be demolished, and a new company raised at Angola, and that part of the coast. "For," says he, "I understand how to navigate a ship, and can soon teach you to steer; and is it not better to do this than to go back to Cape Corso and be hanged and sun-dried?" To which the deponent replying he was not afraid of being hanged,

Scudamore bid him be still, and no harm should come to him; but before the next day evening, which was the designed time of executing this project, this deponent discovered it to the officer, and assured him Scudamore had been talking all the preceding night to the negroes in Angolan language.

Isaac Burnet heard the prisoner ask James Harris, a pirate (left with the wounded in the prize), whether he was willing to come into the project of running away with the ship, and endeavour the raising of a new company, but turned the discourse to horse-racing as the deponent crept nigher; he acquainted the officer with what he had heard, who kept the people under arms all night, their apprehensions of the negroes not being groundless; for many of them having lived a long time in this piratical way, were, by the thin commons they were now reduced to, as ripe for mischief as any.

The prisoner in his defence said he was a forced man from Captain Rolls in October last, and if he had not shown such a concern as became him at the alteration he must remark the occasion to be the disagreement and enmity between them; but that both Roberts and Val. Ashplant threatened him into signing their Articles, and that he did it in terror.

The *King Solomon* and *Elizabeth* medicine-chests he owns he plundered by order of Hunter, the then chief surgeon, who, by the pirates' laws, always directs in this province, and Mr. Child (though acquitted) had, by the same orders, taken out a whole French medicine-chest, which he must be sensible for me as well as for himself we neither of us dared to have denied; it was their being the proper judges made so ungrateful an office imposed. If after this he was elected chief surgeon himself both Comry and Wilson were set up also, and it might have been their chance to have carried it, and as much out of their power to have refused.

As to the attempt of rising and running away with the prize, he denies it altogether as untrue; a few foolish words, but only by way of supposition, that if the negroes should take it in their heads (considering the weakness and ill look-out that was kept), it would have been an easy matter in his opinion for them to have done it; but that he encouraged such a thing was false; his talking to them in the Angolan language was only a way of spending his time, and trying his skill to tell twenty, he being incapable of further talk. As to his understanding navigation, he had frequently acknowledged it to the deponent Child, and wonders he should now so circumstantiate this skill against him. Guilty.

Robert Johnson.

It appeared to the court that the prisoner was one of the twenty men in that boat of the pirates which afterwards robbed the *King Solomon* at an anchor near Cape Appollonia. That all pirates on this and the like service were volunteers, and he, in particular, had contested his going on board a second time, though out of his turn.

The prisoner in his defence called for Harry Glasby, who witnessed to his being so very drunk when he first came among their crew that they were forced to hoist him out of one ship into the other with a tackle, and, therefore, without his consent, but had since been a trusty man, and was placed to the helm in that running battle they made with the *Swallow*.

He insisted for himself likewise, on Captain Turner's affidavit of his being forced, on which others (his shipmates) had been cleared.

The court considering the partiality that might be objected in acquitting one and condemning another of the same standing, thought fit to remark it as a clear testimony of their integrity, that their care and indulgence to each man in allowing his particular defence, was to exempt from the rigour of the law such who, it must be allowed, would have stood too promiscuously condemned if they had not been heard upon any other fact than that of the *Swallow*, and herein what could better direct them than a character and behaviour from their own associates; for though a voluntary entry with the pirates may be doubtful, yet his consequent actions are not, and it is not so material how a man comes among pirates as how he acts when he is there. Guilty.

George Wilson.

John Sharp, master of the *Elizabeth*, in which ship the prisoner was passenger, and fell a second time into the pirates' hands, deposes that he took the said Wilson off from Sestos, on this coast, paying to the negroes for his ransom the value of three pound five shillings in goods, for which he had taken a note, that he thought he had done a charitable act in this, till, meeting with one Captain Canning, he was asked why he would release such a rogue as Wilson was? for that he had been a volunteer with the pirates out of John Tarlton. And when the deponent came to be a prisoner himself he found Thomas, the brother of this John Tarlton, a prisoner with the pirates also, who was immediately, on Wilson's instigation, in a most sad manner misused and beat, and had been shot, through the fury and rage of some of those fellows, if the town-side (*i.e.*, Liverpool) men had not hid him in a stay-sail under the bowsprit, for Moody and Harper with their pistols cocked searched every corner of the ship to find him, and came to the deponent's hammock, whom they had like fatally to have mistaken for Tarlton, but on his calling out they found their error, and left him with this comfortable anodyne, that "he was the honest fellow who brought the doctor." At coming away the prisoner asked about his note, whether the pirates had it or no? Who not being able readily to tell, he replied, "It's no matter, Mr. Sharp, I believe I shall hardly ever come to England to pay it."

Adam Comry, surgeon of the *Elizabeth*, says, that although the prisoner had, on account of his indisposition and want, received many civilities from him before meeting with the pirates, he yet understood it was through his and Scudamore's means that he had been compelled among them. The prisoner was very alert and cheerful, he says, at meeting with Roberts, hailed him, told him he was glad to see him, and would come on board presently, borrowing of the deponent a clean shirt and drawers, for his better appearance and reception; he signed their Articles willingly, and used arguments with him to do the same, saying, they should make their voyage in eight months to Brazil, share six or seven hundred pounds a man, and then break up. Again, when the crew came to an election of a chief surgeon, and this deponent was set up with the others, Wilson told him he hoped he would carry it from Scudamore, for that a quarter share (which they had more than others) would be worth looking after; but the deponent missed the preferment, by the good will of the *Ranger's* people, who, in general, voted for Scudamore, to get rid of him, the chief surgeon being always to remain with the commodore.

It appeared likewise by the evidence of Captain Jo. Trahern, Tho. Castel, and others, who had been taken by the pirates, and thence had opportunities of observing the prisoner's conduct, that he seemed thoroughly satisfied with that way of life, and was particularly intimate with Roberts; they often scoffing at the mention of a man-of-war, and saying, if they should meet with any of the turnip-man's ships, they would blow up and go to h—l all together. Yet setting aside these silly freaks to recommend himself, his laziness had got him many enemies; even Roberts told him, on the complaint of a wounded man, whom he had refused to dress, that he was a double rogue to be there a second time, and threatened to cut his ears off.

The evidence further assured the court, from Captain Thomas Tarlton, that the prisoner was taken out of his brother's ship, some months before, a first time, and being forward to oblige his new company, had presently asked for the pirates' boat to fetch the medicine-chest away, when the wind and current proving too hard to contend with, he was drove on shore at Cape Montzerado.

The prisoner called for William Darling and Samuel Morwel (acquitted), and Nicholas Butler.

William Darling deposed, the first time the prisoner fell into their hands Roberts mistook him for Jo. Tarlton, the master, and being informed it was the surgeon who came to represent him (then indisposed) he presently swore he should be his messmate, to which Wilson replied, he hoped not, he had a wife and child, which the other laughed at; and that he had been two days on board before he went in that boat, which was drove on shore at Cape Montzerado. And at his second coming, in the *Elizabeth*, he heard Roberts order he should be brought on board in the first boat.

Samuel Morwel says that he has heard him bewail his condition while on board the pirate, and desired one Thomas to use his interest with Roberts for a discharge, saying, his employ and the little fortune he had left at home would, he hoped, exempt him the further trouble of seeking his bread at sea.

Nicholas Butler, who had remained with the pirates about forty-eight hours, when they took the French ships at Whydah, deposes that in this space the prisoner addressed him in the French language several times, deploring the wretchedness and ill-fortune of being confined in such company.

The prisoner, desiring liberty of two or three questions, asked whether or no he had not expostulated with Roberts, for a reason of his obliging surgeons to sign their Articles, when heretofore they did not; whether he had not expressed himself glad of having formerly escaped from them; whether he had not said, at taking the ships in Whydah road, that he could like the sport, were it lawful; and whether if he had not told him, should the Company discharge any surgeon, that he would insist on it as his turn? The deponent answered yes to every question separately; and farther, that he believes Scudamore had not seen Wilson when he first came and found him out of the *Elizabeth*.

He added in his own defence, that, being surgeon with one John Tarlton, of Liverpool, he was met a first time on this coast of Guinea by Roberts the pirate, who, after a day or two, told him, to his sorrow, that he was to stay there, and ordered him to fetch his chest (not medicines, as asserted), which opportunity he took to make his escape; for the boat's crew happening to consist of five French and one Englishman, all as willing as himself, they agreed to push the boat on shore and trust themselves with the negroes of Cape Montzerado. Hazardous, not only in respect of the dangerous seas that run there, but the inhumanity of the natives, who sometimes take a liking to human carcases. Here he remained five months, till Thomas Tarlton, brother to his captain, chanced to put into the road for trade, to whom he represented his hardships and starving condition; but was, in an unchristian manner, both refused a release of this captivity, or so much as a small supply of biscuit and salt meat, because, as he said, he had been among the pirates. A little time after this the master of a French ship paid a ransom for him and took him off; but, by reason of a nasty leprous indisposition he had contracted by hard and bad living, was, to his great misfortune, set ashore at Sestos again, when Captain Sharp met him and generously procured his release in the manner himself has related, and for which he stands infinitely obliged. That ill-luck threw him a second time into the pirates' hands, in this ship *Elizabeth*, where he met Thomas Tarlton, and thoughtlessly used some reproaches of him for his severe treatment at Montzerado; but protests without design his words should have had so bad a consequence; for Roberts took upon him, as a dispenser of justice, the correction of Mr. Tarlton, beating him unmercifully; and, he hopes it will be believed, contrary to any intention of his it should so happen, because, as a stranger, he might be supposed to have no influence, and believes there were some other motives for it. He cannot remember he expressed himself glad to see Roberts this second time, or that he dropped those expressions about Comry, as are sworn; but if immaturity of judgment had occasioned him to slip rash and inadvertent words, or that he had paid any undue compliments to Roberts, it was to ingratiate himself, as every prisoner did, for a more civil treatment, and in particular to procure his discharge, which he had been promised, and was afraid would have been revoked, if such a person as Comry did not remain there to supply his room; and of this, he said, all the gentlemen (meaning the pirates) could witness for him.

He urged also his youth in excuse for his rashness. The first time he had been with them (only a month in all), and that in no military employ; but in particular the service he had done in discovering the design the pirates had to rise in their passage on board the *Swallow*. Guilty.

But execution respited till the King's pleasure be known, because the commander of the *Swallow* had declared the first notice he received of this design of the pirates to rise was from him.

Benjamin Jeffreys.

By the depositions of Glasby and Lillburn (acquitted) against this prisoner, it appeared that his drunkenness was what at first detained him from going away in his proper ship, the *Norman* galley; and next morning, for having been abusive in his drink, saying to the pirates there was not a man amongst them, he received for a welcome six lashes from every person in the ship, which disordered him for some weeks, but on recovery was made boatswain's mate; the serving of which, or any office on board a pirate, is at their own option (though elected), because others are glad to accept what brings an additional share in prize.

The deponents further say that at Sierra Leone every man had more especially the means of escaping, and that this prisoner, in particular, neglected it, and came off from that place after the ship was under sail and going out of the river.

The prisoner, in his defence, protests he was at first forced, and that the office of boatswain's mate was imposed on him, and what he would have been glad to have relinquished. That the barbarous whipping he had received from the pirates at first was for telling them that none who could get their bread in an honest way would go on such an account. And he had certainly taken the opportunity which presented at Sierra Leone of ridding himself from so distasteful a life, if there had not been three or four of the old pirates on shore at the same time who, he imagined, must know of him, and would doubtless have served him the same, if not worse, than they since had done William Williams, who, for such a design, being delivered up by the treacherous natives, had received two lashes through the whole ship's company.

The Court observed the excuses of these pirates about want of means to escape, was oftentimes as poor and evasive as their pleas of being forced at first; for here, at Sierra Leone, every man had his liberty on shore, and, it was evident, might have kept it, if he, or they, had so pleased. And such are further culpable, who having been introduced into the society by such uncivil methods as whipping, or beating, neglect less likely means of regaining liberty; it shows strong inclinations to dishonesty, and they stand inexcusably. Guilty.

Jo. Mansfield.

It was proved against this prisoner, by Captain Trahern and George Fenn, that he was one of those volunteers who was at the attack and robbery of the Company's ship called the *King Solomon*. That he bullied well among them who dared not make any reply, but was very easy with his friends, who knew him; for Moody on this occasion took a large glass from him, and threatened to blow his brains out (a favourite phrase with these pirates) if he muttered at it.

From others acquitted it likewise appeared that he was at first a volunteer among them, from an island called

Dominico, in the West Indies, and had, to recommend himself, told them he was a deserter from the *Rose* man-of-war, and, before that, had been on the highway; he was always drunk, they said, and so bad at the time they met with the *Swallow*, that he knew nothing of the action, but came up vapouring with his cutlass, after the *Fortune* had struck her colours, to know who would go on board the prize; and it was some time before they could persuade him into the truth of their condition.

He could say little in defence of himself, acknowledged this latter part of drunkenness; a vice, he says, that had too great a share in ensnaring him into this course of life, and had been a greater motive with him than gold. Guilty.

William Davis.

William Allen deposed he knew this prisoner at Sierra Leone, belonging to the *Ann* galley; that he had a quarrel with, and beat, the mate of that ship, for which, as he said, being afraid to return to his duty, he consorted to the idle customs and ways of living among the negroes, from whom he received a wife, and ungratefully sold her one evening for some punch to quench his thirst. After this, having put himself under the protection of Mr. Plunket, governor there for the Royal African Company, the relations and friends of the woman applied to him for redress, who immediately surrendered the prisoner, and told them he did not care if they took his head off; but the negroes wisely judging it would not fetch so good a price, they sold him in his turn again to Seignior Jessee, a Christain black, and native of that place, who expected and agreed for two years' service from him, on consideration of what he had disbursed for the redemption of the woman. But long before the expiration of this time Roberts came into Sierra Leone river, where the prisoner, as Seignior Jessee assured the deponent, entered a volunteer with them.

The deponent further corroborates this part of the evidence, in that he being obliged to call at Cape Mount, in his passage down hither, met there with two deserters from Roberts's ship, who assured him of the same, and that the pirates did design to turn Davis away the next opportunity as an idle, good-for-nothing fellow.

From Glasby and Lillburn it was evident, that every pirate, while they stayed at Sierra Leone, went on shore at discretion. That Roberts had often assured Mr. Glyn and other traders at that place, that he would force nobody; and, in short, there was no occasion for it; in particular, the prisoner's row-mate went away, and thinks he might have done the same if he had pleased.

The prisoner alleged his having been detained against his will, and says that, returning with elephants' teeth for Sierra Leone, the pirates' boat pursued and brought him on board, where he was kept on account of his understanding the pilotage and navigation of that river.

It was obvious to the court, not only how frivolous excuses of constraint and force were among these people, at their first commencing pirates, but also it was plain to them, from these two deserters, met at Cape Mount, and the discretional manner they lived in at Sierra Leone, through how little difficulty several of them did, and others might have escaped afterwards, if they could but have obtained their own consents for it. Guilty.

This is the substance of the trials of Roberts's crew, which may suffice for others that occur in this book. The foregoing lists show, by a * before the names, who were condemned; those names with a † were referred for trial to the Marshalsea, and all the rest were acquitted.

The following pirates were executed, according to their sentence, without the gates of Cape Corso Castle, within the flood-marks, viz.:—William Magnes, 35, Minehead; Richard Hardy, 25, Wales; David Simpson, 36, North Berwick; Christopher Moody, 28; Thomas Sutton, 23, Berwick; Valentine Ashplant, 32, Minories; Peter de Vine, 42, Stepney; William Philips, 29, Lower Shadwell; Philip Bill, 27, St. Thomas's; William Main, 28; William Mackintosh, 21, Canterbury; William Williams, 40, near Plymouth; Robert Haws, 31, Yarmouth; William Petty, 30, Deptford; John Jaynson, 22, near Lancaster; Marcus Johnson, 21, Smyrna; Robert Crow, 44, Isle of Man; Michael Maer, 41, Ghent; Daniel Harding, 26, Groomsbury in Somersetshire; William Fernon, 22, Somersetshire; Jo. More, 19, Meer, in Wiltshire; Abraham Harper, 23, Bristol; Jo. Parker, 22, Winfred, in Dorsetshire; Jo. Philips, 28, Jersey; James Clement, 20, Bristol; Peter Scudamore, 35, Wales; James Skyrm, 44, Somersetshire; John Walden, 24, Whitby; Jo. Stephenson, 40, Orkneys; Jo. Mansfield, 30, Bristol; Israel Hynde, 30, Aberdeen; Peter Lesley, 21, Exeter; Charles Bunce, 26, Other St. Mary's, Devonshire; Robert Birtson, 30, Cornwall; Richard Harris, 45, Sadbury, in Devonshire; Joseph Nositer, 26 (speechless at execution); William Williams, 30, Holland; Agge Jacobson, 30, Bristol; Benjamin Jeffreys, 21, Topsham; Cuthbert Goss, 21, Plymouth; John Jessup, 20, Plymouth; Edward Watts, 22, Dunmore; Thomas Giles, 26, Minehead; William Wood, 27, York; Thomas Armstrong, 34, London (executed on board the *Weymouth*); Robert Johnson, 32, at Whydah; George Smith, 25, Wales; William Watts, 23, Ireland; James Philips, 35, Antegoa; John Coleman, 24, Wales; Robert Hays, 20, Liverpool; William Davis, 23, Wales.

The remainder of the pirates, whose names are under-mentioned, upon their humble petition to the court, had their sentence changed from death to seven years' servitude, conformable to our sentence of transportation. The petition is as follows:—

"*To the Honourable the President and Judges of the Court of Admiralty, for trying of pirates, sitting at Cape Corso Castle, the 20th day of April,* 1722.

"The humble petition of Thomas How, Samuel Fletcher, &c.

"Humbly showeth—

"That your petitioners being unhappily, and unwarily drawn into that wretched and detestable crime of piracy, for which they now stand justly condemned, they most humbly pray the clemency of the court, in the mitigation of their sentence, that they may be permitted to serve the Royal African Company of England, in this country for seven years, in such a manner as the court shall think proper; that by their just punishment, being made sensible of the error of their former ways, they will for the future become faithful subjects, good servants, and useful in their stations, if it please the Almighty to prolong their lives.

"And your petitioners, as in duty, &c."

The resolution of the court was—

"That the petitioners have leave by this Court of Admiralty, to interchange indentures with the Captain-General of the Gold Coast, for the Royal African Company, for seven years' servitude, at any of the Royal African Company's settlements in Africa, in such manner as he, the said Captain-General, shall think proper.

"On Thursday, the 26th day of April, the indentures being all drawn out, according to the grant made to the petitioners, by the court held on Friday the 20th of this instant, each prisoner was sent for up, signed, sealed and exchanged them in the presence of—

    Captain MUNGO HEARDMAN, President,
    JAMES PHIPPS, Esq.,
    Mr. EDWARD HYDE,
    Mr. CHARLES FANSHAW, and
    Mr. JOHN ATKINS, Registrar."

A Copy of the Indenture.

The Indenture of a person condemned to serve abroad, for piracy, which, upon the humble petition of the pirates therein mentioned, was most mercifully granted by his Imperial Majesty's Commissioners and Judges appointed to hold a Court of Admiralty, for the trial of pirates, at Cape Corso Castle, in Africa, upon condition of serving seven years, and other conditions, are as follows, viz. :—

"This Indenture, made the twenty-sixth day of April, Anno Regni Regis Georgii magnæ Britanniæ, &c. Septimo, Domini Millessimo, Sepcentessimo viginti duo, between Roger Scot, late of the City of Bristol, mariner, of the one part, and the Royal African Company of England, their Captain-General and Commander-in-chief, for the time being, on the other part, witnesseth, That the said Roger Scot doth hereby covenant, and agree, to, and with, the said Royal African Company, their Captain-General, and Commander-in-chief for the time being, to serve him, or his lawful successors, in any of the Royal African Company's settlements on the coast of Africa, from the day of the date of these presents, to the full term of seven years, from hence next ensuing, fully to be complete and ended; there to serve in such employment as the said Captain-General or his successors shall employ him, according to the custom of the country in like kind.

"In consideration whereof, the said Captain-General, and Commander-in-chief, doth covenant and agree to, and with, the said Roger Scot, to find and allow him meat, drink, apparel, and lodging, according to the custom of the country.

"In witness whereof, the parties aforesaid, to these presents, have interchangeably put their hands and seals, the day and year first above written.

"Signed, sealed, and delivered, in the presence of us, at Cape Corso Castle, in Africa, where no stamped paper was to be had.

> Mungo Heardman, President, }
> John Atkins, Registrar,   } *Witnesses.*

In like manner was drawn out and exchanged the indentures of Thomas How, of Barnstaple, in the county of Devon; Samuel Fletcher, of East Smithfield, London; John Lane, of Lombard Street, London; David Littlejohn, of Bristol; John King, of Shadwell parish, London; Henry Dennis, of Bideford; Hugh Harris, of Corf Castle, Devonshire; William Taylor, of Bristol; Thomas Owen, of Bristol; John Mitchel, of Shadwell parish, London; Joshua Lee, of Liverpool; William Shuren, of Wapping parish, London; Robert Hartley, of Liverpool; John Griffin, of Blackwall, Middlesex; James Cromby, of London, Wapping; James Greenham, of Marshfield, Gloucestershire; John Horn, of St. James's parish, London; John Jessup, of Wisbech, Cambridgeshire; David Rice, of Bristol.

But two or three of whom, I hear, are now living; two others, viz., George Wilson and Thomas Oughterlaney, were respited from execution till his Majesty's pleasure should be known; the former died abroad, and the latter came home, and received his Majesty's pardon; the account of the whole stands thus:—Acquitted, 74; executed, 32; respited, 2; to servitude, 20; to the Marshalsea, 17; killed in the *Ranger*, 10; killed in the *Fortune*, 3; died in the passage to Cape Corso, 13; died afterwards in the Castle, 4; negroes in both ships, 70: total, 276.

I am not ignorant how acceptable a relation of the behaviour and dying words of malefactors are to the generality of our countrymen, and therefore shall deliver what occurred worthy of notice in the deportment of these criminals.

The first six that were called to execution were Magnes, Moody, Simpson, Sutton, Ashplant, and Hardy; all of them old standers and notorious offenders. When they were brought out of the hold, on the parade, in order to break off their fetters, and fit the halters, none of them, it was observed, appeared the least dejected, unless Sutton, who spoke faint, but it was rather imputed to a flux that had seized him two or three days before than fear. A gentleman, who was surgeon of the ship, was so charitable at this time, to offer himself in the room of an ordinary, and represented to them, as well as he was able, the heinousness of their sin, and necessity which lay on them of repentance; one particular part of which ought to be acknowledging the justice they had met with. They seemed heedless for the present, some calling for water to drink, and others applying to the soldiers for caps; but when this gentleman pressed them for an answer, they all exclaimed against the severity of the court, and were so hardened as to curse, and wish the same justice might overtake all the members of it as had been dealt to them. "They were poor rogues," they said, "and so must be hanged, while others, no less guilty in another way, escaped."

When he endeavoured to compose their minds, exhorting them to die in charity with all the world, and would have diverted them from such vain discourse by asking them their country, age, and the like, some of them answered,

"What was that to him? They suffered the law, and should give no account but to God." They walked to the gallows without a tear in token of sorrow for their past offences, or showing as much concern as a man would express at travelling a bad road; nay, Simpson, at seeing a woman that he knew, said, "He had lain with that b——h three times, and now she was come to see him hanged." And Hardy, when his hands were tied behind him (which happened from their not being acquainted with the way of bringing malefactors to execution), observed, "That he had seen many a man hanged, but this way of the hands being tied behind them he was a stranger to and never saw before in his life." I mention these two little instances to show how stupid and thoughtless they were of their end, and that the same abandoned and reprobate temper that had carried them through their rogueries, abided with them to the last.

Samuel Fletcher, another of the pirates ordered for execution, but reprieved, seemed to have a quicker sense of his condition; for when he saw those he was allotted with go to execution, he sent a message by the Provost-Marshal to the court, to be "informed of the meaning of it, and humbly desired to know whether they designed him mercy or not? If they did, he stood infinitely obliged to them, and thought the whole service of his life an incompetent return for so great a favour; but that if he was to suffer, the sooner the better, he said, that he might be out of his pain."

There were others of these pirates the reverse of this, and though destitute of ministers or fit persons to represent their sins and assist them with spiritual advice, were yet always employing their time to good purposes, and behaved with a great deal of seeming devotion and penitence; among these may be reckoned Scudamore, Williams,

Philips, Stephenson, Jeffreys, Lesly, Harper, Armstrong, Bunce, and others.

Scudamore too lately discerned the folly and wickedness of the enterprise, that had chiefly brought him under sentence of death, from which, seeing there was no hopes of escaping, he petitioned for two or three days' reprieve, which was granted; and for that time applied himself incessantly to prayer and reading the Scriptures. He seemed to have a deep sense of his sins, of this in particular, and desired, at the gallows, they would have patience with him, to sing the first part of the thirty-first Psalm; which he did by himself throughout.

Armstrong, having been a deserter from his Majesty's service, was executed on board the *Weymouth* (and the only one that was); there was nobody to press him to an acknowledgment of the crime he died for, nor of sorrowing in particular for it, which would have been exemplary, and made suitable impressions on seamen; so that his last hour was spent in lamenting and bewailing his sins in general, exhorting the spectators to an honest and good life, in which alone they could find satisfaction. In the end he desired they would join with him in singing two or three latter verses of the 140th Psalm; and that being concluded, he was, at the firing of a gun, triced up at the fore-yard-arm.

Bunce was a young man, not above twenty-six years old, but made the most pathetic speech of any at the gallows. He first declaimed against the gilded baits of Power, Liberty, and Wealth, that had ensnared him among the pirates, his inexperienced years not being able to withstand the temptation; but that the briskness he had shown, which so fatally had procured him favour amongst them, was not so much a fault in principle as the liveliness and vivacity of his nature. He was now extremely afflicted for the injuries he had done to all men, and begged their's and God's forgiveness, very earnestly exhorting the spectators to remember their Creator in their youth, and guard betimes, that their minds took not a wrong bias, concluding with this apt similitude, "That he stood there as a beacon upon a rock" (the gallows standing on one) "to warn erring mariners of danger."

IV.

CAPTAIN AVERY AND HIS CREW.

Romantic reports of his greatness—His birth—Is mate of a Bristol man—For what voyage designed—Tampers with the seamen—Forms a plot for carrying off the ship—Executes it, and how—The pirates take a rich ship belonging to the Great Mogul—The Great Mogul threatens the English settlements—The pirates steer their course back for Madagascar—Call a council—Put all the treasure on board of Avery's ship—Avery and his crew treacherously leave his confederates—Go to the Isle of Providence in the West Indies—Sell the ship—Go to North America in a sloop—They disperse—Avery goes to New England—From thence to Ireland—Avery afraid to expose his diamonds for sale—Goes over to England—Puts his wealth into merchant's hands of Bristol—Changes his name—Lives at Bideford—The merchants send him no supplies—Importunes them—Goes privately to Bristol—They threaten to discover him—Goes over to Ireland—Solicits them from thence—Is very poor—Works his passage over to Plymouth—Walks to Bideford—Dies a beggar—An account of Avery's confederates—Their settlement at Madagascar—They meet other pirates—An account of them—The pirates deposed, and why—Marooned on the Island Mauritius—Some account of that island—The adventures of the company continued—Angria, an Indian pirate—His strength by land and sea—The East India Company's wars with him—The pirates go the island of Melinda—Their barbarous behaviour there—Hear of Captain Mackra's designs against them—Their reflections thereupon—Sail for Cochin, a Dutch settlement—The pirates and the Dutch very good friends—Mutual presents made between the pirates and the Governor—The pirates in a fright—Almost starved—Take a prize of an immense value—Take an Ostend East Indiaman—A short description of Madagascar—A prodigious dividend made by the pirates—A fellow's way of increasing his diamonds—Some of the pirates quit, and join the remains of Avery—The proceedings of the men-of-war in those parts—Some Dutchmen petition to be among the pirates—The pirates divided in their measures—Break up—What became of them.

NONE of these bold adventurers were ever so much talked of for a while as Avery: he made as great a noise in the world as Meriveis does now, and was looked upon to be a person of as great consequence; he was represented in Europe as one that had raised himself to the dignity of a king, and was likely to be the founder of a new monarchy, having, as it was said, taken immense riches and married the Great Mogul's daughter, who was taken in an Indian ship which fell into his hands; and that he had by her many children, living in great royalty and state; that he built forts, erected magazines, and was master of a stout squadron of ships, manned with able and desperate fellows of all nations; that he gave commissions out in his own name to the captains of his ships and to the commanders of his forts, and was acknowledged by them as their prince. A play was written upon him, called "The Successful Pirate"; and these accounts obtained such belief that several schemes were offered to the Council for fitting out a squadron to take him, while others were for offering him and his companions an Act of Grace and inviting them to England, with all their treasure, lest his growing greatness might hinder the trade of Europe to the East Indies.

Yet all these were no more than false rumours, improved by the credulity of some and the humour of others who love to tell strange things; for while, it is said, he was aspiring at a crown he wanted a shilling, and at the same time it was given out he was in possession of such prodigious wealth in Madagascar he was starving in England.

No doubt but the reader will have a curiosity of knowing

what became of this man, and what were the true grounds of so many false reports concerning him; therefore I shall, in as brief a manner as I can, give his history.

He was born in the West of England near Plymouth, in Devonshire; being bred to the sea, he served as a mate of a merchantman in several trading voyages. It happened before the Peace of Ryswick, when there was an alliance between Spain, England, Holland, &c. against France, that the French in Martinico carried on a smuggling trade with the Spaniards on the continent of Peru, which by the law of Spain is not allowed to friends in time of peace, for none but native Spaniards are permitted to traffic in those parts or set their feet on shore, unless at any time they are brought as prisoners; wherefore they constantly keep certain ships cruising along the coast, whom they call Guarda del Costa, who have the orders to make prizes of all ships they can light of within five leagues of land. Now the French, growing very bold in trade, and the Spaniards being poorly provided with ships, and those they had being of no force, it often fell out that when they light of the French smugglers they were not strong enough to attack them, therefore it was resolved in Spain to hire two or three stout foreign ships for their service, which being known at Bristol, some merchants of that city fitted out two ships of thirty odd guns, and one hundred and twenty hands each, well furnished with provision and ammunition, and all other stores; and the hire being agreed for by some agents for Spain, they were commanded to sail for Corunna—the Groine—there to receive their orders, and to take on board some Spanish gentlemen who were to go passengers to New Spain.

Of one of these ships, which I take to be called the *Duke*, Captain Gibson, commander, Avery was first mate, and being a fellow of more cunning than courage, he insinuated himself into the good will of several of the boldest fellows on board the other ship as well as that which he was on board of. Having sounded their inclinations before he opened himself, and finding them ripe for his design, he at length proposed to them to run away with the ship, telling them what great wealth was to be had upon the coast of India. It was no sooner said than agreed to, and they resolved to execute their plot at ten o'clock the night following.

It must be observed the captain was one of those who are mightily addicted to punch, so that he passed most of his time on shore in some little drinking ordinary; but this day he did not go on shore as usual; however, this did not spoil the design, for he took his usual dose on board, and so got to bed before the hour appointed for the business. The men also who were not privy to the design turned into their hammocks, leaving none upon deck but the conspirators, who, indeed, were the greatest part of the ship's crew. At the time agreed on the *Duchess's* long-boat appeared, which, Avery hailing in the usual manner, was answered by the men in her, "Is your drunken boat-swain on board?" which was the watchword agreed between them, and Avery replying in the affirmative the boat came aboard with sixteen stout fellows and joined the company.

When our gentry saw that all was clear they secured the hatches, so went to work; they did not slip the anchor, but weighed it leisurely, and so put to sea without any disorder or confusion, though there were several ships then lying in the bay, and among them a Dutch frigate of forty guns, the captain of which was offered a great reward to go out after her; but Mynheer, who perhaps would not have been willing to have been served so himself, could not be prevailed upon to give such usage to another, and so let Mr. Avery pursue his voyage whither he had a mind to.

The captain, who by this time was awakened, either by the motion of the ship or the noise of working the tackles, rung the bell. Avery and two others went into the cabin. The captain, half asleep, and in a kind of fright, asked, "What was the matter?" Avery answered coolly, "Nothing." The captain replied, "Something's the matter with the ship. Does she drive? What weather is it?" thinking nothing less than that it had been a storm and that the ship was driven from her anchors. "No, no," answered Avery, "we're at sea, with a fair wind and good weather." "At sea!" says the captain; "how can that be?" "Come," says Avery, "don't be in a fright, but put on your clothes, and I'll let you into a secret. You must know that I am captain of this ship now, and this is my cabin, therefore you must walk out. I am bound to Madagascar, with a design of making my own fortune, and that of all the brave fellows joined with me."

The captain having a little recovered his senses began to apprehend the meaning. However, his fright was as great as before, which Avery perceiving, bade him fear nothing; "for," says he, "if you have a mind to make one of us we will receive you, and if you'll turn sober and mind your business, perhaps in time I may make you one of my lieutenants; if not, here's a boat alongside, and you shall be set ashore."

The captain was glad to hear this, and therefore accepted of his offer; and the whole crew being called up, to know who was willing to go on shore with the captain and who to seek their fortunes with the rest, there were not above five or six who were willing to quit this enterprise. Wherefore they were put into the boat with the captain that minute and made their way to the shore as well as they could.

They proceeded on their voyage to Madagascar; but I

do not find they took any ships in their way. When they arrived at the north-east part of that island they found two sloops at anchor, who, upon seeing them, slipped their cables and run themselves ashore, the men all landing and running into the woods. These were two sloops which the men had run away with from the West Indies, and seeing Avery, they supposed him to be some frigate sent to take them, and therefore not being of force to engage him they did what they could to save themselves.

He guessed where they were, and sent some of his men on shore to let them know they were friends, and to offer they might join together for their common safety. The sloops' men were well armed, and had posted themselves in a wood, with sentinels just on the outside to observe whether the ship landed her men to pursue them, and they observing only two or three men to come towards them without arms, did not oppose them; but having challenged them, and they answering that they were friends, they led them to their body, where they delivered their message. At first they apprehended it was a stratagem to decoy them on board, but when the ambassadors offered that the captain himself and as many of the crew as they should name would meet them on shore without arms, they believed them to be in earnest, and they soon entered into a confidence with one another, those on board going on shore and some of those on shore going on board.

The sloops' men were rejoiced at the new ally, for their vessels were so small that they could not attack a ship of any force, so that hitherto they had not taken any considerable prize; but now they hoped to fly at high game. And Avery was as well pleased at this reinforcement to strengthen them for any brave enterprise, and though the booty must be lessened to each by being divided into so many shares, yet he found out an expedient not to suffer by it himself, as shall be shown in its place.

Having consulted what was to be done, they resolved to sail out together upon a cruise—the galley and two sloops. They therefore fell to work to get the sloops off, which they soon effected, and steered towards the Arabian coast. Near the River Indus the man at the masthead spied a sail, upon which they gave chase, and as they came nearer to her they perceived her to be a tall ship, and fancied she might be a Dutch East Indiaman homeward bound; but she proved a better prize. When they fired at her to bring to she hoisted Mogul's colours, and seemed to stand upon her defence. Avery only cannonaded at a distance, and some of his men began to suspect that he was not the hero they took him for. However, the sloops made use of their time, and coming one on the bow and the other on the quarter of the ship, clapped her on board and entered her, upon which she immediately struck her colours and yielded. She was one of the Great Mogul's own ships, and there were in her several of the greatest persons of his Court, among whom it was said was one of his daughters, who were going on a pilgrimage to Mecca, the Mahometans thinking themselves obliged once in their lives to visit that place; and they were carrying with them rich offerings to present at the shrine of Mahomet. It is known that the Eastern people travel with the utmost magnificence, so that they had with them all their slaves and attendants, their rich habits and jewels, with vessels of gold and silver, and great sums of money to defray the charges of their journey by land; wherefore the plunder got by this prize is not easily computed.

Having taken all the treasure on board their own ships, and plundered their prize of everything else they either wanted or liked, they let her go; she not being able to continue her voyage, returned back. As soon as the news came to the Mogul, and he knew that they were English who had robbed them, he threatened loud, and talked of sending a mighty army with fire and sword to extirpate the English from all their settlements on the Indian coast. The East India Company in England were very much alarmed at it; however, by degrees they found means to pacify him, by promising to do their endeavours to take the robbers and deliver them into his hands; however, the great noise this thing made in Europe as well as in India, was the occasion of all these romantic stories which were formed of Avery's greatness.

In the meantime our successful plunderers agreed to make the best of their way back to Madagascar, intending to make that place their magazine or repository for all their treasure, and to build a small fortification there, and leave a few hands always ashore to look after it and defend it from any attempts of the natives; but Avery put an end to this project, and made it altogether unnecessary.

As they were steering their course as has been said, he sends a boat on board of each of the sloops desiring the chief of them to come on board of him in order to hold a council; they did so, and he told them he had something to propose to them for the common good, which was to provide against accidents; he bade them consider the treasure they were possessed of would be sufficient for them all if they could secure it in some place on shore, therefore all they had to fear was some misfortune in the voyage; he bade them consider the consequences of being separated by bad weather, in which case the sloops, if either of them should fall in with any ships of force, must be either taken or sunk, and the treasure on board her lost to the rest, besides the common accidents of the sea ; as for his part he was so strong he was able to make his party good with any ship they were likely to meet in those seas; that if he met with any ship of such strength, and could not take her, he was safe from being taken, being so well-manned, besides, his ship was a quick sailor, and could carry sail when their sloops could not, wherefore he proposed to them to put the treasure on board his ship, to seal up each chest with three seals, whereof each was to keep one, and to appoint a rendezvous in case of separation.

Upon considering this proposal it appeared so reasonable to them that they readily came into it, for they argued to themselves that an accident might happen to one of the sloops and the other escape, wherefore it was for the common good. The thing was done as agreed to, the treasure put on board of Avery, and the chests sealed ; they kept company that day and the next, the weather being fair, in which time Avery tampered with his men, telling them they now had sufficient to make them all easy, and what should hinder them from going to some country where they were not known and living on shore all the rest of their days in plenty. They understood what he meant, and, in short, they all agreed to bilk their new allies, the sloops' men ; nor do I find that any of them felt any qualms of honour rising in his stomach to hinder them from consenting to this piece of treachery. In fine, they took advantage of the darkness that night, steered another course, and by morning lost sight of them.

I leave the reader to judge what swearing and confusion there was among the sloops' men in the morning when they saw that Avery had given them the slip, for they knew by the fairness of the weather and the course they had agreed to steer, that it must have been done on purpose. But we leave them at present to follow Mr. Avery.

Avery and his men, having consulted what to do with themselves, came to a resolution to make the best of their way towards America, and, none of them being known in those parts, they intended to divide the treasure, to change their names, to go ashore, some in one place some in another, to purchase some settlements and live at ease. The first land they made was the island of Providence, then newly settled; here they stayed some time, and having considered that when they should go to New England the greatness of their ship would cause much inquiry about them, and possibly some people from England who had heard the story of a ship's being run away with from the Groine might suspect them to be the people, they therefore took a resolution of disposing of their ship at Providence. Upon which Avery, pretending that the ship being fitted out upon the privateering account and having had no success, he had received orders from the owners to dispose of her to the best advantage, He soon met with a purchaser, and immediately bought a sloop.

In this sloop he and his companions embarked. They touched at several parts of America, where no person suspected them, and some of them went on shore, and dispersed themselves about the country, having received such dividends as Avery would give them, for he concealed the greatest part of the diamonds from them, which in the first hurry of plundering the ship they did not much regard, as not knowing their value.

At length he came to Boston, in New England, and seemed to have a desire of settling in those parts, and some of his companions went on shore there also, but he changed his resolution, and proposed to the few of his companions who were left to sail for Ireland, which they consented to. He found out that New England was not a proper place for him, because a great deal of his wealth lay in diamonds, and should he have produced them there he would have certainly been seized on suspicion of piracy.

In their voyage to Ireland they avoided St. George's Channel, and sailing north about, they put into one of the northern ports of that kingdom; there they disposed of their sloop, and coming on shore they separated themselves, some going to Cork, and some to Dublin, eighteen of whom obtained their pardons afterwards of King William. When Avery had remained some time in this kingdom he was afraid to offer his diamonds for sale, lest an inquiry into his manner of coming by them should occasion a discovery; therefore, considering with himself what was best to be done, he fancied there were some persons at Bristol whom he might venture to trust; upon which he resolved to pass over into England; he did so, and, going into Devonshire, he sent one of these friends to meet him at a town called Bideford. When he had communicated himself to his friends, and consulted with them about the means of his effects, they agreed that the safest method would be to put them in the hands of some merchants, who, being men of wealth and credit in the world, no inquiry would be made how they came by them. This friend telling him he was very intimate with some who were very fit for the purpose, and if he would but allow them a good commission would do the business very faithfully. Avery liked the proposal, for he found no other way of managing his affairs, since he could not appear in them himself; therefore his friend going back to Bristol and opening the matter to the merchants they made Avery a visit at Bideford, where, after some protestations of honour and integrity, he delivered them his effects, consisting of diamonds and some vessels of gold; they gave him a little money for his present subsistence, and so they parted.

He changed his name and lived at Bideford without making any figure, and therefore there was no great notice taken of him; yet let one or two of his relations know where he was, who came to see him. In some time his little money was spent, yet he heard nothing from his merchants. He wrote to them often, and after much importunity they sent him a small supply, but scarce sufficient to pay his debts; in fine, the supplies they sent him from time were so small that they were not sufficient to give him bread, nor could he get that little without a great deal of trouble and importunity; wherefore, being weary of his life, he went privately to Bristol to speak to the merchants himself, where, instead of money he met a most shocking repulse, for when he desired them to come to an account with him they silenced him by threatening to discover him, so that our merchants were as good pirates on land as he was on sea.

Whether he was frightened by these menaces, or had seen somebody else he thought knew him, is not known; but he went immediately over to Ireland, and from thence solicited his merchants very hard for a supply, but to no purpose, for he was even reduced to beggary. In this extremity he was resolved to return and cast himself upon them, let the consequences be what it would. He put himself on board a trading vessel, and worked his passage over to Plymouth, from whence he travelled on foot to Bideford, where he had been but a few days before he fell sick and died, not being worth as much as would buy him a coffin.

Thus have I given all that could be collected of any certainty concerning this man, rejecting the idle stories which were made of his fantastic greatness, by which it appears that his actions were more inconsiderable than those of other pirates since him, though he made more noise in the world.

Now we shall turn back and give our readers some account of what became of the two sloops.

We took notice of the rage and confusion which must have seized them upon their missing of Avery. However, they continued their course, some of them still flattering themselves that he had only outsailed them in the night, and that they should find him at the place of rendezvous. But when they came there, and could hear no tidings of him there was end of hope. It was time to consider what they should do with themselves; their stock of sea provision was almost spent, and though there was rice and fish, and fowl to be had ashore, yet these would not keep for sea without being properly cured with salt, which they had no conveniences of doing; therefore, since they could not go a-cruising any more, it was time to think of establishing themselves on land; to which purpose they took all things out of the sloops, made tents of the sails, and encamped themselves, having a large quantity of ammunition and abundance of small arms.

Here they met with several of their countrymen, the crew of a privateer sloop which was commanded by Captain Thomas Tew; and, since it will be but a short digression, we will give an account how they came here.

Captain George Dew and Captain Thomas Tew having received commissions from the then Governor of Bermudas to sail directly for the river Gambia in Africa, there, with the advice and assistance of the agents of the Royal African Company, to attempt the taking the French factory at Goorie, lying upon that coast. In a few days after they sailed out, Dew, in a violent storm, not only sprung his mast, but lost sight of his consort; Dew therefore returned back to refit, and Tew, instead of proceeding on his voyage, made for the Cape of Good Hope, and doubling the said Cape, shaped his course for the Straits of

Babel Mandel, being the entrance into the Red Sea. Here he came up with a large ship, richly laden, bound from the Indies to Arabia, with three hundred soldiers on board, besides seamen; yet Tew had the hardiness to board her, and soon carried her; and it is said by this prize his men shared near three thousand pounds a-piece. They had intelligence from the prisoners of five other rich ships to pass that way, which Tew would have attacked, though they were very strong, if he had not been overruled by the quartermaster and others. This differing in opinion created some ill blood amongst them, so that they resolved to break up pirating, and no place was so fit to receive them as Madagascar; hither they steered, resolving to live on shore and enjoy what they got.

As for Tew himself, he, with a few others, in a short time went off to Rhode Island, from whence he made his peace.

Thus have we accounted for the company our pirates met with here.

It must be observed that the natives of Madagascar are a kind of negroes; they differ from those of Guinea in their hair, which is long, and their complexion is not so good a jet; they have innumerable little princes among them, who are continually making war upon one another; their prisoners are their slaves, and they either sell them or put them to death as they please. When our pirates first settled amongst them their alliance was much courted by these princes, so they sometimes joined one, sometimes another, but wheresoever they sided they were sure to be victorious, for the negroes here had no firearms, nor did they understand their use; so that at length these pirates became so terrible to the negroes that if two or three of them were only seen on one side when they were going to engage, the opposite side would fly without striking a blow.

By these means they not only became feared, but powerful; all the prisoners of war they took to be their slaves; they married the most beautiful of the negro women, not one or two, but as many as they liked; so that every one of them had as great a seraglio as the Grand Seignior at Constantinople. Their slaves they employed in planting rice, in fishing, hunting, &c., besides which they had abundance of others who lived, as it were, under their protection, and to be secure from their disturbances or attacks of their powerful neighbours, these seemed to pay them a willing homage. Now they began to divide from one another, each living with his own wives, slaves, and dependents, like a separate prince; and as power and plenty naturally beget contention, they sometimes quarrelled with one another, and attacked each other at the head of their several armies; and in these civil wars many of them were killed; but an ancident happened which obliged them to unite again for their common safety.

It must be observed that these sudden great men had used their power like tyrants, for they grew wanton in cruelty, and nothing was more common than, upon the slightest displeasure, to cause one of their dependents to be tied to a tree and shot through the heart—let the crime be what it would, whether little or great, this was always the punishment; wherefore the negroes conspired together to rid themselves of these destroyers all in one night; and as they now lived separate the thing might easily have been done had not a woman, who had been wife or concubine to one of them, run near twenty miles in three hours to discover the matter to them. Immediately upon the alarm they ran together as fast as they could, so that when the negroes approached them they found them all up in arms; wherefore they retired without making any attempt.

This escape made them very cautious from that time, and it will be worth while to describe the policy of these brutish fellows, and to show what measures they took to secure themselves.

They found that the fear of their power could not secure them against a surprise, and the bravest man may be killed when he is asleep by one much his inferior in courage and strength; therefore, as their first security, they did all they could to foment war between the neighbouring negroes, remaining neuter themselves, by which means those who were overcome constantly fled to them for protection, otherwise they must be either killed or made slaves. They strengthened their party, and tied some to them by interest; when there was no war they contrived to spirit up private quarrels among them, and upon every little dispute or misunderstanding push on one side or other to revenge, instruct them how to attack or surprise their adversaries, and lend them loaded pistols or firelocks to dispatch them with, the consequence of which was that the murderer was forced to fly to them for the safety of his life with his wives, children, and kindred.[1]

Such as these were fast friends, as their lives depended upon the safety of the protectors; for, as we observed before, our pirates were grown so terrible that none of their neighbours had resolution enough to attack them in an open war.

By such arts as these, in the space of a few years their body was greatly increased; they then began to separate themselves and remove at a greater distance from one another for the convenience of more ground, and were divided, like Jews, into tribes, each carrying with him his wives and children (of which by this time they had a large family), as also their quota of dependents and followers. And if power and command be the thing which distinguish a prince, these ruffians had all the marks of royalty about them; nay more, they had the very fears which commonly disturb tyrants, as may be seen by the extreme caution they took in fortifying the places where they dwelt.

In this plan of fortification they imitated one another. Their dwellings were rather citadels than houses; they made choice of a place overgrown with a wood, and situate near a water; they raised a rampart or high ditch round it, so straight and high that it was impossible to climb it, and especially by those who had not the use of scaling ladders; over this ditch there was one passage into the wood; the dwelling, which was a hut, was built in that part of the wood which the prince who inhabited it thought fit, but so covered that it could not be seen till you came to it; but the greatest cunning lay in the passage which led to the hut, which was so narrow that no more than one person could go abreast, and contrived in so intricate a manner that it was a perfect maze or labyrinth, it being round and round, with several little cross-ways, so that a person that was not well acquainted with the way might walk several hours round and cross these ways without being able to find the hut; moreover, all along the sides of these narrow paths certain large thorns which grew upon a tree in that country were struck into the ground with their points uppermost, and the path itself, being made crooked and serpentine, if a man should attempt to come near the hut at night he would certainly have stuck upon these thorns, though he had been provided with that clue which Ariadne gave to Theseus when he entered the cave of the Minataur.

Thus tyrant-like they lived, fearing and feared by all; and in this situation they were found by Captain Woods Rogers when he went to Madagascar in the *Delicia*, a ship of forty guns, with a design of buying slaves, in order to sell to the Dutch at Batavia or New England. He happened to touch upon a part of the island where no ship had been seen for seven or eight years before, where he met with some of the pirates, at which time they had been upon the island above twenty-five years, having a large motley generation of children and grandchildren descended from them, there being about that time eleven of them remaining alive.

Upon their first seeing a ship of this force and burthen they supposed it to be a man-of-war sent to take them; they therefore lurked within their fastnesses; but when some from the ship came on shore without any show of hostility, and offering to trade with the negroes, they ventured to come out of their holes, attended like princes; and since they actually are kings *de facto*, whichis a kind of a right, we ought to speak of them as such.

Having been so many years upon this island it may be imagined their clothes had long been worn out, so that their majesties were extremely out at the elbows; I cannot say they were ragged, since they had no clothes—they had nothing to cover them but the skins of beasts without any tanning, but with all their hair on, nor a shoe nor stocking, so they looked like the pictures of Hercules in the lion's skin; and being overgrown with beard, and hair upon their bodies, they appeared the most savage figures that a man's imagination can frame.

However, they soon got rigged, for they sold great numbers of those poor people under them for clothes, knives, saws, powder and ball, and many other things, and became so familiar that they went aboard the *Delicia*, and were observed to be very curious, examining the inside of the ship, and very familiar with the men, inviting them ashore. Their design in doing this, as they afterwards confessed, was to try if it was not practicable to surprise the ship in the night, which they judged very easy in case there was but a slender watch kept on board, they having boats and men enough at command; but it seems the captain was aware of them, and kept so strong a watch upon deck that they found it was in vain to make any attempt; wherefore, when some of the men went ashore they were for inveigling them and drawing them into a plot for seizing the captain, and securing the rest of the men under hatches when they should have the night-watch, promising a signal to come on board and join them, proposing, if they succeeded, to go a-pirating together, not doubting but with that ship they should be able to take anything they met on the sea. But the captain, observing an intimacy growing between them and some of his men, thought it could be for no good; he therefore broke it off in time, not suffering them so much as to talk together; and when he sent a boat on shore with an officer to treat with them about the sale of slaves, the crew remained on board the boat, and no man was suffered to talk with them but the person deputed by him for that purpose.

Before he sailed away, and they found that nothing was to be done, they confessed all the designs they had formed against him. Thus he left them as he found them, in a great deal of dirty state and royalty, but with fewer subjects than they had, having, as we observed, sold many of them; and if ambition be the darling passion of men, no doubt they were happy. One of these great princes had formerly been a waterman upon the Thames, where, having committed a murder, he fled to the West Indies, and was of the number of those who ran away with the sloops, the rest had been all foremast men, nor was there a man amongst them who could either read or write, and yet their

Secretaries of State had no more learning than themselves. This is all the account we can give of these kingdoms of Madagascar, some of whom it is probable are reigning to this day.

THE END.

www.ingramcontent.com/pod-product-compliance
Lightning Source LLC
Chambersburg PA
CBHW022111290426
44112CB00008B/632